calbizcentral™
presented by CalChamber

HR Handbook

for California Employers

2008 Edition

Published by
California Chamber of Commerce
P.O. Box 1736
Sacramento, CA 95812-1736

ISBN 1-57997-212-8

5 4 3 2 1

The information compiled in this handbook is being provided by CalBizCentral as a service to the business community. Although every effort has been made to ensure the accuracy and completeness of this information, CalBizCentral and the contributors and reviewers of this publication cannot be responsible for any errors and omissions, nor any agency's interpretations, applications and changes of regulations described herein.

This publication is designed to provide accurate and authoritative information in a highly summarized manner with regard to the subject matter covered. It is sold with the understanding that the publisher and others associated with this publication are not engaged in rendering legal, technical or other professional service. If legal and other expert assistance is required, the services of competent professionals should be sought.

This publication is available from:

CalChamber/CalBizCentral
P.O. Box 1736
Sacramento, CA 95812-1736
(916) 444-6670
http://www.calbizcentral.com

Table of Contents

Chapter 7

Chapter 8

What's New for 2008?

This preface lists additions and changes for ***2008 HR Handbook***. These changes are detailed in chapter order.

Getting Started

Access all of your 2008 forms on the Web at ***www.calbizcentral.com/support***. For instructions, see "Online Forms" in Chapter 1, page 4.

Hiring Employees

- The *I-9 Form* was revised in 2007. You must use this version of the I-9 for any employee hired after November 7, 2007. See "What If the Documents I'm Shown Aren't Valid?" on page 28; and
- New forms (for descriptions, see "What Forms and Checklists Do I Use to Hire Employees?" on page 38):
  - *I-9 Form*
  - *Recruiting Checklist*
  - *Emergency Information - Spanish*

Developing Policies

- New forms (for descriptions, see "What Forms and Checklists Do I Use to Develop Policies?" on page 89):
  - *Guest and Visitor Policy*
  - *Guest and Visitor Request Form*
  - *Guest and Visitor Request Form - Spanish*
  - *Telecommuting Agreement*
  - *Telecommuting Policy*
  - *Telecommuting Request*
  - *Telecommuting Request Checklist*
  - *Telecommuting Safety Checklist*
  - *Workplace Violence Policy*

Providing Benefits

New legislation creating a leave of absence for spouses of military personnel. See "What Do I Need to Know About Military Spouse Leave?" on page 118;

- Updated guidelines for predesignating a personal medical doctor (MD), doctor of osteopathic medicine (DO) or medical group. See "Choice of Physician, Chiropractor, or Acupuncturist" on page 134; and
- New forms (for descriptions, see "What Forms and Checklists Do I Use To Provide Benefits?" on page 149):

  COBRA Administration Guide
  - *Employee Letter- FMLA/CFRA Conditionally Granted*
  - *Employee Letter - FMLA/CFRA during Workers' Compensation*
  - *FMLA/CFRA Application - English*
  - *FMLA/CFRA Application - Spanish*
  - *Leave Interaction*
  - *Military Spouse Leave Policy (25 or more employees)*
  - *Military Spouse Request for Leave (25 or more employees)*
  - *Request for Use of Kin Care - Spanish*

- *Temporary Modified Duty Agreement*
- *Workers' Compensation Insurance Shoppers Checklist*

Paying Employees

- Effective January 1, California's minimum wage is $8.00 an hour. See "What Is the Minimum Wage?" on page 169;
- A licensed physician or surgeon primarily engaged in performing duties that require a license is exempt from overtime if paid $64.18. See "What Is the Minimum Salary?" in Chapter 5, page 168;
- A three-year statute of limitations, not one year, applies to the "one additional hour of pay" employers are required to pay employees when meal and/or rest breaks are not provided. See "What Happens If I Fail to Give Non-exempt Employees Meal and Rest Breaks?" on page 188; and
- New forms (for descriptions, see "What Forms and Checklists Do I Use to Help Me Pay Employees?" on page 191):
  - *Absence Request - English*
  - *Absence Request - Spanish*
  - *Makeup Time Request - Spanish*
  - *Meal and Rest Periods Policy*
  - *Meal Break Waiver - English*
  - *Meal Break Waiver - Spanish*
  - *Meal Break Waiver - On Duty*
  - *Meal Break Waiver - Second Meal*
  - *Overtime Request - English*
  - *Overtime Request - Spanish*

Workplace Safety

- New forms (for descriptions, see "What Forms and Checklists Do I Use for Ensuring Workplace Safety?" on page 219):
  - *Code for Safe Practices for Construction Workplaces*
  - *Ergonomics Checklist - Computer and Keyboard Issues*

- *Ergonomics Checklist - Hand Tool Use*
- *Ergonomics Checklist - Manual Handling*
- *Ergonomics Checklist - Task-Work Methods*
- *Ergonomics Checklist - Workstation Layout*
- *Hazard Assessment and Correction Record*
- *Heat Illness Prevention Plan (Outdoor Employees)*
- *Safety Program Self Audit Checklist*
- *Training Sign-In Sheet - Spanish*
- *Worker Training and Instruction Record*

Preventing Discrimination and Harassment

- California's sexual harassment training regulations were finalized in 2007. For an in-depth overview, and answers to frequently asked questions, see "Final Training Regulations" on page 242; and
- New forms (for descriptions, see "What Forms and Checklists Do I Use to Help Me Prevent Discrimination and Harassment?" on page 258):
  - *Harassment Complaint Procedure - English*
  - *Harassment Complaint Procedure - Spanish*

Ending the Employment Relationship

- New forms (for descriptions, see "What Forms and Checklists Do I Use to End the Employment Relationship?" on page 277:
  - *Affidavit to Collect Compensation of Deceased*
  - *Authorization to Release Personnel Records*
  - *Employer Proof of Identity and Disbursement of Final Pay*
  - *Final Paycheck Acknowledgment - English*
  - *Final Paycheck Acknowledgment - Spanish*

Glossary

- Revised to give you better, accurate definitions of employment related terms. See "Glossary of Terms, Laws, and Agencies" on page 285.

Chapter 1

Getting Started with This Product

This simple product makes it easy to find what you need — quickly.

Structure

This book organizes the information into chapters based on topics. If you are not sure what chapter to look in, consult the "Index."

Formatting

This product uses formatting conventions to help you identify important information.

Table 1. ***HR Handbook*** **Formatting**

Bold	This formatting emphasizes important terms.
Italics	This formatting identifies forms and checklists.
	This icon identifies information to which you should pay close attention.
	This icon identifies definitions of terms, as well as helpful advice.
Spot Color	This formatting defines chapters by color and identifies glossary terms and what's new within each chapter.

Does This Employment Law Apply to Me?

Use the chart on the next page to determine if an employment law applies to your company, based on the number of employees you have.

For further information about each law, see the "Index," which refers you to material throughout this product.

Table 2. Does This Employment Law Apply to Me?

Law/Requirement	All employers	4 or more	5 or more	15 or more	20 or more	25 or more	50 or more	75 or more
Affirmative Action							✓	✓
Alcohol/Drug Rehabilitation						✓	✓	✓
Americans with Disabilities Act (ADA)				✓	✓	✓	✓	✓
Cal-COBRA (2–19 employees only)	✓							
California Family Rights Act (CFRA)							✓	✓
Child Labor	✓							
COBRA (health insurance continuation)					✓	✓	✓	✓
Disability Leave			✓	✓	✓	✓	✓	✓
Discrimination and Foreign Workers		✓	✓	✓	✓	✓	✓	✓
Discrimination Laws (State)			✓	✓	✓	✓	✓	✓
Discrimination Laws (Federal)				✓	✓	✓	✓	✓
Domestic Violence/Sexual Assault Victims' Leave	✓							
Employee Safety	✓							
Family and Medical Leave Act (FMLA)							✓	✓
Immigration Reform and Control Act (IRCA)	✓							
Independent Contractors	✓							
Jury/Witness Duty Leave	✓							
Kin Care	✓							
Military Service Leave	✓							

Table 2. Does This Employment Law Apply to Me? ***(continued)***

Law/Requirement	All employers	4 or more	5 or more	15 or more	20 or more	25 or more	50 or more	75 or more
Military Spouse Leave						✓	✓	✓
New Employee Reporting	✓							
Paid Family Leave (PFL)	✓							
Plant Closing (State WARN Act)								✓
Posters and Notices	✓							
Pregnancy Disability Leave (PDL)			✓	✓	✓	✓	✓	✓
Privacy	✓							
School Activities Leave						✓	✓	✓
School Appearance Leave	✓							
Sexual Harassment	✓							
Smoking in the Workplace	✓							
State Disability Insurance (SDI)	✓							
Unemployment Insurance (UI)	✓							
Victims of Crime Leave	✓							
Volunteer Civil Service Leave	✓							
Voting Leave	✓							
Wage and Hour Laws	✓							
Workers' Compensation	✓							

Online Forms

New for 2008

Throughout this book, you'll find references to many forms and checklists. As regulations can change throughout the year, accessing your forms online ensures that you will always have the most current version of each form. Be sure to check ***www.calbizcentral.com/support*** occasionally for updates to forms, as well as descriptions of important mid-year regulatory changes.

To download all of the forms mentioned in this book:

1. Go to ***www.calbizcentral.com/support***.
2. From the list of 2008 product titles, select ***HR Handbook for California Employers***.
3. Enter your product security code in the input field and select "Continue."

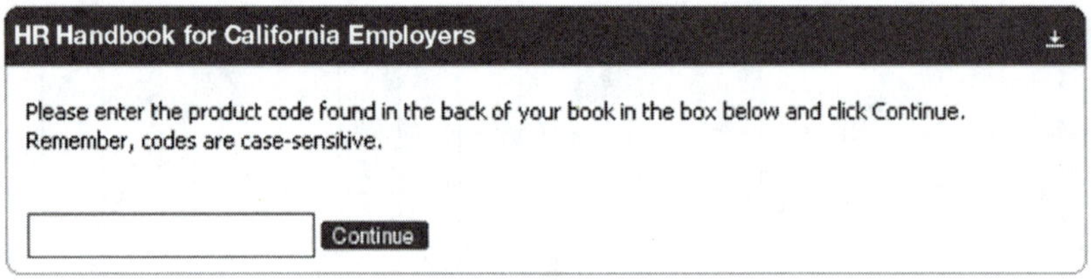

You'll find the product security code on the inside covers of the book.

4. Right-click on the link and select "Save Target As."
5. Save the compressed zip file to the location on your computer where you would like to store your forms.
6. Navigate to the compressed zip file and extract the contents.

To find the form you need easily, open ***_ViewFormsListingFirst.htm***. This page provides links to all downloaded forms, as well as helpful descriptions of each.

About the Editor

Jessica Hawthorne is Employment Law Counsel and a Helpline Consultant for the California Chamber of Commerce. In addition to this book, she is the main contributor to the ***2008 California Labor Law Digest, Labor Law Administration***, and ***Employee Handbook Software***. Jessica also writes the bi-weekly ***HR California Extra*** and has an employment law blog at ***www.hrcalifornia.com***. Her expertise includes topics such as employee handbooks, sexual harassment investigations, family and medical leave, and exempt vs. non-exempt employees.

Jessica graduated from Widener University School of Law and the University of Pittsburgh, and has been admitted to the bar in California. Her previous experience includes labor and employment counseling, education law, and dispute resolution.

About the Editor

[illegible]

Chapter 2

Hiring Employees

If you establish a hiring procedure that covers everything from making the decision to hire someone to welcoming a new employee, you give yourself the best opportunity to avoid litigation and have a smooth, enjoyable hiring experience.

In this chapter, you can find answers to questions about:

- Legal recruiting procedures;
- Required and recommended forms;
- Credit and background checks for applicants;
- Independent contractors; and
- Much more!

Minimum Compliance Elements

1. Hang your *Employer Poster* (available from ***www.calbizcentral.com***), which includes mandatory postings that all applicants and employees must be able to see.

2. Use the *Hiring Checklist* to make sure you fill out all the required paperwork for every new hire. See "Required Forms and Checklists" on page 38.

3. Look at all candidates objectively, in terms of their ability to do the job. See "Interview Candidates" on page 16.

4. Make sure you classify workers properly. See "What's the Difference Between an Exempt and a Non-exempt Employee?" on page 11.

5. Make sure you aren't controlling your independent contractors as if they were employees. See "How Do I Make Sure That the Individual Is Truly an Independent Contractor?" on page 31.

The Basics of Hiring Employees

Many employers find hiring a new employee a complicated and daunting process. You must:

- Find the best employee for the job;
- Fulfill extensive paperwork requirements;
- Avoid violating complex discrimination laws; and
- Avoid creating/violating contracts that open you up to litigation.

To protect yourself from making a costly mistake, consider establishing a hiring policy. Before you begin the hiring process, review your policy to make sure you don't violate it.

> ***Example:*** If your policy states that you open all new positions to existing employees before looking outside the company, and you fail to do so, you could open yourself up to employee complaint, and even legal action.

How Do I Hire an Employee?

Very carefully! Wading through the extensive legal requirements and forms can feel like walking through a minefield of potentially explosive illegal decisions and actions.

To help organize the process of finding and preparing to hire an employee, and to comply with legal requirements, you can use the *Pre-Hire Checklist* and the *Hiring Checklist*, described in Table 8 on page 38.

The following sections provide information to help you:

- "1 — Define Job Requirements with Up-to-Date Information" on page 9
- "2 — Recognize the Need for a New Employee and Determine the Best Type of Employee to Hire" on page 9.
- "3 — Advertise and/or Recruit for the Position" on page 12.
- "4 — Evaluate Potential Candidates" on page 14.
  - "Review Résumés" on page 14 (optional);
  - "Screen Candidates with a Phone Interview" on page 14 (optional);
  - "Receive Applications" on page 15; and
  - "Interview Candidates" on page 16.

- "5 — Conduct Background Checks" on page 18.
- "6 — Make the Hiring Decision and Offer the Position" on page 23.
- "7 — Fill Out Paperwork" on page 24.
- "8 — Welcome Your New Employees" on page 29.

1 — Define Job Requirements with Up-to-Date Information

It is vital that you start the hiring process with up-to-date information about the job requirements. If you need to fill an existing position, locate the existing job description and make sure that it is accurate. If you are creating a new position, write a new job description that clearly outlines the essential functions of the job.

Essential functions are fundamental job requirements of the position or the reason the job exists.

See "What Are Essential Functions?" in Chapter 7, page 236 for tips on documenting the essential functions of a job. You must be sure that applicants who could perform the essential functions of the job are not turned away based on their inability to perform a non-essential function. Beware of creating promises in a job description that you will have to keep later. See "Don't Create a Contract" on page 36.

Writing a job description does not have to be stressful. CalBizCentral has software to make writing job descriptions easier. See "Where Do I Go for More Information?" on page 49.

2 — Recognize the Need for a New Employee and Determine the Best Type of Employee to Hire

The first task in the hiring process is to figure out exactly what kind of help you need and determine the resources available to meet that need.

Do you need a full-time or part-time employee? Would an independent contractor or a temporary employee better suit your needs?

How Do I Know Which Type of Worker to Hire?

There are many types of worker classifications. Consider the nature of the assignment, and what level of supervision will be required before making your decision. For example, do you need a supervisor who runs a retail store during business hours? A worker who replenishes inventory when your store is closed? A worker to fill in for an employee taking medical leave?

Table 3 describes the various types of workers. To read about how workers can be classified for wages, see "What Do I Pay My Workers?" in Chapter 5, page 167.

Table 3. Types of Workers

What type	What it means
Exempt	An exempt employee is not subject to any of the laws pertaining to over-time, uniforms and equipment, meal periods, and rest periods. An exempt employee normally is an executive, managerial, administrative, or professional employee; exempt employees can also be certain artists or outside salespeople. For more information on how to determine whether an employee is exempt or non-exempt, see "What's the Difference Between an Exempt and a Non-exempt Employee?" on page 11.
Non-exempt	A non-exempt employee is subject to all Wage Order rules and wage laws. You must pay non-exempt employees overtime for working more than eight hours in a day or more than 40 in a workweek. Sometimes, salaried employees can still be non-exempt. See Table 44 in Chapter 5, page 167.
Independent contractor	California labor law defines an independent contractor as "any person who renders service for a specified recompense for a specified result, under the control of his principal as to the result of his work only and not as to the means by which such result is accomplished." Make sure that you classify independent contractors properly. See "How Do I Make Sure That the Individual Is Truly an Independent Contractor?" on page 31. What this means is that contractors can have freedoms, such as: • Flexible working conditions, like the ability to set their own hours; • Certain tax advantages; and • Financial and personal rewards of self-employment. For these workers, employers are not required to: • Provide certain statutory employment benefits, such as: – Workers' compensation coverage; – Unemployment benefits; – Overtime payments; and – Minimum wage obligations. • Withhold income taxes from payments for services.

Table 3. Types of Workers *(continued)*

What type	What it means
Full-time	A full-time employee works the number of hours that you designate as "full-time." You may want to define full-time employees as those who work the same number of hours that your health insurer requires for health care coverage.
Part-time	A part-time employee works less than the number of hours that qualify an employee as a full-time employee. Part-time employees may or may not receive the same level of benefits as full-time employees.
Regular	A "regular" employee is someone who has completed the introductory period and who is not employed on a casual basis. Regular employees may be either full-time or part-time employees, depending upon the number of hours they work.
Introductory	An introductory employee is someone new to your company. You may define the introductory period in terms of calendar days or working days. Be sure to reserve the right to extend such periods in appropriate cases.
Temporary	Temporary employees are hired for specific assignments of limited duration. They may work full-time or part-time, but the length of their employment is usually specified. You should reserve the right to extend the duration of temporary employment without implying such employees' rights to benefits during the extension. Benefits established by law, however, generally are applicable to temporary employees who otherwise qualify.
Casual (on call, per diem, irregular)	Casual workers perform intermittent service on an as-needed basis. For example, a retail establishment might have an employee who floats among departments as needed, or a preschool might bring in an additional teacher for a week to make sure state teacher/child ratios are met during attendance peaks, but the teacher isn't on staff all the time.

What's the Difference Between an Exempt and a Non-exempt Employee?

For details about exempt and non-exempt workers, see Table 3 on page 10.

When deciding to hire an employee, you need to determine whether the position merits exempt or non-exempt status. The difference between exempt and non-exempt is that while non-exempt employees are subject to the laws pertaining to overtime, meal periods, and rest periods, exempt employees are not.

! Keep in mind that non-exempt employees may receive a salary. This does not make them exempt. See "What Do I Pay My Workers?" in Chapter 5, page 167 for more information.

In other words, non-exempt employees:

- Earn overtime pay, (see"What Is Overtime and How Does It Affect Me?" in Chapter 5, page 171);
- Are paid at least minimum wage (see "What Is the Minimum Wage?" in Chapter 5, page 169); and
- Must take meal and rest periods (see "What Are the Meal and Rest Break Requirements?" in Chapter 5, page 162).

Whether an employee's status is exempt depends mostly on the employee's duties and responsibilities. Exempt employees typically hold managerial-level positions and are responsible for getting their job duties done regardless of the time it takes them. Thus, exempt employees do not keep time records for purposes of recording overtime. Exempt status is also determined by a minimum salary level; see "What Is the Minimum Salary?" in Chapter 5, page 168. There are five main types of exempt positions:

- Administrative;
- Computer Professional;
- Executive/Managerial;
- Professional; and
- Outside Salesperson.

Use the Exempt Analysis Worksheets (described in Table 8 on page 38) to help you decide how to classify your employee. You can find these in your online Formspack, described in detail in "Online Forms" on page 4.

3 — Advertise and/or Recruit for the Position

You can use a variety of methods to let potential candidates know about the position, for example:

- Advertise in magazines, newspapers, or trade publications;
- Post job announcements on the Internet;
- Recruit in person at trade shows and job fairs; and
- Send a job request to a staffing agency, EDD, or schools.

Whatever method you choose, make sure that the language you use does not:

- Imply a secure contract, overriding employment at-will — Although California is an at-will state, courts have decided that various factors, including employment advertisements and applications, can create an implied contract. For more information, see "Don't Create a Contract" on page 36. At-will is a legal concept, mandated by California law, assuring both employer and employee that either party can terminate the relationship at any time, and for any reason, or no reason.

Avoid advertisements with language that seems to guarantee future employment such as:

- "Secure position";
- "Looking for candidates willing to make a long-term commitment to the company"; and
- "Looking for someone who can grow with the company."

Make sure that recruiters know they do not have the authority to promise job security to applicants.

Example: "Don't worry, we'll find a place for you" creates an oral contract that is just as binding as a written one. For more information, see "Don't Create a Contract" on page 36.

- Violate any state and federal discrimination laws — State and federal law prohibits limiting or excluding someone from employment because they have, or you think they have, certain characteristics. See "What Is Discrimination?" in Chapter 7, page 228 for more details. Make sure to avoid words and phrases that single out characteristics that could belong to a protected class.

Avoid even the appearance of the intent to discriminate by advertising in general interest venues or in a wide range of special interest ones, rather than in publications geared toward one protected class.

! The only time you can use prohibited language is when it identifies a bona fide occupational qualification (BFOQ). For example, an advertising agency looking for a model to advertise men's suits may specify "male model" in a job announcement. Being male is a BFOQ for this job.

4 — Evaluate Potential Candidates

A thorough examination of the potential candidates gives you the best chance of finding an employee who matches well with your company. This person should have the necessary skills to do the job, but you should also find out about his/her work style, personality, and employment-related interests to make sure this employment relationship will be a good "fit" for both of you. Though not required by law, each of the following activities can help you find a high quality employee:

- "Review Résumés" on page 14;
- "Screen Candidates with a Phone Interview" on page 14;
- "Receive Applications" on page 15; and
- "Interview Candidates" on page 16.

Review Résumés

Sometimes an applicant will submit a résumé providing helpful information about his/her education, skills, past work experience, and accomplishments. A résumé is the candidate's marketing tool, and does not contain all of the information you should gather about a potential candidate, but it can give you a way to preview the person before beginning the application process.

You are not required to keep unsolicited résumés. You can:

- Send them back to the applicant along with a note explaining that there are currently no openings for the position sought; or
- Keep the unsolicited résumés in a separate folder as a pool of potential employees.

Screen Candidates with a Phone Interview

Another, more informal way to preview a potential employee is through a phone interview. This gives you a chance to talk over points of his/her résumé or application and clarify anything you want to know more about.

As in all conversations, be careful not to create an implied contract or to open yourself up to a discrimination charge. You might consider developing a script for the person conducting the phone interview. You can use the *Guide for Pre-Employment Inquiries*, described in Table 8 on page 38, to make sure your script doesn't contain any illegal questions. You can also see the *Employment Interview Checklist* described in Table 8 on page 38, for a series of questions you can ask. You can find these forms in your online

Formspack, described in detail in "Online Forms" on page 4. For tips on steering clear of implied contracts, see "Don't Create a Contract" on page 36.

Receive Applications

Applications can provide you with a broad range of standardized information that can help you evaluate applicants more equally. Types of information an application may request include:

- Applicant's availability;
- Experience and skills, including related military experience;
- Licensing and/or certification;
- Employment history;
- Specialized knowledge or training, such as proficiency in a language other than English; and
- Certification that all information provided is true and accurate.

To reduce the possibility of liability for discrimination, compare your own application with the provided sample *Employment Application – Short Form*, and review it using the *Guide for Pre-Employment Inquiries*, both described in Table 8 on page 38, (especially if you use applications created out of state). Also, read "Interview Candidates" on page 16 for more information and tips on correct note-taking techniques.

You should include the following "damage-control" provisions in the application and require the applicant to separately initial each provision.

Table 4. Application Provisions

What	Why
An authorization to check all references listed by the applicant	Since you may be liable for "negligent hiring" if you fail to check an applicant's references, this provision will help protect you from a claim that the applicant's privacy was invaded. It is also easier to gain information from former employers if they are aware that their former employee has authorized disclosure to you. Watch Out! This release cannot protect you against claims of intentional misconduct or employment discrimination (such as asking about protected information like medical history).
A statement that all answers given by the applicant are true, and any omissions or false information are grounds for rejection of the application or for termination	The courts have allowed employers to use an applicant's placement of false information on a job application as evidence in their defense of wrongful termination lawsuits, even when the employer did not discover the information was false until after the employee was terminated.
A statement that any future employment will be on an at-will basis	This helps applicants understand that employment is at-will. State that for any contrary representations to be binding, they must be in writing.

Interview Candidates

Interviewing candidates is your opportunity to learn more about your applicants and to determine which is best for you based on their:

- Skills;
- Suitability for the position;
- Work style;
- Personality; and
- Employment-related interests.

You will probably only select for interviews and/or background checks a small fraction of the candidates who submitted applications.

Be careful of questions that can put you at risk for a discrimination lawsuit and statements that can establish contracts or violate your policies. Read "Don't Create a Contract" on page 36 and the *Employment Interview Checklist*, described in Table 8 on page 38, for more information.

In general, don't ask questions about:

- Marital status or children;
- Age;
- Disabilities; and
- Hobbies and outside activities that might indicate race, religion, age, etc.

The *Guide for Pre-Employment Inquiries*, described in Table 8 on page 38, can guide you in asking appropriate questions. Also see "What Can I Do to Defend Myself Against a Claim?" in Chapter 7, page 257 for exceptions to these guidelines.

! Managers and supervisors who conduct interviews should beware of exaggerating the employment opportunity. California courts continue to award damages to employees who were promised increased compensation, promotions, or job security during the employment process, and the promises were not fulfilled. Damages can reach millions of dollars if the court finds that an employer induced an applicant to leave secure employment by knowingly making false promises regarding the terms of future employment.

There are a number of tips you might consider following when conducting your interviews:

Table 5. Tips for Conducting Interviews

When?	Providing a deadline for applicants to respond to job openings can make it easier to evaluate all of your applicants and offer interviews all at once. Others prefer to leave a position open until filled.
Where?	Invite candidates to visit your office for the interview. This is their chance to learn more about your company and work environment, and to meet potential coworkers. Additionally, it is a professional way to receive applicants; it allows you to select a quiet place for talking with the candidate without distractions.
How long?	Interviews generally last between 30 and 60 minutes, depending on the job requirements and the candidate's experience. Tell the candidate how long the interview will be at the beginning, and allow time to answer any questions the candidate may have.

Table 5. Tips for Conducting Interviews *(continued)*

What?	Using "Don't Create a Contract" on page 36 and the *Employment Interview Checklist*, described in Table 8 on page 38, create a script of questions to ask each applicant, and make sure other interviewing managers understand the guidelines for interviewing.
Notes?	You may take notes during the interview, but you must be very careful how you phrase your written comments, because the notes could be used in a legal claim. See "Don't Create a Contract" on page 36 for more details.

5 — Conduct Background Checks

Before selecting a new employee, do some research on your applicants. Researching your applicant's background can provide you with valuable information, and can make costly litigation far less likely. See "Negligent Hiring" on page 23 for details.

! Researching an applicant's background can, if improperly done, involve an invasion of privacy.

Remember that you are looking for information that will help you evaluate a candidate's job-related abilities. Also remember that records of a credit check, medical exam, etc., must be kept separate from the employee's regular personnel file — keep these records confidential.

You might examine each candidate's:

- Need for a work permit;
- Criminal background;
- Credit history and/or investigative consumer report;
- Drug/alcohol screening results;
- Physical health;
- References; and
- Educational background.

For economic reasons, you may wish to do some of this research post-offer, only on the lead candidate, and make your offer contingent upon satisfactory results.

Table 6. Background Checks

What	Why
Proof of legal working age or work permit	Hiring someone less than 18 years old will probably require a work permit. See “What If the Applicant Is a Minor?” on page 32.
Criminal background check	You can choose not to hire someone based on past felony convictions if you have a legitimate business purpose. Do not automatically deny employment to any applicant who has a record of criminal conviction. The decision not to hire someone on this basis should be job related. The law requires the Department of Justice to send conviction and pending arrest information to the employer and the applicant if he/she is applying for a license, employment, or volunteer position with supervisory or disciplinary power over vulnerable persons under his/her care. This includes the care of minors, the elderly, or the mentally impaired. The request for records must include the applicant’s fingerprints. If you hire an applicant who has been convicted of any of the crimes listed below, you must notify the parents of any minor who will be supervised or disciplined by the employee or volunteer. You must provide the notice at least 10 days prior to the day that the employee or volunteer begins his/her new duties or tasks. The violations that must be reported include: • Assault with intent to commit mayhem, rape, sodomy, or oral copulation; • Unlawful sexual intercourse with a minor; • Rape; • Bodily harm to a child; • Cruel or inhuman corporal punishment to a child; and • Corporal injury to another. The Department of Justice accepts only the electronic submission of fingerprints. If your organization employs or uses volunteers who care for minors, the elderly, or the mentally impaired, consult with your legal counsel about criminal history checks.

Table 6. Background Checks *(continued)*

What	Why
Credit check	If the job description demands that the employee will handle large amounts of money or be responsible for your company's finances, you may want to obtain a consumer credit report. The process requires many mandatory forms, which you can find in your online Formspack, described in detail in"Online Forms" on page 4. The process is as follows: **1.** Written disclosure — Tell the applicant, in writing, that you intend to obtain a consumer report. You can use the *Notice of Intent to Obtain Consumer Report*, described in Table 8 on page 38. **2.** Written Authorization — Obtain the authorizing signature of the applicant. You can use the *Authorization to Obtain Consumer Credit Report*, described in Table 8 on page 38. **3.** Certification to Consumer Reporting Agency — Provide the agency with written certification that disclosure has been made, authorization has been obtained, and that the information will not be used in violation of any federal or state law. You can use the *Certification to Consumer Credit Reporting Agency*, described in Table 8 on page 38. **Adverse action** is an employment decision that has a negative impact on hiring, termination, benefits, or compensation. If the information on the consumer credit report leads you to take some adverse action against the applicant, you must give the applicant written notice of the following: • Name, address, and toll-free telephone number of the agency that provided the report; • A statement that the agency did not make the adverse decision and is unable to explain why the decision was made; • A statement of the applicant's right to obtain (if requested within 60 days) a free disclosure of his/her files from the reporting agency; • A statement of the applicant's right to dispute directly with the consumer reporting agency the accuracy of any information provided by the agency; • A statement to the applicant that the decision to take adverse action was based in whole or part upon the information obtained in the consumer credit report; and • A copy of the *Summary of Your Rights Under the Fair Credit Reporting Act*, described in Table 8 on page 38. You can use the *Pre-Adverse Action Disclosure* and the *Adverse Action Notice*, described in Table 8 on page 38.

Table 6. Background Checks *(continued)*

What	Why
Investigative consumer report	Helps you discover information about an applicant's character, general reputation, personal characteristics, and mode of living, obtained through personal interviews. If you intend to obtain such a report, you are required to provide: **1.** Written disclosure — Tell the applicant, in writing, that an investigative consumer report may be obtained. The disclosure must describe the applicant's right to request additional disclosures of the nature and scope of the investigation, and must include a summary of consumer rights. **2.** Certification to the consumer reporting agency — Provide the agency with written certification that proper disclosure has been made to the applicant. **3.** Additional requested disclosure — If the applicant requests it, you must fully disclose the nature and scope of the requested investigation. The Fair Credit Reporting Act (FCRA) prohibits consumer reporting agencies from providing consumer reports that contain medical information for employment purposes or in conjunction with credit or insurance transactions, without the specific prior consent of the applicant. It is prudent to limit the scope of these investigations to specifically job-related information, since investigative reports that are not job-related may violate federal and state civil rights laws if they have a disparate impact on minority applicants. See "What Is Discrimination?" in Chapter 7, page 228 for details.

Table 6. Background Checks *(continued)*

What	Why
Drug testing	In general, drug testing is not required by law. Certain transportation employees must pass drug tests, and certain companies with state or federal contracts must maintain drug-free workplace programs. See "Where Do I Go for More Information?" on page 49 for helpful resources. If you wish to require drug testing for applicants, you should follow these guidelines: • Decide whether drug testing is required for all positions or just those with potential safety concerns. Be consistent; • Determine the hiring stage at which you will test for drugs, and what levels of what substances will be considered "passing" levels; • Obtain the applicant's signed authorization; and • Use an independent testing facility. Be aware that drug testing employees is limited by law, so if you want to do any drug testing, it needs to happen in the applicant phase. If your offer is contingent on a medical evaluation or a drug test, be sure to note this in the employment letter. The offer should be contingent on passing the exam. If an applicant refuses to take a drug test, you can refuse to hire him/her.
Medical evaluation	The position may require job-related physical fitness, such as being able to lift a certain amount of weight. You may test for necessary qualifications only, and only after you have made an offer of employment. You may not test for an individual's HIV status. If your offer is contingent on a medical evaluation or a drug test, be sure to note this in the employment letter. The offer should be contingent on passing the exam.
Reference check	Though you are not required to check your future employee's references, doing so will make your hiring decision easier. See "Negligent Hiring" on page 23. When contacting your applicant's listed references, you should stick to questions that directly relate to job performance in order to avoid liability for invasion of privacy. You may need written permission from the applicant to obtain salary information.
Education check	This is not required, but verifying an applicant's transcript and a university's accreditation can save headaches later.

Negligent Hiring

The law does not specifically obligate you to check an applicant's references and background. However, a court could hold you liable for negligent hiring if you don't investigate, and the employee commits an offense that you could have predicted had you made a reasonable effort to research that person. A reasonable effort, even if former employers are uncooperative, can protect you from negligent hiring claims.

! If you hire someone whose documented past presents an unreasonable risk of harm to others, specifically, to coworkers and customers, this is considered negligence.

> ***Example:*** If an employee with a record of violent behavior assaults someone in your office, the assaulted person may bring a suit of negligent hiring against you, alleging that you should have known about the employee's violent past and not hired the person.

6 — Make the Hiring Decision and Offer the Position

Once you've done the work of reviewing résumés and applications and interviewing candidates, it's time to make your hiring decision. Make all hiring decisions carefully. To prevent claims of unfair hiring practices:

- Be sure you have valid reasons for making the hiring decision, based on the person's:
  - Qualifications;
  - Experience;
  - Skills;
  - Knowledge; and
  - Education.
- Document the reasons why one person was selected over other candidates; and
- Review documents from hiring supervisors to ensure decisions were based on valid reasons, and that no applicant was rejected for a discriminatory reason.

How Do I Offer the Position to the Successful Applicant?

You can send an employment letter, also called an offer letter, to the applicant you've chosen that clarifies the terms of employment, such as:

- Start date;
- At-will employment status;
- Exempt or non-exempt status (see "What's the Difference Between an Exempt and a Non-exempt Employee?" on page 11);
- Wage or salary — if the employee is exempt, phrase the pay rate in terms of dollars weekly, biweekly, or monthly; if the employee is non-exempt, phrase the pay rate in terms of dollars per hour; and
- Whether or not the offer depends on the applicant passing a medical exam, drug test, or reference or background check.

If you send an offer letter, be sure that the salary for an exempt employee meets the minimum salary requirements for an employee to be exempt. See "What Is the Minimum Salary?" in Chapter 5, page 168.

You don't have to write a letter, but many employees won't want to leave their current jobs until they have something in writing confirming the new job.

Be careful that you don't create a contract in your letter, overriding employment at-will. For more information, read "Don't Create a Contract" on page 36. To see a sample letter that contains no contractual language, read the *Employment Letter*, described in Table 8 on page 38.

How Do I Handle Unsuccessful Applicants?

Although not required, you might consider sending a letter to all applicants not hired after the successful applicant has accepted the position, letting them know that they are no longer under consideration for the position. This is a courtesy to the applicant who has pursued employment with your company. You can send a standard letter to all unsuccessful applicants. To see a sample letter, read the *Letter to Applicants Not Hired*, described in Table 8 on page 38.

7 — Fill Out Paperwork

The paperwork involved with hiring a new employee is extensive. Use a *Hiring Checklist* to help you keep track of which forms/notifications you have provided and processed. This checklist is described in Table 8 on page 38.

Use the following forms throughout the hiring process:

- Applications (see "Receive Applications" on page 15);
- Forms for checking background (see "5 — Conduct Background Checks" on page 18);
- Forms for special types of workers, such as:
  - Minors. See "What If the Applicant Is a Minor?" on page 32; and
  - Independent contractors. See "How Do I Make Sure That the Individual Is Truly an Independent Contractor?" on page 31.

You can find these forms in your online Formspack, described in detail in"Online Forms" on page 4.

Fill Out or Provide These Forms on the Employee's First Day of Work

- Information about benefits and employee rights, such as:
  - Workers' Compensation (see "What Do I Need to Know About Workers' Compensation?" in Chapter 4, page 127);
  - State Disability Insurance (see "What Do I Need to Know About SDI?" in Chapter 4, page 122);
  - COBRA and Cal-COBRA rights notifications;
  - *Paid Family Leave* (see "What Do I Need to Know About Paid Family Leave?" in Chapter 4, page 123);
  - *HIPAA Questionnaire*; and
  - Sexual Harassment forms.
- Safety information, such as:
  - *Emergency Information* form; and
  - *Individual Employee Training Documentation – Initial Safety Training* (see Table 64 in Chapter 6, page 219).
- Government forms, such as:
  - *W-4 Form – Employee's Withholding Allowance Certificate*; and
  - *Report of New Employee(s) (Form DE 34).*
- Personnel policy forms, such as:

- *Confidentiality Agreement*; and
- *Property Return Agreement.*

You can find these forms in your online Formspack, described in detail in "Online Forms" on page 4, or CalBizCentral's ***Required Notices Kit***.

Verify the Employee's Authorization to Work

All new workers must fill out their portion of the *I-9 Form* and provide the documents listed on the back of the *I-9 Form* (described in Table 8 on page 38) within three business days of beginning work.

You may not require more or different identity and work authorization documents than specified by the USCIS.

If the employee doesn't have the documentation, you may still hire him/her. However, he/she must give you:

- A receipt demonstrating that he/she has applied for the required documents, within three days after he/she begins work; and
- The actual documents, within 90 days after he/she begins work.

If the employee works for you for less than three business days, Section 2 of the I-9 Form must be completed at the time employment begins. For a non-citizen, make sure you re-verify expiring work authorization documents before the expiration date noted in Section 1 of the *I-9 Form*. For more information about hiring non-U.S. citizens, see "What If the Applicant Is Not a U.S. Citizen?" on page 34.

Regulations Issued for Electronic I-9 Retention

In 2006, the Department of Homeland Security (DHS) adopted an interim rule establishing standards for electronic signatures and the electronic retention of the *Form I-9*.

This interim rule permits employers and employees to complete, sign, and employers to store I-9 Forms electronically, and to electronically scan and store the I-9, as long as certain performance standards, as set forth in the interim rule for the electronic filing system, are met. The interim rule provides a reasonable set of standards for creating a trustworthy system for Form I-9 completion and storage. The standards are technology neutral, and allow businesses the flexibility to keep records in a manner consistent with other business processes. They also provide DHS investigators with a framework for inspecting the records and assessing their trustworthiness.

The interim rule sets standards for electronic retention of Form I-9. The rule does not limit employers to using one system for the storage of Form I-9 electronically, nor does it identify one method for acceptable electronic signatures. Electronic signatures can be accomplished using various technologies including, but not limited to, electronic signature pads, Personal Identification Numbers (PIN), biometrics, and "click to accept'" dialog boxes. Moreover, as far as DHS can determine at this time, "off the shelf'" computer programs and commercial automated data processing systems in use comply with the standards required by this rule.

An employer that is complying with the current record keeping and retention requirements is not required to take any additional or different action to comply with the revised rules; the revised rules simply offer an additional option.

Whether filled out manually or electronically, an employer representative must still physically examine required identification and work eligibility documentation.

Verify That Social Security Numbers and Names Match

The Social Security Administration (SSA) has created an online program called the Social Security Number Verification System (SSNVS). The only purpose of the SSNVS is to verify that Social Security numbers and names that employers have been provided match and are correct for purposes of completing W-2 forms. An employer can verify up to 10 names and Social Security Numbers and receive immediate results. Additionally, an employer can upload up to 250,000 names and Social Security numbers into the SSA database and receive results the next business day.

The registration and use of the SSNVS is free; you can register through the SSA's Business Services online registration at ***www.socialsecurity.gov/bso/bsowelcome.htm***. SSNVS requires Internet access, a browser with cookies enabled, and Adobe Acrobat Reader©.

Implement and use this service in a non-discriminatory manner. Employers should specify, through policy, what classifications of employees will be submitted to the SSNVS system. The SSA emphasizes that such verifications can only occur after an employee has been hired and that the use of SSNVS is applied to employees consistently.

What If the Documents I'm Shown Aren't Valid?

You are not liable for accepting documents that appear reasonably authentic, unless you know or have reason to know that the documents are false. In fact, you may not refuse to honor documents that appear valid on their face.

For *I-9* purposes, new employees may use one item from List A, or one item from List B and one item from List C of the *I-9 Form*. For example, the individual who uses a California driver's license to establish identity must also present a valid document that establishes his/her right to work in the United States.

New for 2008 The I-9 Form was revised in 2007. This version is available in your online Formspack. You must use the 06/05/07 version of the I-9 for any employee hired after November 7, 2007. The use of any other *I-9 Form* will result in fines.

On the 2007 form, five documents have been removed from List A of the List of Acceptable Documents:

- Certificate of U.S. Citizenship (Form N-560 or N-561)
- Certificate of Naturalization (Form N-550 or N-570)
- Alien Registration Receipt Card (I-151)
- Unexpired Reentry Permit (Form I-327)
- Unexpired Refugee Travel Document (Form I-571)

The Unexpired Employment Authorization Document (I-766) document was added to List A of the List of Acceptable Documents.

All Employment Authorization Documents with photographs have been consolidated as one item on List A:

I-688, I-688A, I-688B, I-766

Instructions for Section 1 of the *I-9 Form* now indicate that the employee is not obliged to provide his or her Social Security number in Section 1 of the I-9, unless he or she is employed by an employer who participates in E-Verify.

E-Verify is an Internet-based system operated by the Department of Homeland Security (DHS), in partnership with the Social Security Administration. It allows employers to electronically verify the employment eligibility of newly hired employees. To find out more, the DHS internet address is ***www.dhs.gov/ximgtn/programs/gc_1185221678150.shtm***.

Employers may now sign and retain Forms I-9 electronically. See "Electronic I-9 Retention" above.

Do not file Form I-9 with U.S. Immigrations and Customs Enforcement (ICE) or USCIS. You must keep the I-9 for either:

- Three years after the date of hire; or
- One year after employment is terminated, whichever is later. The form must be available for inspection by authorized U.S. Government officials (e.g., ICE, Department of Labor).

The Spanish version of *Form I-9* may be filled out by employers and employees in Puerto Rico ONLY. Spanish-speaking employers and employees in the 50 states and other U.S. territories may print this for their reference, but may only complete the form in English to meet employment eligibility verification requirements.Any documents used for I-9 purposes that must be "unexpired" will require you to reconfirm the employee's ability to work in the U.S. once the document expires. You should note when the document is to expire and several months prior to the expiration date, remind your employee that he/she will need to provide new I-9 documentation. The employee does not have to provide the same document again. He/she may provide any document from List A or C that establishes the employee's right to work in the U.S.

8 — Welcome Your New Employees

Your new employee's first day of work is the ideal point in the employment relationship to make sure that your new employee:

- Understands your policies and work rules;
- Is informed of his/her legal rights and obligations; and
- Receives the necessary training to do the job safely and efficiently.

All training and orientation should be documented. Proper records can help protect you from lawsuits. Use the *Employee Orientation* checklist, described in Table 8 on page 38, and keep it in the employee's personnel file.

You might be tempted to designate the first few weeks of work as a "probationary" period, but this could be understood as a promise that, when the probationary period is over, the employee will have permanent status. Calling this time an introductory period is acceptable and won't compromise the idea of at-will employment.

Employee Orientation

Verify that the employee:

- Fills out and returns the required forms (see Table 8 on page 38);
- Takes a tour of the building/facilities and learns the location of the exits;
- Meets managers and other employees;
- Understands information on company processes and resources;
- Receives an employee handbook (see "How Do I Create an Employee Handbook?" in Chapter 3, page 58) and returns a signed *Confirmation of Receipt* (see Table 13 in Chapter 3, page 89);
- Receives a copy of all required pamphlets, including:
  - *Sexual Harassment Information Sheets*;
  - *Workers' Compensation Rights and Benefits*; and
  - *Paid Family Leave*.
- Receives a copy of the company's IIPP (see "Injury and Illness Prevention Program" in Chapter 6, page 199); and
- Gets a chance to ask questions about anything he/she does not completely understand.

You can find these forms in your online Formspack, described in detail in "Online Forms" on page 4.

Employee Training

You must provide all of your employees with the necessary knowledge and training to complete their tasks safely. If an employee gets hurt because you did not take the time to make sure that he/she understood how to operate a machine properly, you will be liable. See "How Should I Cover Safety Training?" in Chapter 6, page 209.

If you have 50 or more employees, you must provide at least two hours of sexual harassment training to all supervisory employees who are employed as of July 1, 2005. After this date, all new supervisory employees must receive training within six months of assuming supervisory positions. For more information, see "Provide Training" in Chapter 7, page 241.

What If I Am Using an Independent Contractor?

Engaging an independent contractor can offer significant advantages over hiring an employee. In an independent contractor relationship, business owners do not have to:

- Provide certain benefits, such as workers' compensation and unemployment insurance;
- Meet overtime and minimum wage obligations; and
- Withhold income taxes from payments.

Be careful! It is not enough that the two parties agree to an independent contractor relationship. You can only classify as an independent contractor an individual who meets the requirements for one.

If you misclassify an employee as an independent contractor, you might have to:

- Pay huge fines imposed by the IRS and the EDD; and
- Pay retroactive employee benefits, such as health insurance, vacations, and retirement plans.

How Do I Make Sure That the Individual Is Truly an Independent Contractor?

Various state and federal agencies have their own tests for whether an individual is an independent contractor. These tests cover concepts that have been used in California for several years.

Be careful in making your decision. Each case is unique, and the penalties for making a mistake can be costly. We recommend you consult your legal counsel to help you determine an individual's status.

Independent Contractor Test

The California Common Law and the "Balancing" tests measure a worker's right to control when, how, and where work is performed. Factors include:

- The employer:
  - Has the right to terminate the contract; and
  - Pays by job and not by time.
- Both parties believe they are creating an independent contractor relationship;
- The worker:

- Engages in a distinct occupational business;
- Possesses significant skills or education required for the particular occupation;
- Supplies the instruments and tools for performing the work;
- Performs services over a short or specified period of time;
- Has opportunity for profit or loss, depending upon his/her own managerial skills; and
- Employs additional help at his/her own expense.

- The work:
  - Usually occurs under the employer's general direction, by a specialist, without supervision; and
  - Is not part of the employer's regular business.

You can also use the *Employment Determination Guide (Form DE 38)* to help you determine if the worker is an independent contractor. This form is described in Table 8 on page 38.

What Special Forms Do I Need for Independent Contractors?

Each independent contractor you hire needs to sign a contract, approved by your legal counsel, that includes the scope of work and the terms of the agreement.

You must also report independent contractors to the EDD's New Employee Registry within 20 days of the start-of-work date. Use the *Report of Independent Contractor(s) (Form DE 542)*, described in Table 8 on page 38, and in your online Formspack, described in detail in"Online Forms" on page 4.

What If the Applicant Is a Minor?

A **minor** is any person under the age of 18 who is required to attend school, or any person under the age of six.

When you employ a minor, you must comply with child labor laws designed to help young people acquire work experience and income, while safeguarding their scholastic advancement and physical well-being. You can use the *Checklist for Employing Minors* as a guide, described in Table 8 on page 38.

To employ a minor, you must have a work permit on file year-round, even when school is not in session. You must have the permit on file the day the minor begins work.

A **work permit** sets limits on the maximum number of days and hours of work as well as the spread of hours allowed for that minor. It may also contain limitations on other aspects of the minor's work.

This rule applies to any minor, even:

- High school dropouts;
- Emancipated minors (minors who declare independence from their parents for IRS purposes), although they can apply for one without their parent's permission;
- Minors who are not state residents, such as children who live out of state with one parent during the school year and visit the other parent in California during the summer; and
- Children who work for their parents.

What Circumstances Don't Require a Work Permit?

Direct all questions regarding the need for work permits to the minor's school district (or the school district in which the minor would go to school, if he/she does not currently attend).

You do not need a work permit for minors who:

- Have graduated from high school (In certain hazardous occupations, however, even these minors need a work permit, unless they have completed a certificate program for that industry.);
- Work irregularly at odd jobs, such as yard work and babysitting in private homes;
- Participate in any horseback riding exhibition, contest, or event;
- Are self-employed;
- Are at least 14 years of age and deliver newspapers to consumers; and
- Work for a parent or guardian in connection with property he/she owns, operates, or controls for:
  - Agriculture;
  - Horticulture;
  - Viticulture; and

- Domestic labor.

How Do I Obtain a Work Permit?

1. Complete a *Statement of Intent to Employ Minor and Request for Work Permit (Form B1-1),* described in Table 8 on page 38. The minor's supervisor and parent/ guardian must both sign the form.

2. File Form B1-1 with the minor's school district.

3. The minor's school district completes and issues a *Permit to Employ and Work (Form B1-4),* described in Table 8 on page 38.

Keep the work permit on file the entire length of employment.

For more information on the handling of these forms, see Table 8 on page 38.

What If the Applicant Is Not a U.S. Citizen?

There is nothing wrong with hiring a non-U.S. citizen. However, you may not knowingly hire, contract for labor, recruit, retain, or refer for a fee for employment, an unauthorized alien. If you do, you could face progressive fines from $250 up to $10,000 per alien. Repeat offenders can face up to six months in jail for each violation.

How Do I Protect Myself?

You must verify that every person you hire is either:

- A U.S. citizen; or
- Authorized to work in the U.S.

See "Verify the Employee's Authorization to Work" on page 26 for instructions on the verification process.

If you later discover that the employee is an unauthorized alien, you may not continue to employ him/her.

What Other Things Should I Be Careful of When Employing Aliens?

You may not:

- Adopt an English-only policy; or
- Discriminate against any employee who has valid documents of eligibility, on the basis of:
  - National origin;
  - Citizenship status; or
  - Future expiration date of verifying documents.

An **English-only policy** prohibits the use of other languages in the workplace. It is illegal in California unless certain conditions are met, including business necessity and employee notice.

The Hitches, Glitches, and Pitfalls of Hiring Employees

Understanding the potential for lawsuits will help you avoid them. The most important thing you can do is watch your language to avoid:

- Creating a contract that may lead to a wrongful termination lawsuit at the end of the employment relationship; and
- Making an employment decision or acting in any way that may lead to a claim of discrimination.

See "How Can I Avoid a Discrimination/Harassment Claim?" in Chapter 7, page 240 for guidelines on non-discriminatory employment decisions.

Don't Create a Contract

California is an at-will employment state. This means that, as long as you don't break a law or violate a specified public policy, you can hire or terminate an employee whenever you want, and workers can accept or leave employment whenever they want.

In every employment relationship there is an implied covenant requiring you to exercise good faith and fair dealing in the employment relationship. An employment contract can have express limitations on when, and under what circumstances, you can terminate the relationship.

Essentially, **good faith and fair dealing** means that you should make decisions on a fair basis, and treat in like manner employees who are similarly situated.

A contract may override the presumption of at-will employment because it usually creates a promise that you will only terminate an employee for just cause.

Just cause means a fair and honest cause or reason, acted on in good faith by the employer.

Contracts can be written, oral, or implied.

Table 7. Types of Contracts

What kind?	What about it?
Written contracts are the most obvious. An employee with a written and signed contract has the right to have that contract honored.	Written contracts can work to your benefit if your contract states that your right to discharge is unrestricted and that the employment is at-will. You should also consider having these provisions: • Specify the duration of the contract and the time period required for notice for termination of the contract; • State that the contract can be renewed at the option of the company; and • State that the written document constitutes the entire agreement, that no representations or promises other than those documented can be relied upon, and that it can be modified only in writing signed by a corporate officer. The main disadvantages of written contracts are that they are less flexible and that any inadvertent omissions or ambiguities will be construed against you rather than the employee.
Oral contracts, based on conversations between employer and employee, are not as obvious, but are just as binding as signed written contracts.	Watch what you say to an employee in every phase of the employment relationship. Promises like, "as long as you do a good job, you will have a job here," create oral contracts. See "Don't Create a Contract" on page 36 for details.
Implied contracts are based upon the length of employment and indicators of job security that an employee has received.	The courts determine whether an implied contract exists on a case-by-case basis. The best defense against an implied contract claim is a signed at-will agreement. You should also have an express at-will employment policy in your employee handbook. See Table 11 in Chapter 3, page 61.

Be Aware of the Laws That Apply

Though employment in California is considered at-will, federal and state laws require that you treat all qualified candidates equally. You cannot make hiring decisions based (in whole or in part) on an applicant's race, gender, nationality, sexuality, marital status, religion, disabilities, medical condition, age, union activity, past bankruptcy, or status as an authorized immigrant or a veteran. California's laws are stricter than the federal laws. The definition of disability is broader, and more classes are included as protected.

If an aggrieved person files a discrimination lawsuit, you will have to be able to prove that you had legitimate reasons for not hiring that individual. This might be tougher than it sounds. Any documents or notes on documents will be used either to defend you or to accuse you. Only constant vigilance and consistent behavior will protect you!

See "How Can I Avoid a Discrimination/Harassment Claim?" in Chapter 7, page 240 for more details.

What Forms and Checklists Do I Use to Hire Employees?

The following tables describe required and recommended forms associated with the hiring process.

You can find these forms in your online Formspack, described in detail in"Online Forms" on page 4.

Table 8. Required Forms and Checklists

Notification/ Form	What do I use it for?	When do I use it?	Who fills it out?	Where does it go?
Adverse Action Notice	To take adverse action (such as not hiring an applicant or terminating an employee) based on a credit report you have obtained.	When you know you are taking adverse action based on information in the credit report (see "5 — Conduct Background Checks" on page 18).	You do.	Give to employee. Keep a copy in a private file away from personnel file. Restrict access to the form to a "need to know" basis.
Authorization to Obtain Consumer Credit Report	To obtain a credit report of any type.	Before you obtain the report (see "5 — Conduct Background Checks" on page 18).	You and the employee or applicant fill out respective sections of the form.	Keep in personnel file. Restrict access to the form to a "need to know" basis.

Table 8. Required Forms and Checklists *(continued)*

Notification/ Form	What do I use it for?	When do I use it?	Who fills it out?	Where does it go?
Checklist for Employing Minors	Tracking legal issues to consider when hiring a minor.	During the recruiting and hiring processes.	You do.	Keep the checklist in the minor's personnel file.
Confidentiality Agreement	Obtaining employee acknowledgement that there is information necessary for his/her job that he/she may not disclose.	At the time of hire or change in duties of an employee.	You prepare the agreement and have it reviewed by an attorney. Employee signs the agreement.	The original agreement should go in the employee's personnel record. Provide the employee a copy.
Emergency Information	Recording important medical information and contacts in case of an emergency.	At the time of hire. Keep the form updated throughout employment.	Employee	Keep emergency information readily accessible. You may keep the forms in your personnel records, but you might want to use a separate binder for quicker access.
Emergency Information - Spanish **New for 2008**	Recording important medical information and contacts in case of an emergency for employees whose primary language is Spanish.	At the time of hire. Keep the form updated throughout employment.	Employee	Keep emergency information readily accessible. You may keep the forms in your personnel records, but you might want to use a separate binder for quicker access.
Employee Orientation	Tracking completed orientation tasks.	In the first weeks of employment.	Manager	Keep in the employee's personnel file.

Table 8. Required Forms and Checklists *(continued)*

Notification/ Form	What do I use it for?	When do I use it?	Who fills it out?	Where does it go?
Employment Application – Short Form	Gathering key work history information from an applicant, obtaining authorization to check references and background, and certification that all information is truthful.	During the recruiting process.	Applicant	Keep in the employee's personnel file, if the applicant is hired. If you don't hire the applicant, keep the paperwork for two years.
Employment Determination Guide (Form DE 38)	Determining employee versus independent contractor status.	During the hiring process.	You do.	Keep in the applicant's file, or if the applicant is hired, in the personnel file.
Employment Interview Checklist	Listing which questions to ask applicants during an interview.	During the applicant's interview.	Interviewer	Keep in the employee's personnel file, if hired. If you don't hire the applicant, keep the paperwork for two years.
Employment Letter	Informing an applicant that he or she has been selected for employment.	When the employment decision has been made.	You do.	Mail to the applicant. Keep a copy in the employee's personnel file.
Exempt Analysis Worksheet – Administrative Exemption	Determining whether an employee's duties meet the requirements for exempt status.	During the hiring process.	You do.	Keep in the employee's personnel file.

Table 8. Required Forms and Checklists *(continued)*

Notification/ Form	What do I use it for?	When do I use it?	Who fills it out?	Where does it go?
Exempt Analysis Worksheet – Computer Professional Exemption	Determining whether an employee's duties meet the requirements for exempt status.	During the hiring process.	You do.	Keep in the employee's personnel file.
Exempt Analysis Worksheet – Executive/Managerial Exemption	Determining whether an employee's duties meet the requirements for exempt status.	During the hiring process.	You do.	Keep in the employee's personnel file.
Exempt Analysis Worksheet – Professional Exemption	Determining whether an employee's duties meet the requirements for exempt status.	During the hiring process.	You do.	Keep in the employee's personnel file.
Exempt Analysis Worksheet – Salesperson Exemption	Determining whether an employee's duties meet the requirements for exempt status.	During the hiring process.	You do.	Keep in the employee's personnel file.
Guide for Pre-Employment Inquiries	Outlining what you can and can't ask during the recruiting process.	During the recruiting process.	No filling out needed.	Use as a reference.
Hiring Checklist	Tracking completion of recommended and required hiring procedures and forms.	During the recruiting and hiring process.	Manager or other person in charge of hiring employees.	Keep in the employee's personnel file.

Table 8. Required Forms and Checklists *(continued)*

Notification/ Form	What do I use it for?	When do I use it?	Who fills it out?	Where does it go?
Letter to Applicants Not Hired	Informing an applicant that he or she has not been selected for employment.	When the employment decision has been made.	You do.	Mail to the applicant. You should keep a list of the applicants to whom the letter is mailed.
Pre-Hire Checklist	Organizing the process of finding and preparing to hire an employee.	During the recruiting process.	You do.	Keep the checklist in the employee's personnel file, if the applicant is hired.
Property Return Agreement	Obtaining employee acknowledge that he/she has received property of yours (tools, uniforms, etc.) and agrees to return the property.	When your property is issued to the employee.	Employee signs the form.	Keep the original agreement in your personnel records.
Certification to Consumer Credit Reporting Agency	To obtain a credit report of any type.	Before you obtain the report (see "5 — Conduct Background Checks" on page 18).	You do	Send form to the agency creating the report. Keep in personnel file. Restrict access to the form to a "need to know" basis.

Table 8. Required Forms and Checklists *(continued)*

Notification/ Form	What do I use it for?	When do I use it?	Who fills it out?	Where does it go?
Direct Deposit Authorization - English **New for 2008**	To get permission from employees to deposit paychecks directly into their bank account instead of receiving a paper check.	As part of the hiring process or whenever an employee requests direct deposit.	The employee.	Keep in personnel and/or payroll file (if separate).
Direct Deposit Authorization - Spanish **New for 2008**	To get permission from employees whose primary language is Spanish to deposit paychecks directly into their bank account instead of receiving a paper check.	As part of the hiring process or whenever an employee requests direct deposit.	The employee.	Keep in personnel and/or payroll file (if separate).
HIPAA Questionnaire	To respond to a *Certificate of Group Health Plan Coverage* (a HIPAA Certificate) from a new group health plan participant.	On the day the employee enrolls for the benefit.	Prior employer or plan administrator fills out Question 6. Current employer or plan administrator fills out the rest of the form.	Send the *HIPAA Questionnaire* to the prior employer or plan administrator. Keep a copy of the questionnaire in your personnel records.

Table 8. Required Forms and Checklists *(continued)*

Notification/ Form	What do I use it for?	When do I use it?	Who fills it out?	Where does it go?
I-9 Form **New for 2008**	To verify the immigration status of **all** employees.	Section 1: at the time of hire. Section 2: within three business days after the employee's first day of work. Section 3: on or before the expiration date in Section 1.	Section 1: employee fills out. Section 2: you fill out. Section 3: you fill out if necessary for updating or reverifying.	Keep the forms for all employees in a common file rather than separate personnel records.
General Notice of COBRA Continuation Coverage Rights (California Employees)	To inform California employees of their rights to continuation of health care coverage. Applies only to employers with 20 or more employees, and only to employees in California.	On the day the employee enrolls for the benefit.	No filling out needed.	Include this notice in the group health plan's Summary Plan Description. Send a copy of the notice to the spouse of a married employee, preferably by registered mail. Keep a record of the mailing and/or distribution at hire of this notice to both employee and spouse on the *Hiring Checklist*.

Table 8. Required Forms and Checklists *(continued)*

Notification/ Form	What do I use it for?	When do I use it?	Who fills it out?	Where does it go?
General Notice of COBRA Continuation Coverage Rights (Outside California)	To inform employees outside California of their rights to continuation of health care coverage. Applies only to employers with 20 or more employees, and only to employees outside California.	On the day the employee enrolls for the benefit.	No filling out needed.	Include this notice in the group health plan's Summary Plan Description. Send a copy of the notice to the spouse of a married employee, preferably by registered mail. Keep a record of the mailing and/or distribution at hire of this notice to both employee and spouse on the *Hiring Checklist*.
Notice of Intent to Obtain Consumer Report	To obtain a credit report of any type.	Before you obtain the report (see "5 — Conduct Background Checks" on page 18).	You do.	Keep in personnel file. Restrict access to the form to a "need to know" basis.
Paid Family Leave pamphlet	To provide notice to employees of their rights to paid family leave benefits.	Give it to all new employees and any employees taking leave for a covered reason.	No filling out needed.	Give it to employees and make sure they understand its contents.

Table 8. Required Forms and Checklists *(continued)*

Notification/ Form	What do I use it for?	When do I use it?	Who fills it out?	Where does it go?
Pre-Adverse Action Disclosure	To notify an employee or potential employer of the possibility of adverse action.	When you know you are taking adverse action based on information in the credit report (see "5 — Conduct Background Checks" on page 18).	You do.	Give to employee. Keep a copy in a private file away from personnel file. Restrict access to the form to a "need to know" basis.
Permit to Employ and Work (Form B1-4)	To obtain permission to employ a minor.	Before the minor begins working [and after the *Statement of Intent to Employ Minor and Request for Work Permit (Form B1-1)*] has been approved; see the form's description following in this table).	Minor's school district fills out and issues the permit.	Keep form (permit) on file as long as the minor is employed. Keep it in your personnel records or in a common binder for all minor employees.
Recruiting Checklist **New for 2008**	Use this checklist to guide you through the recruiting process for new and existing positions.	When you need to advertise and recruit for a new position.	You do.	In your files.

Table 8. Required Forms and Checklists *(continued)*

Notification/ Form	What do I use it for?	When do I use it?	Who fills it out?	Where does it go?
Report of Independent Contractor(s) (Form DE 542)	All new independent contractors. The District Attorney uses the information in this form to locate parents who owe child support funds.	As soon as possible after signing the contract.	You do.	Mail or fax the form to: Employment Development Department P.O. Box 997350 MIC 99 Sacramento, CA 95899-7350 Fax: (916) 255-3211
Report of New Employee(s) (Form DE 34)	All new employees. Permits registered domestic partners to file joint state income tax and have their earnings treated as community property on par with married couples. The District Attorney uses the information in this form to locate parents who owe child support funds.	Within 20 days of hire.	You do.	Mail or fax the form to: Employment Development Department P.O. Box 997016, MIC 23 West Sacramento, CA 95799-7016 Fax: (916) 255-0951
Sexual Harassment Information Sheets	This form describes the problem and the penalties of sexual harassment.	Whenever you hire a new employee, or engage an independent contractor, etc.	No filling out needed.	Give it to your workers and make sure they understand its contents.

Table 8. Required Forms and Checklists *(continued)*

Notification/ Form	What do I use it for?	When do I use it?	Who fills it out?	Where does it go?
Statement of Intent to Employ Minor and Request for Work Permit (Form B1-1)	To obtain permission to employ a minor. Be sure to finish the permit process with the *Permit to Employ and Work (Form B1-4)*, supplied by the minor's school.	Before the minor begins working.	Each completes the appropriate part: • Minor; • Employer; • Parent; and • School.	File it with the minor's school district. Keep a copy in your personnel records.
Summary of Your Rights Under the Fair Credit Reporting Act	To obtain a credit report of any type.	When you give the employee a copy of the credit report.	No filling out needed.	Give it to applicant.
W-4 Form – Employee's Withholding Allowance Certificate	All employees.	Before employee's first pay date.	Employee	Keep the form in the employee's personnel record. If you sent the original to payroll, keep a copy of the form.
Workers' Compensation Rights and Benefits pamphlet	To provide notice to employees of their right to workers' compensation benefits should they sustain an on-the-job injury.	Give it to all new employees at hire and again to any employee who is injured at work.	Employee fills out the *Personal Physician or Personal Chiropractor Predesignation Form*, then gives it to his/her physician to sign, accepting the predesignation; the rest is informational.	Put the predesignation form in the employee's regular personnel file and send a copy to your contact at your insurer or claims administrator. The employee keeps the rest of the brochure for reference.

Where Do I Go for More Information?

CalBizCentral and the federal and state governments have a variety of resources to help you hire employees in compliance with the law.

Table 9. Additional Resources

For information on	Check out these resources
General	From CalBizCentral: • The ***2008 California Labor Law Digest***, the most comprehensive, California-specific resource to help employers comply with complex federal and state labor laws and regulations; • ***http://www.calbizcentral.com***; and • ***http://www.hrcalifornia.com***.

Table 9. Additional Resources *(continued)*

For information on	Check out these resources
Equal opportunity	The Equal Employment Opportunity Commission (EEOC) has prepared guidelines for the types of disability-related pre-employment questions that you may and may not ask of a job applicant under the ADA. The guidelines also address the effect of the ADA on medical examinations given to applicants and employees. Enforcement Guidelines at ***http://www.eeoc.gov/policy/guidance.html*** Or, you can request publications at no cost to you, including posters, fact sheets, manuals, pamphlets, and enforcement guidelines. For a list of EEOC publications, or to order publications, write, call, or fax: U.S. Equal Employment Opportunity Commission Publications Distribution Center P.O. Box 12549 Cincinnati, Ohio 45212-0549 Toll-free: 1-800-669-3362 TTY: 1-800-800-3302 FAX: 513-489-8692 The Department of Fair Employment and Housing (DFEH) also has informational material on discrimination in employment. Its reach is generally much broader in California than that of the EEOC. Department of Fair Employment and Housing, Sacramento District Office 2000 O Street, Suite 120 Sacramento, CA 95814-5212 Telephone: 916 445-5523 Toll-free: 800 884-1684 *Disability Under the Fair Employment & Housing Act: What you should know about the law (DFEH-208 DH)* at ***http://www.dfeh.ca.gov/Publications/Disability%20Handbook%204-8-02.pdf***
Consumer reporting agencies	Federal Trade Commission Consumer Response Center 600 Pennsylvania Ave, NW Room H-130 Washington, DC 20580 (202) 382-4357 ***http://www.ftc.gov*** *Using Consumer Reports: What Employers Need to Know* at ***http://www.ftc.gov/bcp/conline/pubs/buspubs/credempl.htm***

Table 9. Additional Resources *(continued)*

For information on	Check out these resources
Immigration	The USCIS has established a 24-hour toll-free hotline to provide information regarding the IRCA. Call (800) 255-8155 or (800) 362-2735 (hearing impaired). ***http://uscis.gov/graphics/index.htm*** Handbook for Employers at ***http://uscis.gov/graphics/lawsregs/handbook/hand_emp.pdf***
Workers' compensation	California Workers' Compensation Institute 1111 Broadway, Suite 2350 Oakland, CA 94607 Telephone: (510) 251-9470 FAX: (510) 251-9485 ***http://www.cwci.org***
Fingerprinting Information	California Department of Justice ***http://caag.state.ca.us/fingerprints/index.htm***

CalBizCentral also provides many ongoing and comprehensive educational opportunities for small business owners, HR beginners, and experienced HR professionals alike. These include online sexual harassment training, videos, and special HR seminars. For more information, please visit our Web site at ***http://www.calbizcentral.com***.

Chapter 3

Developing Policies

Every company has policies. You have particular ways of doing things and rules about what employees can and cannot do at work. However, policies that are informal and inconsistent can create potential for big problems later. Developing carefully considered polices and communicating them clearly to your workers leads to effective workforce management and helps avoid lawsuits.

An employee handbook is the best tool for communicating company policy. If you don't currently have a handbook, look at the sample *Employee Handbook* in your online Formspack. You can quickly fill in the blanks and use this as a handbook for your employees; it contains the minimum recommended language.

If you already have a handbook, the information in this chapter will help you make it a strong legal document that will protect your interests and your employees'.

To understand the importance of creating and communicating your company's policies, or if you don't know what the law requires you to tell your employees, read on!

In this chapter, you can find answers to questions about:

- Basic employment policies and practices;
- Creating an employee handbook;
- Keeping employee records; and
- Much more!

Minimum Compliance Elements

1. Hang your *Employer Poster* (available from ***www.calbizcentral.com***), which includes mandatory postings that all employees must be able to see.

2. Adapt the sample *Employee Handbook* to fit your company's needs, and follow the policies consistently for every employee (see Table 13 on page 89).

3. Give each employee a copy of your handbook.

4. Get a signed *Confirmation of Receipt* from each employee, indicating that he or she has read the handbook (see Table 13 on page 89).

The Basics of Developing Policies

This chapter will help you get the most out of your personnel policies. Only a few written policies are required by law, but writing down all of your policies and distributing them to your employees in the form of a handbook is a good practice.

What Information *Must* I Provide to Employees?

State and federal laws require you to:

- Post information in public areas in a language your employees can understand. The *Employer Poster* (located in the ***Required Notices Kit*** associated with this product) includes all the basic required information:
  - Wages — the minimum wage, pay dates, and where to pick up paychecks;
  - Safety — hazardous material information, emergency contact information, and notices of any violations or inspections for violations; and
  - Discrimination — equal employment opportunity (EEO) statements, unlawful harassment notices, and your company's sexual harassment policy.

  You can order additional posters in English and Spanish from CalBizCentral at ***http://www.calbizcentral.com***.

- Give employees certain notices and brochures when you want to hire someone. These include:
  - *Workers' Compensation Rights and Benefits* pamphlet;
  - *Paid Family Leave* pamphlet; and

  - *Sexual Harassment Information Sheets.*
- Notify employees of their legal rights and entitlements, such as:
  - *General Notice of COBRA Continuation Coverage Rights (California Employees)* or *General Notice of COBRA Continuation Coverage Rights (Outside California)*;
  - *State Disability Insurance Provisions*; and
  - *For Your Benefit, California's Program for the Unemployed.*

For a comprehensive list of these notices, see the "Forms and Checklists" tables in Chapter 2, "Hiring Employees"; Chapter 7, "Preventing Discrimination and Harassment"; and Chapter 8, "Ending the Employment Relationship."

What Information *Should* I Provide to Employees?

If your company has a certain policy or benefit that is governed by legal requirements, you may need to communicate these requirements to avoid misunderstandings and potential lawsuits.

> ***Example:*** Paid vacation is not a legal mandate, but if you provide it, you must follow controlling legal requirements, and you should clearly communicate your vacation policy to any employee affected by it.

Why Should I Establish and Write Down Company Policies?

You may not realize the need for formal and comprehensive policies and procedures until you encounter an unanticipated problem. Don't wait until you find yourself in a lawsuit!

Properly conceived, written, and communicated policies can help you:

- Comply with complex federal and state regulations;
- Ensure fair and consistent treatment of employees;
- Avoid misunderstandings that could potentially lead to lawsuits;
- Orient new employees;
- Educate supervisors and managers; and
- Establish legal protections.

Many small- and medium-sized companies find effective workforce management challenging. If your company doesn't have an experienced personnel administrator, you can especially benefit from written policies.

Are There Any Special Circumstances I Should Be Aware of?

Written policies are legal documents, and you should write them with precision. Some circumstances merit special treatment in written policies.

Table 10. Special Circumstances

Changing laws	Employment laws change over time; your policies should too. Review and revise your policies accordingly.
Specialized industries	The policies recommended in this chapter cover the most commonly encountered subjects. Your company may need to develop additional policies based on its unique characteristics, such as including rules about child/teacher ratios for a preschool or waste handling guidelines for a medical office. Check with your trade association to see what resources are available.
Government contractors	Government contractors must comply with a multitude of federal and state laws and regulations, such as strict drug-free workplace rules and affirmative action obligations. If you are a government contractor, consult with legal counsel for assistance in drafting appropriate policies and procedures.
Local ordinances	Cities and counties sometimes legislate in traditional employment practice areas, such as domestic partner benefits and "living wage" ordinances. Consult with legal counsel to determine whether additional local mandates impact your employment policies.
Unionized workers	Unionized employers may have a duty to negotiate before implementing written policies. If you are a unionized employer, regardless of whether the specific policies cover unionized employees, consult a competent labor relations attorney.

How Can I Communicate Company Policies?

You can use a variety of methods to communicate company policies to managers, supervisors, and employees:

- Along with the notices and posters required by law, you can post your company policies in a place where employees have access to them;
- Conduct training sessions with written materials. You can go over the policy point by point, answering any questions as they come up;
- Send written communication to all employees in at least one of the following methods:
  - Sending policies in an email;
  - Mailing them to the employee's home address;
  - Including them in paychecks;
  - Hand delivering; and
  - Putting them in employee mail boxes.
- Draft and distribute an employee handbook. An employee handbook, sometimes called an employee manual, combines your policies in one document and provides employees with an overview of your:
  - Personnel policies;
  - Work rules;
  - Standards of performance; and
  - Benefits.

  You can also explain operational functions, such as:
  - Dealing with customers;
  - Production methods; and
  - Health, safety, and housekeeping practices.
- Consider having a special manual for supervisors and managers that explains in greater detail personnel procedures that the average employee doesn't need to know.

How Do I Create an Employee Handbook?

To prepare an effective handbook, you need to understand your current policies (both written and oral), past practices, and anticipated future needs. Remember that, as a legal document, your handbook must adapt to the ever-changing needs of your company and the laws that govern employment practices. You can find a sample of this form in your online Formspack, described in detail in "Online Forms" on page 4.

1 — Assess Your Current Policies

Written or not, your company does have policies and practices. Current policies provide a foundation for your handbook. To find your current policies:

- Gather all existing written policies;
- Survey managers and supervisors to determine unwritten policies and practices;
- Review payroll and business practices and personnel record maintenance procedures;
- Obtain copies of benefit plans; and
- Review any recent litigation documents (for example, wrongful termination claims, discrimination lawsuits, Cal/OSHA citations, etc.).

2 — Determine Your Need for New Policies

Looking at what you have, you may identify issues for which you don't have clear policies. To help make sure you've got everything, interview employees to consider long-range goals and identify operational needs that you haven't addressed.

3 — Begin the Drafting Process

If you find the thought of writing an important document intimidating, take heart! The sample *Employee Handbook* contains sample language for the most common handbook policies that you can use as-is, or use as a model for your own handbook. "You can find these forms in your online Formspack, described in detail in "Online Forms" on page 4." on page 89 lists other resources that can guide you as you write your handbook.

The important thing to remember is that the ideal handbook contains policies that are:

- Carefully and clearly worded — make sure you don't accidentally go against at-will employment or give up your right to make updates to policies;
- Accurate reflections of your policy — don't make promises you don't intend to keep, because these policies could be used against you in any legal action by an employee;
- Consistent with applicable legal requirements — your policies cannot violate state or federal law; and
- Understood by the audience — if no one understands your policy, they cannot follow it.

Detailed guidelines for supervisors concerning the treatment, management, and discipline of employees belong in a supervisor's manual given to managers and supervisors, rather than to regular employees.

4 — Review Your Document

It may take several drafts to get your handbook just right. Because your managers will implement these polices, ask them to review the initial draft, and incorporate their recommendations into the document.

Before you distribute your handbook to employees, have it reviewed by legal counsel. Your handbook provides structure for employees and guidance for managers, but it is primarily a legal document. Make sure that you have not violated the law, or put yourself in a vulnerable position with the language you have used.

5 — Distribute Your Handbook

Carefully and thoughtfully orchestrate distribution of your handbook to underscore its importance. Orientation presents the perfect opportunity to give a new hire the handbook. For existing employees, either meet with them, or prepare a cover letter to accompany the handbook when you distribute it. Encourage employees to ask questions, and explain any provisions about which they express uncertainty or skepticism.

Each employee should sign a *Confirmation of Receipt* of an employee handbook. Keep the signed form in the employee's personnel file.

6 — Monitor Your Handbook's Effectiveness

You must verify that the terms in the handbook are uniformly applied throughout the company and that employees, supervisors, and managers are following them.

7 — Revise Your Handbook Periodically

Have managers, supervisors, and legal counsel review your handbook periodically. Determine if you need to terminate or revise certain provisions or create additional ones due to a change in the law or a compelling business need.

Issue any changes in writing, and make sure you state that this version supersedes all previous versions. Keep a copy of all changes and new policies in a central file, so you can track and reference them easily.

! If the changes are substantial, employees should sign new confirmation of receipt forms.

What Policies Must I Include in My Handbook?

The following table contains policies required by California and federal law or to provide you with legal protection. If you have an employee handbook, you must have these policies in writing and available for your employees:

Table 11. Mandatory Policies for a Handbook

Policy	What should it say?	Why should I have it?
At-Will Employment Status	Clearly state that: • Employment is at-will; and • You or the employee can terminate the employment relationship at any time, with or without cause.	A written at-will employment policy is critical in defending wrongful discharge claims because it can rebut an employee's claim that he/she could be fired only if you had just cause.
Right to Revise	Clearly state that: • You have the right to change the policies and procedures contained in the handbook; and • The handbook embodies the entire agreement between you and the employee, and that no other oral or written agreements exist. Describe the procedure for changing policies.	Though not required by law, this policy makes your other policies (and your handbook as a whole) solid legal documents. This gives you the flexibility you need to cope with unforeseen changing circumstances and protects you against an employee claim that he/she is not governed by the handbook policies, but has a prior or different agreement.
Confirmation of Receipt	Clearly state that the employee: • Has received; • Read; and • Is aware of the policies and procedures as described in your company's handbook. Include at-will language to reinforce at-will employment status. A Confirmation of Receipt form that does not include such language may leave you more vulnerable to a suit for wrongful discharge.	Retain signed forms in each employee's personnel file, as a written record of the employee's receipt of the handbook.

Table 11. Mandatory Policies for a Handbook *(continued)*

Policy	What should it say?	Why should I have it?
Introductory Statement	This brief introduction should: • Welcome new employees; • Describe the working conditions for different sets of employees; • Specifically state that the new handbook supersedes any previously issued handbooks, policies, or benefit statements that are inconsistent with policies in the new handbook; and • Explain the handbook's purpose. You may also wish to provide a brief overview of company history and/or philosophy. Avoid using terms such as "permanent" or "long-term" employment," or suggesting the prospect of "a promising career with the company." Such promises or statements are inconsistent with the concept of at-will employment.	This statement precludes employees from claiming that the terms of their employment were defined in other documents previously issued.

Table 11. Mandatory Policies for a Handbook *(continued)*

Policy	What should it say?	Why should I have it?
Equal Employment Opportunity **Equal employment opportunity** ensures that all applicants and employees receive equal treatment without regard to race, sex, etc.	Clearly state your commitment to equal employment opportunity for all persons. Describe the procedure for filing complaints relating to perceived discrimination. If you have government contracts, you must include an affirmative action provision that states your commitment to equal opportunity and the steps you take to encourage opportunities for women and minorities. ! Draft your policy carefully to assure that it expresses the promise to comply with the law but does not inadvertently create additional equal employment rights. Recent legislation provides domestic partners with the same protection from discrimination given on the basis of marital status.	State and federal law requires you to communicate with your employees about your commitment to equal opportunity for everyone. For more information on EEO, see Chapter 7, "Preventing Discrimination and Harassment."

Table 11. Mandatory Policies for a Handbook *(continued)*

Policy	What should it say?	Why should I have it?
Unlawful Harassment **Harassment** is any behavior toward a person that a reasonable person would find unwelcome or hostile.	Clearly describe the kinds of conduct that constitute harassment of a protected class. Clearly state that: • Such conduct violates your rules and state and federal law; and • You will take forceful and appropriate measures to punish offenders and redress the harm done to their subjects. Tell employees: • They have the right to complain about harassment; • They can resist such harassment without fear of retaliation; • The procedure for making harassment complaints; and • That you will promptly, fully, and objectively investigate complaints of harassment. Legislation prohibiting sexual harassment includes "gender" in the definition of sex. You must allow employees to appear or dress consistently with their gender identity. Registered domestic partners now have the same rights as spouses. This includes the right to be free from harassment on the basis of registered domestic partner status.	California law requires you to provide information about harassment and your company's complaint process. You may be liable for sexual harassment by non-employees if you, your agents, or supervisors knew or should have known of the harassment and you failed to take immediate and appropriate corrective action. For more information, see "How Should I Handle a Discrimination/Harassment Complaint?" in Chapter 7, page 248.

What Policies Are Recommended for a Handbook?

Table 12 contains important policy topics and provisions that, although not technically required by law, are good to define for all employees. The sample *Employee Handbook*, in your online Formspack, contains sample language for the most important policies.

Table 12. Recommended Policies for a Handbook

Policy	What should it say?	Why should I have it?
Hiring		
Arbitration **Arbitration** is a non-court procedure for resolving disputes using one or more neutral third parties to evaluate the issues and make a decision.	State which circumstances will be covered by arbitration.	To avoid lengthy and costly litigation. ! This is a very dynamic area of law. Be sure to talk to legal counsel if you wish to use arbitration agreements.
Employee Classification	Clearly and unambiguously define employee classifications both in your handbook and for each individual you hire. Take care not to indicate anything other than at-will employment. Establish no more classes than are reasonably necessary. The most common employee classes are: • Full-time; • Part-time; • Regular; • Introductory; • Temporary; • Exempt; • Non-exempt; • Commissioned; and • Casual. For descriptions of these classes, see Table 3 in Chapter 2, page 10.	Employee classifications affect eligibility for benefits, duration of employment, compensation, and expectations regarding employment.

Table 12. Recommended Policies for a Handbook *(continued)*

Policy	What should it say?	Why should I have it?
Job Duties	Clearly state that you: • May occasionally require employees to work on special assignments in addition to normal job duties; and • Reserve the right to change job responsibilities, transfer job positions, or assign additional job duties at any time.	This policy preserves your flexibility in assigning job duties that differ from job descriptions at any time during employment.
Leaves of Absence		
Leaves of Absence **Leaves of absence** are temporary absences from work without loss of employment status. Some specific types are: • Pregnancy disability leave; • Family medical leave; • Disability leave; • Sick leave; and • Personal leave.	Tell employees: • Eligibility requirements; • Conditions for using the leave; • Procedures for: – Requesting leave; – Extending leave; and – Returning to work. • Whether and under what conditions the leaves are paid; • What period of time the leave covers; and • Effects of the leave on benefit accrual.	Stating the terms of these benefits will prevent misunderstandings and comply with legal requirements. You can choose to provide a generic policy that only discusses basic concepts, or you can provide separate policies that detail specific types of leaves. For more information, see Chapter 4, "Providing Benefits."

Table 12. Recommended Policies for a Handbook *(continued)*

Policy	What should it say?	Why should I have it?
Vacation	Tell employees: • Eligibility requirements; • Accrual rate; • Conditions for using accrued vacation; • Payment for unused accrued vacation; • Carryover and caps on accrual of vacation; • The effect of holidays or sickness during vacation; and • Vacation accrual during leaves of absence. Most employees, at companies of all sizes, are eligible for Paid Family Leave (PFL). You may require that an employee use up to two weeks of paid vacation before receiving PFL benefits.	You are not required to provide any vacation benefits; however, if you do, you must comply with laws that regulate vacation policies, requiring you to treat accrued vacation as wages due an employee upon termination. Stating the terms of this benefit will prevent misunderstandings by employees. For more information, see "What Do I Need to Know About Vacation?" in Chapter 4, page 135.
Paid Time Off (PTO) Some employers use PTO to consolidate different types of time off into time off without condition. You can consolidate vacation and sick pay while continuing to provide paid holidays, or use some other combination.	Tell employees: • Eligibility requirements; • Accrual rate; • Conditions for using accrued PTO; • Payment for unused accrued PTO; • Carryover and caps on accrual of PTO; and • PTO accrual during leaves of absence.	If you provide this benefit, you must comply with laws that regulate vacation policies, requiring you to treat accrued PTO as wages due an employee upon termination. Stating the terms of this benefit will prevent misunderstandings. For more information, see "What Do I Need to Know About PTO?" in Chapter 4, page 141.

Table 12. Recommended Policies for a Handbook *(continued)*

Policy	What should it say?	Why should I have it?
Leave for Protected Activities Like other leaves of absence, these leaves are temporary absences from work without loss of employment status. Some protected types of leave are: • Jury duty/witness leave; • Domestic violence leave; • Military leave; • Volunteer civil service leave; • School activities leave; and • Time off for voting.	Tell employees: • Conditions for using the leave; • Procedures for using the leave; and • That you will not discriminate against an employee who must take a protected leave.	State and federal law prevents you from discriminating or discharging employees who must take off time from work for protected activities. This policy provides consistency in the treatment of your employees. Having this policy informs your employees of their rights. For more information, see Chapter 4, "Providing Benefits."

Table 12. Recommended Policies for a Handbook *(continued)*

Policy	What should it say?	Why should I have it?
Benefits		
Insurance Benefits	Provide general descriptions and refer employees to the insurance plan booklets for further information. You are not required to provide this benefit, but if you do, don't put complete information in your handbook. Just distribute the plan description booklets provided by the insurance company. Insurance carriers must provide domestic partner benefits at the same level as those provided for a spouse. It is unlikely that insurance carriers will offer benefits for a spouse only. For more information, see "Domestic Partners and Health Plans" in Chapter 4, page 145.	This policy provides consistency in the treatment of your employees and informs them of their rights.
Insurance Benefits *(Continued)*	Provide no more than general statements that: • Recognize the existence of such plans; • Outline available benefits; and • Identify which employees are eligible. You do not have to fully describe these benefits in your handbook, but you must distribute summary plan descriptions (SPDs) to participants and beneficiaries of all ERISA plans.	This policy provides consistency in the treatment of your employees and informs them of their rights. For more information, see""What Do I Need to Know About Retirement or Pension Plans?" in Chapter 4, page 147.

Table 12. Recommended Policies for a Handbook *(continued)*

Policy	What should it say?	Why should I have it?
Workers' Compensation	Most employers are required to provide workers' compensation. Tell your employees: • Where they will receive emergency medical care; • How to report injuries and accidents on the job; and • Their rights to care, compensation, and rehabilitation.	This policy informs your employees of their rights, provides basic information about the benefit, and notifies employees about the penalties for workers' compensation fraud. For more information, see "What Do I Need to Know About Workers' Compensation?" in Chapter 4, page 127.
Holidays	Tell employees: • Which holidays you recognize; • Who can take paid holidays; • Any conditions that qualify for holiday pay; • The holiday pay rate; and • What happens if a holiday falls on a weekend, on an employee's normal days off, and during vacations or other leaves of absence.	You are not required to provide paid time off for holidays or premium pay for work performed on holidays. However, if you do, stating the terms of this benefit will prevent misunderstandings.
External Employee Education	If you reimburse employees for voluntary training programs, your policy should describe what the employee needs to do to: • Get approval for the training; and • Be reimbursed.	Stating the terms of this benefit will prevent misunderstandings.

Table 12. Recommended Policies for a Handbook *(continued)*

Policy	What should it say?	Why should I have it?
Management		
Personnel Records	Tell employees: • That personnel records are confidential; • Who to contact to access their records; and • Any restrictions on access, such as times of the day, who must be present, etc. Be sure that employees understand their obligation to update their names and addresses whenever changes occur.	To inform employees of their rights and prevent misunderstandings. Many laws govern personnel records retention. For more information, see *Records Retention Requirements*, described in Table 13 on page 89 and in your online Formspack, described in detail in"Online Forms" on page 4.
Performance Evaluations	Tell employees: • When and how often performance evaluations occur; • What criteria you use to evaluate performance; • Who will give the evaluations; and • What happens to the evaluations (placed in file, signed copies, etc.). If you have a policy of regular evaluations, communicate the timing to employees so they don't have unrealistic expectations. However, if you are not going to stick to the schedule, don't have a policy.	This policy advises employees of performance expectations.

Table 12. Recommended Policies for a Handbook *(continued)*

Policy	What should it say?	Why should I have it?
Employment of Relatives	Clearly state that you will review decisions regarding potential employment of relatives individually. Describe: • The types of circumstances and relationships prohibited; and • Any circumstances that might qualify as exceptions to the policy. ! You cannot prohibit the employment of relatives. You can, for reasons of security, morale, or conflict of interest, prohibit one relative from reporting to another. A blanket prohibition against the employment of relatives can expose you to liability for marital status and national origin discrimination, so make sure to phrase your policy carefully. See "What Is Discrimination?" in Chapter 7, page 228 for more details. Registered domestic partners are now entitled to the same rights and protections as spouses.	Employing relatives of current employees can often lead to morale problems such as favoritism or conflicts of interest, particularly when one family member supervises another.
Employee Property	State that you reserve the right to inspect employee's personal property under certain circumstances. If you have reasonable suspicion that the employee has stolen your property, then you have the right to search their personal property. Define the employee's property that is subject to inspection, such as packages, purses, and backpacks.	You must notify employees of this right in advance of an inspection.

Table 12. Recommended Policies for a Handbook *(continued)*

Policy	What should it say?	Why should I have it?
Telecommuting	Define: • The equipment required and who must provide it; • How to keep information and/ or shared data secure; and • Policies that will change as a result of telecommuting. You are not required by law to provide equipment for telecommuters if the telecommuting is done for the employee's convenience.	If you permit telecommuting, this policy will clarify basic conditions for it.
Company Property		
Employer Property	List the company-owned facilities and property available for the employees to use. State that the property: • Belongs to the company; and • Is subject to inspection by the company at any time. Tell employees what they can and cannot use your property for.	This policy helps avoid a claim that you committed an invasion of privacy by searching the property.
Off-Duty Use of Facilities	State specifically that employees may not: • Remain on company premises while not on duty; and • Use company property for their personal uses while not on duty.	This policy can protect you from workers' compensation liability if your supervisors consistently enforce it.

Table 12. Recommended Policies for a Handbook *(continued)*

Policy	What should it say?	Why should I have it?
Personal Use of Company Cell Phone	State whether or not you allow employees to use company-provided cell phones for personal use. If you do permit employees to make personal calls using a company phone, describe any restrictions on such use.	This policy can protect you from having to pay cell phone charges for an employee's personal calls.
Prohibiting Use of Company Cell Phone While Driving	State that you prohibit the use of cell phones while driving on company business and/or in a company vehicle.	This policy protects the safety of your employees and other drivers. It also helps you avoid liability should your employee kill or injure someone due to driving while using a cell phone for company business.
Prohibiting Camera Phones in the Workplace	State that you prohibit camera phones: • Anywhere in the workplace; • In specified areas; or • In "secure" areas.	This policy prevents employees from using a camera phone in an area where other employees have an expectation of privacy, or in a sensitive or secure area.
Use of Electronic Media	List the electronic media that your company uses. State that: • This media belongs to the company; • The media communications and files are subject to inspection by the company at any time; • Employees must use this media for company business; and • Employees may not use this media in any manner that conflicts with your discrimination/harassment policies.	This policy prevents employees from misusing your electronic media, and helps avoid a claim that you committed an invasion of privacy by searching the files.

Table 12. Recommended Policies for a Handbook *(continued)*

Policy	What should it say?	Why should I have it?
Bulletin Boards	If you have bulletin boards available, tell your employees: • The approval process, if any, for hanging materials; and • Any limitations on postings (size, content, etc.).	This policy helps you maintain control over the types of material posted in the workplace.
Solicitation and Distribution of Literature	Tell employees when and where they may solicit and distribute literature. You can ban non-employees from soliciting/distributing literature on company property at any time. You can also ban employees from distributing literature in working areas at any time. You cannot, however, prohibit employees from soliciting/distributing literature in nonworking areas of company property during nonworking hours.	This policy will help you prohibit solicitation and distribution of literature by unions, salespeople, and others.
Housekeeping	State your expectations about the cleanliness of employee workstations and common areas.	This policy promotes safe working conditions and efficiency in the workplace.
Parking	State: • Whether or not you provide parking; • Whether or not you take responsibility for damage that occurs in the parking lot; and • If there are any spots reserved for clients, guests, etc.	This policy will help prevent misunderstandings.
Smoking	Tell employees where the designated smoking areas are.	No federal law prohibits smoking in private workplaces; however, state law substantially limits smoking in enclosed places of employment in California. Many city laws have regulations that restrict smoking even further.

Table 12. Recommended Policies for a Handbook *(continued)*

Policy	What should it say?	Why should I have it?
Employee Conduct		
Prohibited Conduct	• List your rules of conduct; • Define the rules as "conduct that will not be tolerated"; and • State that the examples of conduct cited are illustrative and not all-inclusive.	Having a prohibited conduct policy preserves your right to take action for violations of company rules.
Off-Duty Conduct	Explain what types of off-duty conduct you prohibit and what types you allow. You may not discriminate against an employee for lawful activities outside work. For more information, see Table 66 in Chapter 7, page 230.	This type of policy protects your legitimate business interests.

Table 12. Recommended Policies for a Handbook *(continued)*

Policy	What should it say?	Why should I have it?
Drug and Alcohol Abuse	Clearly state your company's: • Concerns about the use of drugs and alcohol in the workplace; • Prohibition against their use; • Specific rules and regulations concerning drugs and alcohol, including the consequences of failure to comply with the company's drug and alcohol policy; • Exceptions to these rules; for example, if your company: – Permits parties on company property or allows sales staff to entertain clients during working hours; or – Has employees taking prescription medication that may affect their ability to safely perform their jobs; and • Commitment to reasonably accommodate any employee who wishes to participate in an alcohol or drug rehabilitation program.	This policy lets your employees know the consequences of not abiding by your workplace policy. This policy is required if you have government contracts. California law requires a company with 25 or more employees to reasonably accommodate any employee who wishes to participate in an alcohol or drug rehabilitation program, as long as the accommodation does not impose an undue hardship on the employer. Because of the current uncertain and transient state of the law, consult legal counsel before implementing any alcohol and drug abuse policies and testing or screening programs.
Punctuality and Attendance	Tell employees: • Who to report to in the event of absence or tardiness; • What constitutes excessive tardiness or absenteeism; and • The consequences of excessive tardiness or absenteeism. Clearly state if excessive tardiness or absenteeism can result in termination.	This policy lets employees know what is expected of them when they are going to be late or absent, and what the consequences can be if they fail to call in or report to work.

Table 12. Recommended Policies for a Handbook *(continued)*

Policy	What should it say?	Why should I have it?
Conducting Personal Business	State how you expect employees to use their time while on the job, for example, whether or not you want them to: • Devote all of their time to performing their company job assignments; and • Refrain from conducting personal business or business for another company while on duty.	This type of policy protects your legitimate business interests.
Dress Code and Other Personal Standards ! Dress codes are one place where men and women can be treated differently and expected to wear different types of clothing.	Explain your general or specific clothing and appearance standards: • General — properly groomed and wearing appropriate apparel; and • Specific — certain types of clothing or uniforms, even separate standards for different classes of employee. If you observe a "casual dress" day, describe: • The standard of casual dress; and • When casual dress days are observed. You must allow an employee to appear or dress consistently with his/her gender identity. Make sure that your dress codes can accommodate an employee's religious creed that affects his/her style of dress.	Having this policy will help avoid inconsistencies.

Table 12. Recommended Policies for a Handbook *(continued)*

Policy	What should it say?	Why should I have it?
Customer Relations	Describe: • How employees should interact with customers; and • The procedures for handling problems or extraordinary events.	This policy stresses the importance of customer satisfaction.
Business Conduct and Ethics	Outline what constitutes unethical behavior or the appearance of unethical behavior.	Gifts, entertainment, or money from an external organization or business may influence your employee's business decisions. This policy seeks to prevent businesses from using gifts to interfere with and/or influence employees.

Table 12. Recommended Policies for a Handbook *(continued)*

Policy	What should it say?	Why should I have it?
Confidentiality	Tell employees: • The type of information that they must not disclose; • Your reasons for prohibiting disclosure; • Any circumstances under which they may divulge such information; • Whether they must obtain permission before disclosing confidential information, and from whom they should ask permission; and • What disciplinary action will result if they use confidential information in violation of the policy. To enhance enforceability, carefully tailor your confidentiality statement to describe the actual information and work process you want protected. Under state law, you may not prohibit employees from disclosing the amount of their wages or other information about their working conditions. This prohibition against disclosure does not include proprietary or trade secret information. Consult with legal counsel before implementing such a policy.	To protect confidential company information. You can draft a standalone agreement that the employee signs at time of hire. For more information, see "7 — Fill Out Paperwork" in Chapter 2, page 24.

Table 12. Recommended Policies for a Handbook *(continued)*

Policy	**What should it say?**	**Why should I have it?**
Conflicts of Interest A **conflict of interest** is a conflict between the private interests and the official responsibilities of a person in a position of trust.	Tell employees: • What types of activities are prohibited, such as: – Directly competing with the employer; and – Using company time or resources for anything other than company business. • What corrective action can be taken if an employee is involved in an activity that creates a conflict of interest. Clearly state that the rule addresses job related concerns or problems with employee morale.	This type of policy protects your legitimate business interests.
Wages		
Payment of Wages	Specify: • Pay days; • Pay periods; • Location where paychecks are available; and • Time paychecks are available. Indicate when paychecks will be available for scheduled paydays that fall on a Saturday, Sunday, or company holiday. If you offer automatic payroll deposit, notify employees of this service. ! You may not make automatic payroll deposit mandatory.	To inform employees of their rights and prevent misunderstandings. For more information, see Chapter 5, "Paying Employees."

Table 12. Recommended Policies for a Handbook *(continued)*

Policy	What should it say?	Why should I have it?
Pay Differentials Many employers offer premium wages to workers who work undesirable shifts.	Tell employees: • Which employees and which shifts are eligible for pay differentials; • The amounts of the differentials; and • The circumstances under which differentials may be granted.	This policy will prevent misunderstandings by explaining your choice whether or not to pay premium rates.
Advances	State that you do not advance wages or lend money.	Recent opinion letters from the state Labor Commissioner's office indicate that it is very difficult, and perhaps even impossible, to require and enforce the repayment of a "loan." If you want to advance money to employees, consult with legal counsel before doing so.
Miscellaneous Time This can be: • Makeup time; • Travel time; • Time for mandatory meetings and training; and • Call-in time.	Briefly define the type of time and circumstances that it applies to. Tell employees: • The criteria/procedure to qualify for the time; and • Pay rates if applicable.	This policy provides the conditions for makeup time, if available, and helps prevent misunderstandings about how these types of time will be paid. For more information on how to pay employees for time spent not working, see "How Do I Handle Time Spent Traveling, on Rest Breaks, or Between Shifts?" in Chapter 5, page 164.

Table 12. Recommended Policies for a Handbook *(continued)*

Policy	What should it say?	Why should I have it?
Overtime (for non-exempt employees only) **Overtime** means any hours worked beyond eight hours per day or 40 hours per week. For employees with an alternative workweek, see "What Are My Scheduling Options?" in Chapter 5, page 160.	State that: • You comply with all state and federal overtime requirements; • Time off with pay for any reason will not accrue toward overtime calculation; and • Non-exempt employees must get overtime authorized in advance. You must define a workday and workweek for use in computing overtime.	This policy will help prevent misunderstandings with regard to overtime hours and payments. For more information, see the "Work Schedules" policy in this table, and "How Do I Set Up Work Schedules?" in Chapter 5, page 158.
Work Schedules	Tell employees: • Normal office and/or production work hours; • Whether you permit employees to exchange work schedules; and • The process for requesting an exchange of work schedules. For the purposes of overtime calculation, define the: • 24-hour period that makes a workday; and • 7-day period that makes a workweek. If you have different workdays, workweeks, or work shifts for different employees, describe those as well.	This policy will help prevent misunderstandings with regard to work hours. For more information, see "How Do I Set Up Work Schedules?" in Chapter 5, page 158.

Table 12. Recommended Policies for a Handbook *(continued)*

Policy	What should it say?	Why should I have it?
Timekeeping Requirements	Clearly define timekeeping practices, including the need to keep accurate records worked by non-exempt employees. Warn employees of the consequences for: • Falsification, destruction, modification, or removal of time records; • Late or early recording of time; and • Recording another employee's time records. Specify the: • Classes of employees who must record their time; • Date and time the timesheet is due; and • Appropriate methods of recording.	To inform employees of their rights, prevent misunderstandings, and notify them about the penalties for fraud.
Expense Accounts	Tell employees the schedule and deadlines for submitting business expense reports for reimbursement.	You must reimburse employees for reasonable business expenses they incur while performing their work.
Health and Safety		
Health and Safety	• Express your company's commitment to healthful and safe conditions for all employees; and • Refer employees to your Injury and Illness Prevention Program (IIPP) guide for specific details.	Having an IIPP is required by law, but your IIPP should be a standalone document. A simple reference to this document in your handbook alerts employees that the IIPP exists and must be followed. For more information, see "Injury and Illness Prevention Program" in Chapter 6, page 199.

Table 12. Recommended Policies for a Handbook *(continued)*

Policy	What should it say?	Why should I have it?
Ergonomics **Ergonomics** is the scientific study of the relationship between people and their work environments.	• Establish your policy on workplace ergonomics; and • Notify employees of your company's commitment to the prevention of repetitive motion injuries (RMIs).	You are not required to have an ergonomics policy, but the Cal/OSHA ergonomics standard for minimizing workplace RMIs does require your company to have an ergonomics program if certain conditions are met. For more information, see "Repetitive Motion Injuries (Ergonomics)" in Chapter 6, page 205.
Security and Workplace Violence	• Discuss potential security threats, such as theft or violence; • Discuss the presence of strangers on company premises; • Describe procedures for reporting any suspicious activity to the company; and • Encourage employees to report such activity.	This policy permits your company to express concern for employee welfare and safety, and supports your IIPP. Depending on the risk factors in a particular workplace, you may be required by law to address workplace violence in your IIPP. For more information, see "Injury and Illness Prevention Program" in Chapter 6, page 199.
Recreational Activities and Programs	If your company sponsors voluntary recreational activities (for example, a softball team) you should have a policy that protects you from liability for injuries incurred at such activities. State that: • Employees are under no pressure to participate; and • You are not responsible for injuries incurred.	This policy will help you avoid workers' compensation claims that arise out of non-work activities.

Table 12. Recommended Policies for a Handbook *(continued)*

Policy	What should it say?	Why should I have it?
Employees Who Are Required to Drive	Tell employees who must drive their own vehicles on company business: • That you require each driver to show proof of license and insurance; and • The rate at which you reimburse their mileage.	This policy lets employees know what to expect when they drive their own vehicle or a company vehicle.
Termination		
Termination	• State that employment with the company is at-will and can be terminated at any time, with or without notice, and with or without cause; • Exclude any statements suggesting that cause is required for termination; • Define conduct that constitutes a voluntary termination; and • Require terminated employees to return all company property. You cannot unilaterally deduct payments for unreturned company property from an employee's final paycheck.	Having an established termination procedure can help you avoid costly mistakes when you end the employee relationship. For more information, see Chapter 8, "Ending the Employment Relationship."

Table 12. Recommended Policies for a Handbook *(continued)*

Policy	What should it say?	Why should I have it?
Progressive Discipline	If you want to establish a progressive discipline system, clearly state that: • Employment with the company is at-will and can be terminated at any time, with or without notice, and with or without cause; • You use a disciplinary process, but do not describe the stages and consequences in detail; • Employees are subject to immediate termination under certain circumstances within your company's sole discretion; and • Any listing of infractions that may result in discipline is not all-inclusive and is meant only to illustrate examples. ! Avoid listing "cardinal offenses" that could lead to termination. California courts have held that this could be used to limit the effectiveness at-will employment status.	This policy: • Demonstrates your company's fairness and good faith efforts to assist employees; and • Notifies employees regarding your expectations and the consequences of failing to meet them.
Employee References	Tell employees: • Where to direct requests for references; • Who can release references; and • The information provided in a reference.	This policy can reduce your risk of liability for defamation. For more information, see "How Should I Handle Employee References?" in Chapter 8, page 276.

The Hitches, Glitches, and Pitfalls of Developing Policies

Written policies serve a variety of important purposes, but can also cause problems if you aren't careful.

What Do I Need to Watch Out for When I Create Policies/Handbooks?

- Don't create policies that violate federal or state laws. To read about some of the laws you should be aware of, see "Glossary of Terms, Laws, and Agencies" on page 285.
- Don't override the employment-at-will relationship by promising fairness or equity in termination decisions or setting forth discipline or termination procedures that conflict with employment-at-will.

  Include precisely written at-will language (see page 12) in your handbook, making sure that the language is consistent with other policies as well as statements in employment applications (see "3 — Advertise and/or Recruit for the Position" in Chapter 2, page 12), employment contracts (see "6 — Make the Hiring Decision and Offer the Position" in Chapter 2, page 23), and other materials.
- Don't open yourself to claims that a secondary or pre-existing agreement defines an employee's terms and conditions of employment. See "Right to Revise" in Table 11 on page 61.

  Include a statement in the introduction of your current handbook that specifically states that the new handbook supersedes any previously issued handbooks or policy or benefit statements that are inconsistent with policies described by the new handbook edition.

  Include an integration clause that states that the current handbook embodies the entire agreement between employer and employee and that no other oral or written agreements exist.
- Don't forget to allow room for change.

  Include a right to revise provision that states you have the right to change the policies and provisions contained in the handbook. See Table 11 on page 61.

What Do I Need to Watch Out for When I Update Policies/Handbooks?

If you do change or terminate a policy:

- Communicate the change to all employees, and obtain written acknowledgement that employees have read and understood the changes; and
- Do not interfere with employees' vested benefits.

What Forms and Checklists Do I Use to Develop Policies?

The following table describes forms associated with policy development.

You can find these forms in your online Formspack, described in detail in "Online Forms" on page 4.

Table 13. Forms and Checklists

Form Name	What do I use it for?	When do I use it?	Who fills it out?	Where does it go?
Confirmation of Receipt	Use to document that the employee has received and understands your company policies.	When hiring a new employee, or when you make a significant change to your handbook.	The employee signs it.	Keep in each employee's personnel file.
Employee Handbook	Use as a guide when drafting and reviewing your own policies. You don't have to use our sample as a guide, but the sample language is representative of clear and correct policy statements.	Not required by law. If you publish one, all employees should have a copy. Be sure to provide a copy to every new hire. You can distribute the handbook via your company intranet.	You create the handbook. You should have it reviewed by your legal counsel.	Employees keep the completed handbook in their possession. You should keep a copy of the sample to use as reference when making updates.

Table 13. Forms and Checklists *(continued)*

Form Name	What do I use it for?	When do I use it?	Who fills it out?	Where does it go?
Guest and Visitor Policy **New for 2008**	Notifying employees regarding your policy on bringing guests or visitors to work.	Not required by law, but should be part of your employee handbook or distributed to employees upon hire.	No filling out needed.	Employees keep their own copies. You should keep a copy as part of your employee handbook or personnel policies file.
Guest and Visitor Request Form **New for 2008**	Give to employees who wish to bring a guest or visitor to work.	When employees request to bring a guest or visitor to work.	Employees fill it out and you sign it.	In the employee's personnel file and in your files. You should also provide a copy of this form to your receptionist or security team.
Guest and Visitor Request Form - Spanish **New for 2008**	Give to employees whose primary language is Spanish who wish to bring a guest or visitor to work.	When employees request to bring a guest or visitor to work.	Employees fill it out and you sign it.	In the employee's personnel file and in your files.
Records Retention Requirements	To check how long to keep personnel records.	For reference.	No filling out needed.	NA
Telecommuting Agreement **New for 2008**	Use this form to describe the expectations your company has of employees who telecommute.	After a telecommuting relationship has been approved.	You do.	In the employee's personnel file and in your files.

Table 13. Forms and Checklists *(continued)*

Form Name	What do I use it for?	When do I use it?	Who fills it out?	Where does it go?
Telecommuting Policy **New for 2008**	Use this sample to communicate your company's policy regarding telecommuting and inform employees on how telecommuting plans will be reviewed and implemented.	Not required by law, but should be part of your employee handbook or distributed to employees upon hire.	No filling out needed.	Employees keep their own copies. You should keep a copy as part of your employee handbook or personnel policies file.
Telecommuting Request **New for 2008**	Provide this form to employees who request to telecommute. This form will help you understand why they wish to telecommute and whether such accommodation is appropriate.	When an employee requests a telecommuting arrangement.	The employee.	In the employee's personnel file and your files.
Telecommuting Request Checklist **New for 2008**	This checklist should be completed to evaluate whether telecommuting is appropriate for the individual and the job an employee performs.	After receiving a request for telecommuting plan	You do.	In the employee's personnel file and your files.

Table 13. Forms and Checklists *(continued)*

Form Name	What do I use it for?	When do I use it?	Who fills it out?	Where does it go?
Telecommuting Safety Checklist **New for 2008**	Use this form in conjunction with your company's safety checklist for your work-place to ensure the telecom-muter's work-space is safe.	After approving a telecommuting plan.	You do.	In your files.
Workplace Violence Policy **New for 2008**	To communicate your company's policy against workplace violence.	Not required by law, but should be part of your employee hand-book or distrib-uted to employees upon hire.	No filling out needed.	Employees keep their own copies. You should keep a copy as part of your employee handbook or personnel poli-cies file.

Where Do I Go for More Information?

CalBizCentral and the federal and state governments have a variety of resources to help you develop written employee policies.

Table 14. Additional Resources

For information on	Check out these resources
General	From CalBizCentral: • ***2008 California Labor Law Digest***; • ***2008 Employee Handbook Software***; • ***http://www.calbizcentral.com***; and • ***http://www.hrcalifornia.com***.
Equal Employment Opportunity	Complete regulations with OFCCP summaries at ***http://www.dol.gov/esa/ofccp/index.htm***
Workplace Violence and Security	Cal/OSHA's Guidelines for Workplace Security at ***http://www.dir.ca.gov/DOSH/dosh_publications/worksecurity.html***

Table 14. Additional Resources *(continued)*

For information on	Check out these resources
Drugs and Alcohol	Rules for drug and alcohol testing at ***http://www.dot.gov***
Legal Counsel	American Bar Association at ***http://www.abanet.org***

CalBizCentral also provides many ongoing and comprehensive educational opportunities for small business owners, HR beginners, and experienced HR professionals alike. These include online sexual harassment training, videos, and special HR seminars. For more information, please visit our Web site at ***http://www.calbizcentral.com***.

Chapter 4

Providing Benefits

One of the most complicated areas of employment law is employee benefits. Benefits include anything that's part of an employee's compensation package that isn't a wage or salary. Federal and California laws mandate some benefits, such as unemployment insurance. Others, like health care or paid vacation, are optional. However, if you offer these optional benefits, you must comply with certain legal guidelines that expand your employees' rights to use them.

This chapter describes the different benefits you can—or *must*— provide, and guides you through the processes of providing them.

In this chapter, you can find answers to questions about:

- Vacation, holidays, and sick leave;
- Unemployment insurance;
- Workers' compensation;
- Pregnancy and family/medical leave; and
- Much more!

Minimum Compliance Elements

1. Hang your *Employer Poster* (available from ***www.calbizcentral.com***), which includes mandatory postings that all of your employees must be able to see.

2. Give employees information on their workers' compensation, paid family leave, and disability insurance benefits (all located in the ***Required Notices Kit***, available from ***www.calbizcentral.com***).

3. Pay particular attention to the overlapping requirements of pregnancy disability leave, family/medical leave, and workers' compensation; see:
   - "What Do I Need to Know About PDL?" on page 97;
   - "What Do I Need to Know About Family and Medical Leaves?" on page 101;
   - "What Do I Need to Know About Workers' Compensation?" on page 127;
   - "What Do I Need to Know About SDI?" on page 122;
   - "What Do I Need to Know About Paid Family Leave?" on page 123; and
   - "How Do Different Types of Leave Interact?" on page 108.

The Basics of Providing Benefits

There are some benefits that you must provide to your employees, and many more that you can offer at your discretion.

Federal and California laws require that you provide certain benefits to your employees. Not every employer is required to provide all of these benefits — some are only required for companies over a certain size. See "Does This Employment Law Apply to Me?" in Chapter 1, page 1.

Other benefits are optional. However, if you do offer them, California law regulates how you apply them and the way you provide them.

Table 15. Benefits

Required benefits	Optional benefits
Benefits	
• Pregnancy disability leave (PDL), page 97; • Family and medical leave, page 101; • Disability leave, page 107; • Domestic violence leave, page 111; • School activities leave, page 115; • Jury/witness duty leave, page 116; • Military service leave, page 116; • Victims of violent crime leave, page 113; • Volunteer civil service leave, page 119; and • Voting leave, page 120.	• Vacation, page 135; • Holidays, page 137; • Floating holidays and personal days, page 138; • Sick leave, page 139; • Paid time off, (PTO) page 141; • Compensatory time off, (CTO) page 141; • Bereavement leave, page 141; and • Personal leaves of absence, page 142.
Insurance/Type of Payment	
• State Disability Insurance (SDI), page 122; • Unemployment Insurance (UI), page 125; • Workers' Compensation, page 127; and • Paid Family Leave (PFL), page 123.	• Health care, page 145; • Voluntary disability insurance, page 147; • Bonuses, page 147; and • Retirement and pension plans, page 147.

What Do I Need to Know About PDL?

Pregnancy disability leave (PDL) is covered by a California law created to protect pregnant employees against discrimination and to allow for time off from work for pregnancy, childbirth, and related medical conditions. PDL is not for baby bonding.

See "What Do I Need to Know About Family and Medical Leaves?" on page 101 for information on baby bonding leave.

Table 16. Pregnancy Disability Leave

Question	Answer
Do I have to provide this benefit?	You are required to provide PDL if you: • Have five or more full- or part-time employees; or • Are the State of California, its counties, or any other political or civil subdivisions of the state and cities. If you refuse to provide PDL to an eligible employee, or discriminate against an employee exercising her right to PDL, you can be penalized. See "What Are the Penalties for Discrimination/Harassment?" in Chapter 7, page 256.
Is this time off paid?	Only if you also pay for other temporary disability leaves. Consult your lawyer. ! You can require employees to use accrued sick pay during PDL, before using unpaid PDL. The employee may elect to use accrued vacation (see page 135) or PTO (see page 141) during PDL, before using unpaid PDL. If the employee becomes disabled, she may be eligible for SDI benefits. See "What Do I Need to Know About SDI?" on page 122 for more information.
Who's eligible?	All pregnant employees, regardless of length of service.
How does this start?	When the employee's health care provider determines that she is disabled by pregnancy, childbirth, or related medical conditions. This time off also covers severe morning sickness and prenatal care. **Disabled by pregnancy** Disabled by pregnancy means that an employee is unable to work, perform one of her essential duties, suffers from severe morning sickness, or is in need of prenatal care. The employee must provide you with verbal or written notice of the need for PDL, when it will start, and approximately how long it will last. If possible, she must provide 30 days' notice whenever the PDL is foreseeable.

Table 16. Pregnancy Disability Leave *(continued)*

Question	Answer
How long does it last?	PDL covers the actual period of disability, up to four months, even if your policy for other temporary disability leaves allows less. In addition, if your policy provides for a longer period of leave, you must allow the employee the extra time off. The law requires that the employee can use the leave intermittently, in increments as small as one hour. The four months' leave is actually the number of days the employee would work in a four-month period. ***Example:*** If the employee works full time (22 work days in a month, times four months, times 8 hours, or 704 hours), she is entitled to up to 704 hours of leave. If the employee works part time, then she is entitled to part of 704 hours of leave (an employee working 20 hours a week would be entitled to 352 hours of leave).
What's the process like?	**1.** Your employee notifies you that her health care provider has determined she is disabled by her pregnancy, childbirth, or related medical condition. **2.** Respond to the request as soon as possible, but no later than 10 calendar days after the request. Give the employee a copy of the *Employee Letter – PDL Only*, described in Table 38 on page 149. If you are subject to Family and Medical Leave (see page 101), and the employee is eligible for FMLA running concurrently with PDL, give the employee a copy of the *Employee Letter – PDL/FMLA*, described in Table 38 on page 149. **3.** You can require a medical certification for the leave if you also require certifications for other disability leaves. See the *Certification of Physician or Practitioner for PDL or PDL/FMLA*, described in Table 38 on page 149. You can also require a medical release to allow the employee to return to work if you require releases for other disability leaves. See the *Certification of Physician or Practitioner for Employee Return to Work*, described in Table 38 on page 149. **4.** When the PDL is over, you must reinstate the employee to the same position.

Table 16. Pregnancy Disability Leave *(continued)*

Question	Answer
What if the employment relationship ends?	If the employee decides to leave the company (voluntary quit), PDL ends. If you need to fire an employee who is taking PDL, consult legal counsel. If you need to lay off an employee who is taking PDL, remember that the employee has the same rights and seniority that she would have had she been at work. See "Layoff" in Chapter 8, page 270 for more information.
What other benefits are related/can be affected?	**Family Leaves** See "How Do Different Types of Leave Interact?" on page 108. **Health Benefits** Employees taking PDL are entitled to the following health benefits: • Same access to participation in health and benefits plans as with any other unpaid disability leave. If you provide health insurance during other disability leaves, you are required to do so for PDL; and • COBRA coverage, if triggered by PDL. Contact your insurance provider for information. **Employee Benefits** The following employee benefits are covered by PDL: • Seniority — Employees continue to accrue seniority as with your paid and unpaid leave policies; • Holidays — Regular holidays when your business is closed count as PDL days; • Company closures — If your business closes for an extended vacation (such as summer vacation), or other reasons, such as for maintenance, inventory, or remodeling, this time does not count toward PDL days; and • Sick leave, vacation, and PTO — if the employee is on company-paid leave, these benefits continue to accrue; if on unpaid leave, they only accrue if your other disability policies allow.

What Do I Need to Know About Family and Medical Leaves?

Family and medical leaves cover time off for:

- Bonding with a newborn or adopted child;
- Caring for a family member with a serious health condition; and
- Caring for the employee's own serious health condition.

For more information about FMLA and CFRA, see "Glossary of Terms, Laws, and Agencies" on page 285.

In California, the following rules are common to the FMLA (federal) and the CFRA (state).

Table 17. Family and Medical Leave

Question	Response
Do I have to provide this benefit?	You must provide family and medical leave if you: • Have 50 or more employees; or • Are a public agency. If you fail to comply with these laws, you can be subject to civil lawsuits, including: • Compensatory and punitive damages; • Reinstatement; and • Back pay, court costs, and attorneys' fees.
Is this time off paid?	Family and medical leaves are generally unpaid, although you can, as a matter of policy, require or allow employees to substitute accrued sick pay, vacation, or PTO for unpaid leave. ! Although FMLA and CFRA are unpaid, the employee may be eligible for Paid Family Leave (PFL). See "What Do I Need to Know About Paid Family Leave?" on page 123 for more information. ! If the employee is pregnant, she may also be covered by PDL. See "What Do I Need to Know About PDL?" on page 97 for information about paying employees on PDL. ! If the employee becomes disabled, he/she may be eligible for SDI benefits. See "What Do I Need to Know About SDI?" on page 122 for more information.

Table 17. Family and Medical Leave *(continued)*

Question	Response
Who's eligible?	Employees eligible for family and medical leave are those who have worked: • For a covered employer for at least 12 months (this time does not have to be consecutive); • At least 1,250 hours in the past 12 months; and • At a worksite where there are at least 50 or more company employees within a 75 mile radius. In California, if you do not inform the employee at the time of request of his/her ineligibility for family and medical leave, the employee is presumed eligible for these benefits.
How does this start?	Once the employee informs you that he/she needs leave, you must provide up to 12 weeks of family or medical leave. Generally, you can require that employees give you 30 days' notice when requesting family or medical leave (for example, expected birth of a child or a planned medical treatment). If the condition is not planned or foreseeable, however, employees must provide the notice as soon as practical. Employees must state the reason for the leave request. In both situations, you must respond to the employee's request, at least verbally, within two business days. See the *Employee Letter – FMLA/CFRA*, described in Table 38 on page 149. If the employee is eligible for both PDL and FMLA concurrently, see the *Employee Letter – PDL/FMLA* and the *Employee Letter – CFRA Leave Taken after FMLA/PDL*, described in Table 38 on page 149.

Table 17. Family and Medical Leave *(continued)*

Question	Response
How long does it last?	FMLA and CFRA both provide for up to 12 weeks of leave, but they run concurrently, unless the leave involves PDL (see page 97). If the employee is eligible for FMLA/CFRA leave, the total leave is a maximum of 12 weeks. Registered domestic partners have the same rights under the law as a spouse. Thus, an eligible employee who needs time off to care for his/her registered domestic partner would be entitled to a maximum of 12 weeks of leave under CFRA. For more information on domestic partner rights, see "Domestic Partners and CFRA" on page 106. The employee may take the leave all at once, or in shorter increments of hours, days, or weeks. ***Example:*** If the employee works full time, (5 days a week times 12 weeks, 60 days, or 40 hours a week times 12 weeks, 480 hours) he/she is entitled to up to 60 days or 480 hours of leave. If the employee works part time, then he/she is entitled to part of 480 hours or 60 days of leave. The individual who works 20 hours a week would be eligible for 30 days or 240 hours of leave. For more information on how these different leaves interact, see "How Do Different Types of Leave Interact?" on page 108.

Table 17. Family and Medical Leave *(continued)*

Question	Response
What's the process like?	**1.** Inquire as to if the employee is seeking FMLA/CFRA leave, because the employee does not have to ask specifically for family and medical leave. You are responsible for designating the leave as family or medical leave; if you do not notify the employee that the leave is qualified as such, it doesn't count against the 12 weeks. **2.** You must notify employees of the method you use to calculate the 12-month period in which the 12 weeks of entitlement occurs. The method that allows you the most control uses a "rolling" 12-month period measured backward from the date the employee first uses any leave. **3.** You can require medical certification within 15 calendar days of your request. If you wish, you may require a second opinion of the employee's illness, but you must pay for it. See the *Medical Certification – FMLA/CFRA* form, described in Table 38 on page 149. **4.** You must reinstate the employee to his/her position either by an agreed-upon date, or within two days of the employee's notification of readiness to return. You can require a medical release to allow the employee to return to work if you also require releases for other disability leaves. See the *Certification of Physician or Practitioner for Employee Return to Work*, described in Table 38 on page 149.

Table 17. Family and Medical Leave *(continued)*

Question	Response
What if the employment relationship ends?	If the employee decides to leave the company (voluntary quit), family and medical leave ends. If you need to fire an employee who is taking family and medical leave, consult legal help. If you need to lay off an employee who is taking family and medical leave, remember that the employee has the same rights and seniority that he/she would have had he/she been at work. See "Layoff" in Chapter 8, page 270 for more information.
What other benefits are related/can be affected?	Several other benefits can be affected by an employee taking family and medical leaves: **Health benefits** Employees taking family and medical leaves are entitled to the following health benefits: • Continued group health plan coverage at the same level and under the same conditions as when the employee was working (including dental, eye, mental health, and dependent coverage); and • Continuation of benefits as provided by any disability leave and/or COBRA. **Other benefits** The following employee benefits are covered by family leave laws: • Seniority — Employees continue to accrue seniority as with your paid and unpaid leave policies; • Holidays — Regular holidays when your business is closed count as family leave days; • Company closures — If your business closes for an extended vacation (such as summer vacation), or other reasons, such as for maintenance, inventory, or remodeling, this time does not count toward family leave days; and • Sick leave, vacation, and PTO — if the employee is on company paid leave, these benefits continue to accrue; if on unpaid leave, they only accrue if your other disability policies allow.

Domestic Partners and CFRA

The federal Family and Medical Leave Act (FMLA) does not provide domestic partners with leave. However, in California, registered domestic partners have the same legal rights as a spouse. Therefore, an eligible employee would be entitled to up to 12 weeks of leave that is CFRA only, to care for his/her domestic partner. This does not affect the employee's FMLA entitlement.

Potential for Discrimination

In one circumstance, the new state law appears to provide registered domestic partners with more leave than single or married employees.

If, before taking any FMLA leave, a registered domestic partner takes CFRA leave (up to 12 weeks) to care for his/her domestic partner, he/she would still have 12 weeks of FMLA leave available during that 12-month period. The employee could then use FMLA leave to care for his/her own serious health condition or that of a parent or child.

In contrast, a married employee who takes leave to care for a spouse is entitled to the same 12 weeks of CFRA leave, but it runs concurrently with FMLA leave because a spouse is covered under FMLA. If that married employee later needs leave to care for his/her own serious health condition or that of a parent or child, he/she is not entitled to any more leave in the same 12-month period. This creates the potential for a claim of discrimination on the basis of marital status — because the individual is married, he/she is denied a benefit that is available to a registered domestic partner.

Your company could voluntarily remedy this by providing additional leave to the married employee whose first absence is to care for a spouse, and who then needs additional time to care for his/her own serious health condition or that of a parent or child.

This legislation's effect on FMLA rights for married couples is an unsettled area of the law. Consult legal counsel before granting or denying FMLA leave or an additional leave of absence to any employee.

For more information about domestic partner rights, see "What Do I Need to Know About Domestic Partner Rights?" on page 143.

Concurrently means that as a week of Leave Type A is used up, so is a week of Leave Type B.

Table 19. How Different Types of Leave Interact

This leave	Runs concurrently with	Under these conditions
PDL (see page 97)	FMLA	Always, if you notify the employee.
	CFRA	Never.
	Workers' Compensation	Never.
	Disability	If your disability policy says so (it should).
FMLA (see page 101)	CFRA	For all leaves except due to pregnancy disability or to care for a registered domestic partner; see "Domestic Partners and CFRA" on page 106.
	Workers' Compensation	If there is a work-related injury or illness, the employee cannot work, and you notify the employee.
	Disability	If your disability policy says so (it should) and you notify the employee.
	PDL	If the employee is on leave due to pregnancy disability and you notify the employee.
CFRA (see page 101)	FMLA	For all leaves except due to pregnancy disability or to care for a registered domestic partner; see "Domestic Partners and CFRA" on page 106.
	Workers' Compensation	If there is a work-related injury or illness, the employee cannot work, and you notify the employee.
	Disability	If your disability policy says so (it should) and you notify the employee.
	PDL	Never.

Table 19. How Different Types of Leave Interact *(continued)*

This leave	Runs concurrently with	Under these conditions
Workers' compensation (see page 127)	FMLA/CFRA	Always, if there is a work-related injury or illness, the employee cannot work, and you notify the employee.
	Disability	If your disability policy says so (it should) and you notify the employee.
	PDL	Never.
Disability (see page 107)	FMLA/CFRA	If you are covered, your disability policy says so (it should), and you notify the employee.
	Workers' Compensation	If your disability policy says so (it should) and you notify the employee.
	PDL	If your disability policy says so (it should) and you notify the employee.

An employee who is a victim of domestic violence may request time off from work to ensure his/her health, safety or welfare, or that of his/her child.

What Do I Need to Know About Domestic Violence Leave?

Table 20. Domestic Violence Leave

Question	Response
Do I have to provide this benefit?	All employers must grant leave for employees to obtain a restraining order or other court assistance. If you have 25 or more employees, you must also grant leave for employees to: • Seek medical attention for injuries, including counseling; • Obtain services from a domestic violence shelter or rape crisis center; and • Take action to protect him/herself from future domestic violence, including relocation and safety planning.
Is this time off paid?	For exempt employees, it depends on the duration of the absence and whether he/she has available sick leave, vacation, or PTO. You must pay exempt employees for any day in which they perform any work. For non-exempt employees, you decide.
Who's eligible?	Any employee who is a victim of domestic violence.
How does this start?	Your employee becomes a victim of domestic violence. He/she will notify you in some way.
How long does it last?	An employee can take anywhere from a few hours (to obtain a restraining order) to 12 weeks (for recovering physically/mentally). You can determine whether his leave runs concurrently with leave granted by FMLA/CFRA. See "What Do I Need to Know About Family and Medical Leaves?" on page 101.

Table 20. Domestic Violence Leave *(continued)*

Question	Response
What's the process like?	**1.** Your employee gives you reasonable advance notice, unless it isn't feasible for him/her to do so. If he/she can't give notice prior to an absence, within a reasonable time, he/she must provide one of the following: • A police report regarding the domestic violence; • A court order protecting or separating the employee from the abuser; • Evidence that he/she appeared in court; and • Documentation from a medical professional, domestic violence advocate, health advocate, health care provider, or counselor that the employee underwent treatment for injuries resulting from domestic violence. **2.** Keep all requests for time off as a result of domestic violence confidential. **3.** Make the necessary adjustments to the work schedule and paycheck of the affected employee. If the request is for ongoing leave (for example counseling appointments once a week, or several court appointments) this may mean planning for long-term adjustments.
What if the employment relationship ends?	If the employee decides to leave the company (voluntary quit), domestic violence leave ends. If you need to fire an employee who is taking domestic violence leave, consult legal help. If you need to lay off an employee who is taking domestic violence leave, remember that the employee has the same rights and seniority that he/she would have, had he/she been at work. See "Layoff" in Chapter 8, page 270 for more information.
What other benefits are related/can be affected?	Rather than taking unpaid time, an employee may use available vacation, personal leave, or PTO.

What Do I Need to Know About Leave for Victims of Violent Crimes?

An employee who is a victim of a violent crime, or whose immediate family member is a victim, may take time off to attend judicial proceedings related to that crime.

Table 21. Violent Crime Victim Leave

Question	Response
Do I have to provide this benefit?	All employers must grant leave for eligible employees to attend judicial proceedings.
Is this time off paid?	For exempt employees, it depends on the duration of the absence and whether he/she has available sick leave, vacation, or PTO. You must pay exempt employees for any day in which they perform any work. Exempt and non-exempt employees may choose to take accrued paid vacation, personal leave, sick leave, or unpaid time off.
Who's eligible?	Any employee who is the victim of a violent crime, or who is an immediate family member of a victim, a registered domestic partner of a victim, or the child of a registered domestic partner of a victim. Immediate family members include: • Spouse • Child • Stepchild • Brother • Stepbrother • Sister • Stepsister • Mother • Stepmother • Father • Stepfather
How does this start?	Your employee notifies you in some way that he/she or someone else listed above is the victim of a violent crime.
How long does it last?	There are no restrictions on the length of time. However, the time off from work must be in order to attend judicial proceedings related to the violent crime.

Table 21. Violent Crime Victim Leave *(continued)*

Question	Response
What's the process like?	Your employee gives you reasonable advance notice, unless it isn't feasible for him/her to do so. As documentation for the absence, the employee must provide you with a copy of the notice of each scheduled proceeding that is provided to the victim by the agency responsible for providing notice. If advance notice is not feasible, you should not take any action against the employee if, within a reasonable time after the absence, he/she provides you with documentation of the judicial proceeding from one of the following entities: • The court or government agency setting the hearing; • The district attorney or prosecuting attorney's office; or • The victim/witness office that is advocating on behalf of the victim.
What if the employment relationship ends?	If the employee decides to leave the company (voluntary quit), the violent crime leave ends. If you need to fire an employee who is taking violent crime leave, consult legal help. If you need to lay off an employee who is taking violent crime leave, remember that the employee has the same rights and seniority that he/she would have, had he/she been at work. See "Layoff" in Chapter 8, page 270 for more information.
What other benefits are related/can be affected?	An employee may elect to use accrued paid vacation, personal leave, sick leave, or unpaid time off.

What Do I Need to Know About Time Off for School Activities?

Parents or guardians of a child in school may occasionally need to participate in school activities, such as parent/teacher conferences, field trips, or meetings.

Table 22. Time Off for School Activities

Questions	Response
Do I have to provide this benefit?	Yes, all employers are covered. You must grant time off: • To any employee who must appear at a school in connection with his/her child who has been suspended; and • For other school activities if you have 25 or more employees at the same location.
Is this time off paid?	For exempt employees, it depends on the duration of the absence. You must pay exempt employees their full week's salary for any week in which they perform any work. For non-exempt employees, you decide.
Who's eligible?	Any employee who is the parent or legal guardian of a child in grades K–12, or attending a licensed day care facility.
How does this start?	NA
How long does it last?	You must provide up to 40 hours off per calendar year for school activities; however, you can limit the use of this time off to no more than eight hours in any one calendar month.
What's the process like?	**1.** Your employee will notify you that he/she wants to take time off to participate in a school activity. You might want to have a form for requesting time off. **2.** You either approve the requested time or ask the employee to reschedule. **3.** You may require documentation from the school as proof that the employee participated in the activity on a specific date and at a specific time.
What if the employment relationship ends?	Nothing. This is not an accrued benefit.
What other benefits are related/can be affected?	If the employee is on company paid leave, then sick pay, vacation, and PTO continue to accrue. If on unpaid leave, they only accrue if your other policies require.

What Do I Need to Know About Time Off for Jury/Witness Duty?

According to state law, a person called to serve jury duty or participate as a witness in a trial must do so, unless the court releases him/her from service.

Table 23. Time Off for Jury/Witness Duty

Question	Response
Do I have to provide this benefit?	Yes, all employers are covered. You may not discharge or discriminate against any employee who takes time off to serve as a juror or a witness, provided he/she gives reasonable notice.
Is this time off paid?	This depends on the employee's status as exempt or non-exempt. • Non-exempt — No. You do not have to pay wages while he/she serves on jury duty or as a witness; or • Exempt — If an employee performs any work in a workweek, you must pay him/her for the full week. You do not need to pay him/her for a workweek when he/she performs *no* work.
Who's eligible?	Any employee who has been called to serve.
How does this start?	Your employee gets a summons for jury duty or a subpoena to appear in court as a witness.
How long does it last?	It depends on how long the court proceeding lasts, or how long his/her responsibilities as a witness last.
What's the process like?	**1.** Your employee gives you notice. **2.** Make the necessary changes to the work schedule and paycheck of the affected employee.
What if the employment relationship ends?	Nothing. This is not an accrued benefit.
What other benefits are related/can be affected?	Rather than taking unpaid leave, a non-exempt employee may use any available vacation or PTO. If the employee is on company paid leave, then sick pay, vacation, and PTO continue to accrue. If on unpaid leave, they only accrue if your other policies require.

What Do I Need to Know About Military Leave?

When your employees serve in the military, you must protect their jobs. There are several government resources available to explain the details of this benefit. See "You can find these forms in your online Formspack, described in detail in"Online Forms" on page 4." on page 149.

Table 24. Military Leave

Question	Response
Do I have to provide this benefit?	Yes, all employers are covered. When your employees serve in the military during their employment, you are required to either hold their jobs or reemploy them in similar positions when they return. The Veterans Benefits Improvement Act, enacted by Congress in December 2004, requires all employers to provide a notice of rights under the Uniformed Services Employment and Reemployment Rights Act (USERRA) to all persons entitled to rights and benefits under USERRA. The most efficient way to comply is to post the notice in a prominent place where employees customarily check for such information. The notice is part of CalBizCentral's all-in-one ***Employer Poster***. You can order this product, in English and Spanish, from CalBizCentral at ***www.calbizcentral.com***.
Is this time off paid?	• Non-exempt — No; or • Exempt — If an employee performs any work in a workweek, you must pay him/her for the full week. You do not need to pay him/her for a workweek when he/she performs no work.
Who's eligible?	Virtually anyone who has been absent from work due to "service in the uniformed services" is protected. "Service" includes active duty, active duty for training, initial active duty for training, inactive duty training, full-time National Guard duty, and examinations to determine fitness for duty. "Uniformed services" include: • The Army, Navy, Air Force, Marine Corps, Coast Guard (and the Reserves for each of those branches); • The Army National Guard, Air National Guard, and commissioned corps of the Public Health Service; • National Disaster Medical System; and • Any other category of persons designated by the President in time of war or emergency.
How does this start?	Have your employee notify you as soon as he/she learns of the need for military leave.
How long does it last?	Military leave may be almost any length, with a maximum of a cumulative five years.

Table 24. Military Leave *(continued)*

Question	Response
What's the process like?	**1.** Your employee will notify you before he/she leaves. **2.** When the service is over, he/she will provide notice of intent to return. **3.** Under most circumstances, you must reinstate the employee. For exceptions, see the Uniformed Services Employment and Reemployment Rights Act (USERRA) website, listed in "You can find these forms in your online Formspack, described in detail in"Online Forms" on page 4." on page 149.
What if the employment relationship ends?	If the employee decides to leave the company (voluntary quit), military leave ends. If you need to fire an employee who is taking military leave, consult legal help. If you need to lay off an employee who is taking military leave, remember that the employee has the same rights and seniority that he/she would have had he/she been at work. See "Layoff" in Chapter 8, page 270.
What other benefits are related/can be affected?	The employee is entitled to all rights and benefits as if he/she had remained continuously employed. The employee can also elect COBRA-like health care coverage.

What Do I Need to Know About Military Spouse Leave?

New for 2008 In October 2007, Governor Arnold Schwarzenegger signed emergency legislation creating a new leave of absence for spouses of military personnel.

Table 25. Military Spouse Leave

Question	Response
Do I have to provide this benefit?	All California employers with 25 or more employees are covered.
Is this time off paid?	• Non-exempt — No; or • Exempt — If an employee performs any work in a workweek, you must pay him/her for the full week. You do not need to pay him/her for a workweek when he/she performs no work.

Table 25. Military Spouse Leave *(continued)*

Question	Response
Who's eligible?	Employees who work an average of 20 hours or more per week who have a spouse in the United States Armed Forces, National Guard, or Army Reserve who has been deployed during a period of military conflict.
How does this start?	The employee must provide the employer with notice within two business days of receiving official notice that their spouse will be on leave from deployment.
How long does it last?	The leave lasts for up to 10 days.
What if the employment relationship ends?	Employers subject to this law cannot retaliate against an employee who requests or takes this leave.
What other benefits are related/can be affected?	You can allow employees to use sick and or vacation/PTO during this leave but cannot require them to do so.

What Do I Need to Know About Time Off for Volunteer Civil Service?

You may employ people who also provide volunteer emergency services. They may be called away during work hours to help in an emergency or go through training.

Table 26. Time Off for Volunteer Civil Service Duty

Question	Response
Do I have to provide this benefit?	Yes. All employers must provide the time off for emergency service. Employers with 50 or more employees must also provide up to 14 days per year for training.
Is this time off paid?	For exempt employees, it depends on the duration of the absence. You must pay exempt employees their full week's salary for any week in which they perform any work. For non-exempt employees, you decide.
Who's eligible?	Firefighters, peace officers, and emergency rescue personnel, whether he/she is a volunteer or partly/fully paid while providing emergency services.
How does this start?	Your employee notifies you as soon as he/she learns of the need for volunteer civil service duty.

Table 26. Time Off for Volunteer Civil Service Duty *(continued)*

Question	Response
How long does it last?	For the duration of the civil or required service.
What's the process like?	Ask employees to give as much notice as possible.
What if the employment relationship ends?	If the employee decides to leave the company (voluntary quit), the leave ends. If you need to fire an employee who is on volunteer civil service leave, consult legal help. If you need to lay off an employee who is on volunteer civil service leave, remember that the employee has the same rights and seniority that he/she would have had he/she been at work. See "Layoff" in Chapter 8, page 270 for more information.
What other benefits are related/can be affected?	If the employee is on company paid leave, then sick pay, vacation, and PTO continue to accrue. If on unpaid leave, they only accrue if your other policies require.

What Do I Need to Know About Time Off for Voting?

Registered voters have a right to vote in local, statewide, and national elections.

Table 27. Time Off for Voting

Question	Response
Do I have to provide this benefit?	Yes, all employers are covered.
Is this time off paid?	Yes.
Who's eligible?	Any registered voter who does not have sufficient time outside of working hours to vote in a statewide election.
How does this start?	Your employee notifies you as soon as he/she learns of the need for time off to vote.
How long does it last?	Up to two hours on election days.

Table 27. Time Off for Voting *(continued)*

Question	Response
What's the process like?	**1.** The employee notifies you at least two working days in advance to arrange a voting time. **2.** You grant time at the beginning or end of the regular working shift, whichever allows the most free time for voting and the least time off from working.
What if the employment relationship ends?	Nothing. This is not an accrued benefit.
What other benefits are related/can be affected?	None.

What Do I Need to Know About SDI?

State Disability Insurance (SDI) is not a leave of absence, it is a partial wage-replacement plan for California workers *during* a leave of absence. SDI provides short-term benefits to eligible workers who suffer a loss of wages when they are unable to work due to a non-work-related illness or injury, or when they are medically disabled due to pregnancy or childbirth.

Table 28. State Disability Insurance

Question	Response
Do I have to provide this benefit?	Yes, almost every employer is covered. You must withhold part of an employee's pay and send it to the SDI program, which is administered by EDD. Penalties for failing to comply are steep. When you register with EDD, they will give you a registration number and information concerning your tax and reporting requirements. You can rely on their regulations and advice. See EDD's website, listed in "You can find these forms in your online Formspack, described in detail in"Online Forms" on page 4." on page 149 for more information.
Is this time off paid?	Any benefits are paid through SDI. The employee may choose to take accrued vacation or PTO, or you may require that the employee do so. Payment of vacation or PTO does not affect the employee's SDI benefits. If you pay out accrued sick leave, the employee's SDI benefits are reduced by the amount of sick pay. To avoid reduction of SDI benefits, you may coordinate the payment of sick leave with SDI benefits.
Who's eligible?	Everyone is eligible. EDD administers the benefit uniformly.
How does this start?	Your employee becomes disabled. He/she will notify you in some way.
How long does it last?	SDI benefit payments cannot exceed 52 times the employee's weekly benefit amount, or the total wages subject to SDI tax paid in the base period, whichever is less.
What's the process like?	**1.** Provide the employee with a copy of the *For Your Benefit, California's Program for the Unemployed* pamphlet (located in the ***Required Notices Kit*** associated with this product). **2.** Keep records of employee pay as required by state and federal law. **3.** When an employee files an SDI claim, EDD will contact you and provide you with the appropriate paperwork. You fill out the employer portion of the form; EDD does the rest.

Table 28. State Disability Insurance *(continued)*

Question	Response
What if the employment relationship ends?	You are not required to hold the employee's job merely because he/she is collecting SDI benefits. However, laws that do protect the employee's job (such as family leave, PDL, workers' compensation, or the ADA) may apply.
What other benefits are related/can be affected?	SDI covers loss of earnings not covered by workers' compensation. If someone is receiving workers' compensation, then he/she is only eligible for SDI benefits in the amount of the difference between normal wages and workers' compensation. If a person receives UI benefits, he/she cannot receive SDI benefits for the same period. When employees receive full pay, they are ineligible for SDI benefits during that time. Employers can coordinate sick leave and PTO benefits, or other pay (excluding vacation) with EDD to maximize SDI payments. Receipt of vacation pay does not affect SDI payments. Vacation pay does not affect SDI benefits. For information about specific leave benefits, see: • "How Do Different Types of Leave Interact?" on page 108; • "What Do I Need to Know About PDL?" on page 97; • "What Do I Need to Know About Family and Medical Leaves?" on page 101; • "What Do I Need to Know About Disability Leave?" on page 107; and • "What Do I Need to Know About Workers' Compensation?" on page 127.

What Do I Need to Know About Paid Family Leave?

Paid Family Leave (PFL) is not a leave of absence; it is a partial wage-replacement plan for California workers during an absence. PFL provides short-term benefits to eligible workers who suffer a wage loss when they are unable to work because of the need to:

- Care for a seriously ill child, spouse, parent, or domestic partner;
- Bond with the employee's new child or the new child of the employee's spouse or domestic partner; or

- Bond with a child in connection with the adoption or foster care placement of the child with the employee or the employee's spouse or domestic partner.

Table 29. Paid Family Leave

Question	Response
Do I have to provide this benefit?	Yes, almost every employer is covered. You must withhold part of an employee's pay and send it to the PFL program, which is administered by EDD. Penalties for failing to comply are steep. When you register with EDD, they will give you a registration number and information concerning your tax and reporting requirements. You can rely on their regulations and advice. See EDD's website, listed in "You can find these forms in your online Formspack, described in detail in"Online Forms" on page 4." on page 149 for more information.
Is this time off paid?	Benefit payments are approximately 55% of the employee's regular wages and may be used for a maximum of six weeks in a 12-month period.
Who's eligible?	Everyone is eligible. EDD administers the benefit uniformly.
How does this start?	Your employee will be absent for a reason that qualifies for PFL benefits. He/she will notify you in the same way.
How long does it last?	Employees are eligible for benefit payments for a maximum of six weeks in a 12-month period.
What's the process like?	**1.** Provide all new employees, and employees who are absent for a qualifying reason, with a copy of the *Paid Family Leave* pamphlet (located in the ***Required Notices Kit*** available from ***http://www.calbizcentral.com***). **2.** Keep records of employee pay as required by state and federal law. **3.** When an employee files a PFL claim, EDD will contact you and provide you with any paperwork required from you. EDD does the rest.

Table 29. Paid Family Leave *(continued)*

Question	Response
What if the employment relationship ends?	You are not required to hold the employee's job merely because he/she is collecting PFL benefits. However, laws that do protect the employee's job (such as family leave and kin care) may apply.
What other benefits are related/can be affected?	PFL covers loss of earnings not covered by workers' compensation and SDI benefits. If a person receives UI benefits, he/she cannot receive PFL benefits for the same period. If the employee is receiving full replacement wages, such as sick leave and PTO, then he/she is ineligible for PFL benefits during that time. Employers can coordinate sick leave and PTO benefits with EDD to maximize PFL payments. Vacation pay does not affect PFL benefits. However, employers may require that employees take up to two weeks of accrued, unused vacation before PFL payments begin. The first week of vacation would be the 7-day waiting period for PFL payments. For information about specific leave benefits, see Table 15 on page 97.

What Do I Need to Know About UI?

Unemployment Insurance (UI) is a tax that you pay that is held in reserve for your employees when they become unemployed. The UI system is a combination of federal and state programs. You pay taxes to both, and together they make sure that people who are unemployed through no fault of their own have money to live on between jobs. The tax rate increased in 2005. Make sure you are working with current information.

Table 30. Unemployment Insurance

Question	Response
Do I have to provide this benefit?	Yes. Almost all California employers are required to pay the tax. Penalties for failing to pay your share are steep. Almost all California employers are covered. See "What Do I Need to Know About SDI?" on page 122. If your employees work in multiple states, contact legal counsel or EDD to determine how to file. Check out the EDD's website: ***http://www.edd.cahwnet.gov/employer.htm.***
Is this time off paid?	This is not time off from work. Employees must be unemployed or have a reduction in hours in order to receive UI benefits.
Who's eligible?	To be eligible for UI, a claimant must: • Have made a claim for benefits in accordance with the regulations; • Be unemployed through no fault of his/her own; • Have earned $1,300 in one quarter, or have high quarter wages of $900 and total base period earnings of 1.25 times that amount; • Be able to work and be available for work (including part-time work, if appropriate); • Be actively looking for work; and • Have registered for work and conducted a search for suitable work as directed. A claimant is ineligible if he/she is out of work for one of the following reasons: • Voluntary quit without just cause; • Discharge for misconduct; and • Refusal to perform suitable work. See Chapter 8, "Ending the Employment Relationship" for further information.
How does this start?	EDD will notify you of your tax rate, and you will pay quarterly into your reserve account. The EDD sets an initial rate of 3.4% of payroll. After three years in business, your rate goes up or down depending on the cost of the claims submitted.

Table 30. Unemployment Insurance *(continued)*

Question	Response
How long does it last?	UI benefits may be paid for a maximum of 26 weeks. However, there are often extensions of this time, depending on the unemployment situation.
What's the process like?	An employee may file for UI benefits when he/she is out of work, or has had his/her hours significantly reduced. Respond to EDD's request for information. There is a new penalty for providing false information in connection with a UI claim as to the reason for an employee's termination. See "What Is the Basic Process for Ending the Employment Relationship?" in Chapter 8, page 267 for the steps to follow when the employment relationship ends. UI benefits are paid every two weeks (after a one-week waiting period) for up to 26 weeks. Keep records of employee pay as required by state and federal law. See "What Sorts of Records Must I Retain?" in Chapter 5, page 184 for more information. If you disagree with EDD's determination, you can protest the claim. You must appeal in a timely manner. You can use *Responding to a Claim for Unemployment Insurance*, *Appealing a UI Claim to an Administrative Law Judge*, and *Appealing a UI Claim to the UI Appeals Board*, described in Table 73 on page 277.
What if the employment relationship ends?	N/A
What other benefits are related/can be affected?	An unemployed person cannot draw both UI and SDI benefits. See "What Do I Need to Know About SDI?" on page 122 for details.

What Do I Need to Know About Workers' Compensation?

You must carry workers' compensation insurance, which provides payments, without regard to fault, for any injury or death "arising out of and in the course of employment." Injured workers must receive the necessary medical care, at no cost to them, to cure or relieve the effects of the injury. Employees generally give up their rights to sue you for civil damages in exchange for certain, though limited, benefits which may include pay for time away from work.

For information on preventing injuries at work, see Chapter 6, "Ensuring Workplace Safety.

Table 31. Workers' Compensation

Question	Response
Do I have to provide this benefit?	Yes. You must have coverage at all times while your business is in operation. If you fail to provide coverage, and an injury occurs, you still have to pay the employee's medical costs, in addition to penalties and the possibility of lawsuits. Every employer is covered, including non-profit organizations, governments, and every person employing another person.
Is this time off paid?	The employer does not pay for the time off directly. The workers' compensation carrier is responsible for paying the injured employee.
Who's eligible?	Just about everybody, including aliens, casual workers (if they work at least 52 hours in a 90-day period), and minors. Independent contractors are excluded. See Table 3 in Chapter 2, page 10 for more information about independent contractors. You can refute a claim if the employee was: • Under the influence of alcohol or drugs at the time of the injury; • Intentionally inflicting the injury or committing suicide; • Engaging in an "altercation" in which he/she was the initial physical aggressor; • Committing a felony for which he/she has been convicted; • Engaging in horseplay; • Voluntarily participating in off-duty recreational, social, or athletic activity not constituting his/her work-related activities, unless those activities are expected of employees; and • Going to or coming from work, unless you control the route or mode of transportation.

Table 31. Workers' Compensation *(continued)*

<table>
<tr><th>Question</th><th>Response</th></tr>
<tr><td>How does this start?</td><td>Employees are protected as soon as they start performing work on your behalf.

As of August 1, 2004, you must provide all new employees with the updated Workers' Compensation Rights and Benefits pamphlet, described in Table 8 in Chapter 2, page 38, and located in the Required Notices Kit available from www.calbizcentral.com.

Workers' compensation law covers four types of injuries:
• Specific physical injury;
• Cumulative physical injury;
• Specific mental/psychiatric injury; and
• Cumulative mental/psychiatric injury.

Any one of these injuries is covered under workers' compensation law, regardless of whether first aid or surgery is required, or if the injury is work-disabling, even if no medical treatment is required.

An injury is deemed job-related when:
• It arises out of and in the course of employment;
• The job has played an "active" role and has been a "positive" factor in the injury;
• The injury was caused only by something to which the employee was exposed in his/her employment period;
• The employment brought the employee to the place where the accident occurred; or
• The injury happened at home, if the employee's work duties require tasks at home.

Typically, courts will resolve any reasonable doubt about whether or not an injury occurred in the course of employment in favor of the injured claimant.

Psychiatric injuries have slightly different standards. Work-related stress must be "predominant as to all causes of the psychiatric injury combined." Unless a "sudden and extraordinary" employment condition is involved, the employee must have worked for you for at least six months.</td></tr>
</table>

Table 31. Workers' Compensation *(continued)*

Question	Response
How does this start? (continued)	Work-related stress (not stress from the employee's family, heath, etc.) must account for more than half of the employee's injury. Psychiatric injuries must meet *all* of the following criteria: • Diagnosis as a mental disorder, based on the published criteria of the American Psychiatric Association; • Determination that the mental disorder results in disability or requires medical treatment; and • Proof that the "actual events of employment were predominant as to all causes combined," except in situations involving a significant violent act. As soon as you get worker's compensation insurance, you should identify health care providers and hospital facilities that have been designated by the insurance company and/or are familiar with occupational injuries and the workers' compensation system. In most circumstances, you may designate the treating physician for at least the first 30 days following an injury. For more on designating physicians, see "Choice of Physician, Chiropractor, or Acupuncturist" on page 134. Regulatory activity continues in the area of workers' compensation. For up-to-date information on this and other employment-related issues, subscribe to the California Chamber's free newsletter, ***HR California Extra*** at ***www.hrcaliforniaextra.com***.
How long does it last?	This is determined by the workers' compensation carrier and the treating physician.
What's the process like? Need help finding a medical provider? Check out ***http://www.scif.com/MedFinder/medfinder_fset.htm***	**1.** Should a work-related injury or illness occur, your company's first duty is to provide the employee with first aid or emergency medical care, if needed. Even where your company has designated a medical provider and the employee has not predesignated his/her own physician, you can lose the right to control the medical care if you fail to promptly provide medical care when requested. For more on designating physicians, see "Choice of Physician, Chiropractor, or Acupuncturist" on page 134.

Table 31. Workers' Compensation *(continued)*

Question	Response
What's the process like? (continued)	**2.** If the injury requires more than first aid, give the employee the *Employee's Claim for Workers' Compensation Benefits (DWC 1)* as soon as possible after the incident. Although you have the right to postpone acceptance of a workers' compensation claim for up to 90 days, pending an investigation to determine if the injury is work-related, you must provide all appropriate medical care immediately upon learning of the injury. Your potential liability for medical care costs is limited to $10,000 for treatment prior to the decision to accept or reject the claim. **3.** File the *Employer's Report of Occupational Injury or Illness* with your insurance company. **4.** Conduct an investigation into the circumstances surrounding the injury. Document any findings, and use this information to prevent future injuries. **5.** If you are required to record and report injuries on the Cal/OSHA *Log 300* forms, do so. See "How Do I Report and Record Work-Related Injuries and Illnesses?" in Chapter 6, page 211 to find out if these requirements apply to you. **6.** Communicate with your injured employee, and focus on his/her recovery and return to work. Make sure the employee knows what benefits are available to him/her and when the benefit services will be furnished. Make sure that employees are receiving the benefit checks to which they are entitled. Stay informed. **7.** Take corrective action to eliminate any workplace hazards that were discovered in the injury investigation. **8.** Respect employee confidentiality. Like most types of medical information, workers' compensation claim information must be kept private.

Table 31. Workers' Compensation *(continued)*

Question	Response
What if the employment relationship ends?	Do not take adverse action against an employee involved in a workers' compensation claim, unless you have consulted an attorney. You are expressly prohibited from discharging, threatening, or discriminating in any way against an employee because he/she has received an award from, has filed, or intends to file a workers' compensation claim. If the employee decides to leave the company (voluntary quit), workers' compensation leave ends. If you need to fire an employee who is taking workers' compensation leave, consult legal help. If you need to lay off an employee who is taking workers' compensation leave, remember that the employee has the same rights and seniority that he/she would have had he/she been at work. See "Layoff" in Chapter 8, page 270 for more information.

Table 31. Workers' Compensation *(continued)*

<table>
<tr><th>Question</th><th>Response</th></tr>
<tr><td>What other benefits are related/can be affected?</td><td>Workers' compensation leave may run concurrently with family and medical leave for eligible employees. During the time workers' compensation leave runs concurrently with family and medical leave, the employee may receive the following health benefits:
• Same access to participation in health and benefits plans as with any other unpaid disability leave. If you provide health insurance during other disability leaves, you are required to do so for workers' compensation; and
• COBRA coverage, if triggered by workers' compensation. Contact your insurance provider for information.
The following employee benefits are covered by workers' compensation:
• Seniority — Employees continue to accrue seniority as with your paid and unpaid leave policies;
• Holidays — You determine whether or not an employee on workers' compensation leave receives holiday pay. Treat the employee on workers' comp the same as you treat employees on other types of disability leave;
• Company closures — If your business closes for an extended vacation (such as summer vacation), or other reasons, such as for maintenance, inventory, or remodeling, this time does not count toward workers' compensation days; and
• Sick leave, vacation, and PTO — if the employee is on company-paid leave, these benefits continue to accrue. If on unpaid leave, they only accrue if your other disability policies allow.
You may allow the use of sick pay (page 139), vacation (page 135), or PTO (page 141) to supplement workers' compensation benefits.
The employee may now be a "qualified person with a disability" requiring reasonable accommodation. See "What Is Reasonable Accommodation?" in Chapter 7, page 235.</td></tr>
</table>

Choice of Physician, Chiropractor, or Acupuncturist

New for 2008 Although an employees have the right to notify you that they have a personal medical doctor (MD), doctor of osteopathic medicine (DO) or medical group, specific rules govern this predesignation. Employees make a valid physician pre-designation if:

- Your employer offers group health coverage;
- The doctor is your regular physician, who shall be either a physician who has limited his or her practice of medicine to general practice or who is a board-certified or board-eligible internist, pediatrician, obstetrician-gynecologist, or family practitioner, and has previously directed your medical treatment, and retains your medical records;
- Your "personal physician" may be a medical group if it is a single corporation or partnership composed of licensed doctors of medicine or osteopathy, which operates an integrated multi-specialty medical group providing comprehensive medical services predominantly for non-occupational illnesses and injuries;
- Prior to the injury your doctor agrees to treat you for work injuries or illnesses;
- Prior to the injury you provided your employer the following in writing:
  - Notice that you want your personal doctor to treat you for a work-related injury or illness; and
  - Your personal doctor's name and business address.
- A physician pre-designation made before March 14, 2006 is valid if all of the above conditions are met.

Employers must notify employees of the right to pre-designate a personal physician and provide new employees with physician pre-designation form upon hire or by the end of the first pay period. Employees that have properly pre-designated a personal physician are entitled to be treated by that physician whether or not the employee would otherwise be treated within a Medical Provider Network. If emergency or first aid treatment is required, you must provide it, but employees can get follow-up treatment with their pre-designated personal physician.

The new rules also require employers whose employees are not treated by a Medical Provider Network to provide their employees with a form for pre-designating a chiropractor or acupuncturist, upon hire or by the end of the first pay period. A valid personal chiropractor or personal acupuncturist pre-designation requires the chiropractor or acupuncturist to have previously directed treatment of the employee and retain the employee's treatment records and history. The chiropractor or acupuncturist must also be licensed under the Business and Professions Code. There is no requirement for acceptance as there is with the personal physician. These employers must notify employees in writing of their right to request a change to a treating physician of their choice 30 days after reporting an injury if the original treating physician was selected by the employer or its insurer.

What Do I Need to Know About Vacation?

Vacation is paid time away from work that is typically planned in advance. Many employers offer two or three weeks of paid vacation per year.

Table 32. Vacation

Question	Response
Do I have to provide this benefit?	No. If you choose to offer paid vacation, there are important rules to follow. Vacation can accrue or vest on an hourly, daily, weekly, or monthly basis. ***Example:*** If your employees earn three weeks of vacation a year (120 hours), then vacation accrues at a rate of approximately 0.45 hours daily. Any employer who offers vacation must offer it in accordance with these regulations.
Is this time off paid?	Vacation can be paid or unpaid. If it is paid, vacation is treated like wages. Once it is earned, it cannot be taken away. You cannot have a "use it or lose it" policy, but you can require that your employees cash out their unused vacation once a year, or that they stop accruing vacation after reaching a certain cap. For more information about vacation policies, see "Vacation" in Table 12 in Chapter 3, page 65.
Who's eligible?	You get to decide who is eligible to accrue vacation. Be consistent. Employees who are similarly situated should be accruing vacation at the same rate.
How does this start?	You can allow your employees to start accruing vacation from the day they start work. Or, you can choose to make your employees wait a reasonable period (30 days, 90 days) before vacation begins to accrue.
How long does it last?	You get to decide. Your policy may offer an employee three weeks of vacation per year, and may forbid employees from taking it all at once. You have the authority to approve and deny any given vacation schedule. For non-exempt employees, you can decide whether vacation is taken in days, hours, or half hours. For exempt employees, you may decide whether vacation is taken in four hour increments or more, or in full day increments only.

Table 32. Vacation *(continued)*

Question	Response
What's the process like?	**1.** Your employee will notify you that he/she wants to take vacation. You might want to have a form for this that your employees can use. **2.** You either approve the requested day(s) or ask the employee to reschedule. **3.** When the employee takes the day(s), be sure to subtract the time from the amount of his/her accrued vacation.
What if the employment relationship ends?	If you offer paid vacation, when an employee leaves, you must include any accrued but unused vacation in the final paycheck, paid at the rate the employee was earning at the time of termination. See "How Do I Calculate a Final Paycheck?" in Chapter 5, page 175.
What other benefits are related/can be affected?	You can require employees to use their accrued vacation for some types of leave. For other leaves, you cannot require employees to use vacation, but they have the option of doing so if they want to. See: • "Pregnancy Disability Leave" on page 97; • "Family and Medical Leave" on page 101; • "Disability Leave" on page 107; • "Paid Family Leave" on page 123; and • "Workers' Compensation" on page 127.

What Do I Need to Know About Holidays?

Common holidays include New Year's Day, Presidents' Day, Memorial Day, the Fourth of July, Labor Day, Thanksgiving and the Friday after, and Christmas.

Table 33. Holidays

Question	Response
Do I have to provide this benefit?	No. However, you may need to accommodate religious holidays in certain circumstances. See "Religion" in Chapter 7, page 233. If you have a policy of giving a paid day off, the courts will construe that as an obligation.
Is this time off paid?	Not necessarily. For non-exempt employees, you are not required to pay for holiday time, although many employers do. For exempt employees, you must pay them their full weekly salary for any week in which they perform any work. For more information about holiday policies, see "Holidays" in Table 12 in Chapter 3, page 65.
Who's eligible?	You get to decide who is eligible for holidays. All employees who are similarly situated should receive the same holiday benefits.
How does this start?	NA
How long does it last?	Typically, one day at a time.
What's the process like?	Create a holiday policy and provide it to your employees. See "Holidays" in Table 12 in Chapter 3, page 65. Tell employees at the beginning of each year which holidays will be granted and whether they will be paid.

Table 33. Holidays *(continued)*

Question	Response
What if the employment relationship ends?	Employees cannot accrue or vest holiday pay, like they can with vacation; therefore, you don't need to pay a departing employee for any future holidays.
What other benefits are related/can be affected?	Holidays don't directly affect other types of leave, although employees may want to take vacation or other time off on days before or after a holiday to extend their time away from work. Certain leaves may have an affect on holidays. See: • "Pregnancy Disability Leave" on page 97; • "Family and Medical Leave" on page 101; • "Disability Leave" on page 107; and • "Workers' Compensation" on page 127.

What Do I Need to Know About Floating Holidays/Personal Holidays/ Personal Days?

The way your policy defines floating holidays/personal days determines how you need to treat the time off.

- You must treat time off associated with an event as a holiday. See "What Do I Need to Know About Holidays?" on page 137; and
- You must treat time off that an employee may take any time and for any reason as vacation. See "What Do I Need to Know About Vacation?" on page 135.

Just as with vacation, you may place a cap on the accrual of these days off, but you must give employees reasonable opportunity to take the days off so that they can stay below the cap.

What Do I Need to Know About Sick Leave?

Sick leave is an optional benefit many employers provide to their employees to take care of themselves and family members during illness.

Table 34. Sick Leave

Question	Response
Do I have to provide this benefit?	No, but if you do, you must also allow employees to use one-half of their annual sick leave to care for family members. See "What's the process like?" below for more information about kin care.
Is this time off paid?	For non-exempt employees, you decide. Unlike vacation, accrued but unused sick leave need not be paid out at termination. For exempt employees, you need not provide sick leave, but if you do not, you will not be able to deduct for any complete days of absence due to illness. See "Deductions from an Exempt Employee's Salary" in Chapter 5, page 180.
Who's eligible?	Anyone you decide. Make sure that employees who are similarly situated are similarly eligible.
How does this start?	You decide. Your policy should make clear what the employee needs to do in order to use a sick day.
How long does it last?	You decide. You also are not required to allow accrual of sick leave, so unused sick leave can be forfeited at the end of a designated period (i.e., annually, or every quarter).

Table 34. Sick Leave *(continued)*

Question	Response
What's the process like? **Kin care** includes care of a sick child, parent, spouse, registered domestic partner, or child of a registered domestic partner.	If you choose to offer sick leave, document your policy, and provide this information to all employees (even if they're not eligible). You should document absences for sick leave. Consider requiring a medical excuse for extended absences. Keep a copy of the excuse in the employee's medical file. Document time off for payroll purposes. For more information, see "Deductions from an Exempt Employee's Salary" in Chapter 5, page 180. **Kin Care** If you offer sick leave, you must also allow employees to take up to half of their annual accrued sick leave for kin care. You should require employees to designate time off for kin care as such. See the *Request for Use of Kin Care*, described in Table 38 on page 149. Keep the documentation in the employee's medical file. Denying an employee this right, or discriminating against an employee who exercises this right, can cause you problems. This includes having to reinstate an employee to a previous position, and paying back wages, other damages, and attorney fees. You may not discipline, discharge, demote, or suspend an employee for taking time off for kin care. You also may not count time off for kin care against an employee in accordance with any absence control policy you may have.
What if the employment relationship ends?	Regardless of how the relationship ends, you are not required to pay an employee for unused sick leave.
What other benefits are related/can be affected?	If you offer sick leave, you must also provide kin care benefits. If you offer sick leave as part of a PTO policy, allow your employees to take up to half of their annual accrued PTO as kin care leave. Any sick leave payment you provide your employees can reduce the amount of SDI benefits they receive. For more information, see "What Do I Need to Know About SDI?" on page 122. Employees who are pregnant must be allowed to use accrued sick leave during PDL. For more information, see "What Do I Need to Know About PDL?" on page 97.

What Do I Need to Know About PTO?

Paid time off (PTO) may be a combination of sick pay, holiday pay, and/or vacation. Employees can take planned and unplanned days off. California law treats PTO like vacation. See "What Do I Need to Know About Vacation?" on page 135. If you offer PTO, you must allow employees to use half of their annual PTO accrual for kin care. See "Paid Time Off (PTO)" in Chapter 3, page 67 for more information.

What Do I Need to Know About CTO?

Compensatory time off (CTO or "comp time") is time off given in exchange for extra hours worked.

> ***Example:*** An employee might work an extra two hours and ask for "comp time" of three hours off at a later date.

It is illegal for all private employers to provide CTO, not only in California, but nationwide. If you are a private employer, you may not provide it under any circumstances. For more on CTO, see "Can I Offer Compensatory Time Off Instead of Overtime?" in Chapter 5, page 174.

Do not confuse CTO with makeup time, which is permitted in California. See "How Can I Use Makeup Time?" in Chapter 5, page 166.

What Do I Need to Know About Bereavement Leave?

When an employee experiences the death of a family member or friend, he/she may request time off for a funeral or for mourning.

Table 35. Bereavement Leave

Question	Response
Do I have to provide this benefit?	No. This is entirely a matter of company policy.
Is this time off paid?	For non-exempt employees, you get to decide. Many employees want to take the time off even if it is unpaid. For exempt employees, you need not pay the employee for time missed if it was a complete day.

Table 35. Bereavement Leave *(continued)*

Question	Response
Who's eligible?	You can determine eligibility requirements for this leave. You might designate bereavement leave as applicable only to family deaths, or you might extend it for other circumstances.
How does this start?	Your employee notifies you as soon as he/she learns of the need for bereavement leave.
How long does it last?	You can determine how much time you want to give for this type of leave.
What's the process like?	A request for this type of leave may come up suddenly. **1.** Document the circumstances and how much leave is granted. You may want to have the employee fill out a request for time off form. **2.** Make the necessary adjustments to the work schedule and paycheck of the affected employee.
What if the employment relationship ends?	Nothing. This is not an accrued benefit.
What other benefits are related/can be affected?	You may require non-exempt employees to use sick leave, vacation, or PTO for this purpose. For exempt employees, see "Deductions from an Exempt Employee's Salary" in Chapter 5, page 180.

What Do I Need to Know About Personal Leaves of Absence?

An employee may wish to take a leave of absence for personal reasons.

Table 36. Leaves of Absence

Question	Response
Do I have to provide this benefit?	No. This is entirely a matter of company policy. However, a personal leave may be a form of reasonable accommodation. See "What Is Reasonable Accommodation?" in Chapter 7, page 235 for more information.
Is this time off paid?	For non-exempt employees, you decide. Many employees want to take the time off, even if it is unpaid. For exempt employees, see "Deductions from an Exempt Employee's Salary" in Chapter 5, page 180.

Table 36. Leaves of Absence *(continued)*

Question	Response
Who's eligible?	You can determine eligibility requirements for this leave. ! If you provide this benefit for one employee, you set a precedent for other employees and could create a potential for discrimination claims if you deny another employee's request for the same type of leave.
How does this start?	An employee requests time off.
How long does it last?	You can determine how much time you want to give for this type of leave.
What's the process like?	A request for this type of leave may come up suddenly. **1.** Document the circumstances and how much leave is granted. You may want to have the employee fill out a request for time off form. **2.** Make the necessary adjustments to the work schedule and paycheck of the affected employee.
What if the employment relationship ends?	Nothing. This is not an accrued benefit.
What other benefits are related/can be affected?	Depending on the reason for the leave, it may qualify as family leave, sick leave, or some other type, therefore placing it under the regulations for those types of leave. When your employee requests the time off, inquire about the reason to determine if it qualifies.

What Do I Need to Know About Domestic Partner Rights?

The California Domestic Partner Rights and Responsibilities Act of 2003 became effective January 1, 2005. The Act:

- Gives domestic partners the same rights, protections, and benefits as are granted to, and imposed upon, spouses;
- Subjects domestic partners to the same responsibilities, obligations, and duties under law, whether they derive from statutes, administrative regulations, court rules, government policies, common law, or any other provisions or sources of law, as are granted to and imposed upon spouses;
- Grants registered domestic partners, with respect to a child of either of them, the same rights and obligations as those of a child of a spouse; and

- Gives domestic partners the same rights for leave under the California Family Rights Act (CFRA) as that given to spouses and their children. See "Domestic Partners and CFRA" on page 106.

Employers with state contracts for $100,000 or more must certify that they are in compliance with legislation[1] regarding benefits. If you want to contract with the state, you must provide the same benefits to domestic partners of employees as are provided to spouses of employees. If you do business with the state, consult with your legal counsel and benefits advisor.

A law passed in 2006 adds sexual orientation to existing classifications protected from discrimination by recipients of state funds and expands the definition of discrimination to include the perception that the victim is a member of a protected class.

This law adds sexual orientation to existing law that prohibits discrimination on the basis of race, national origin, ethnic group identification, religion, age, sex, color, or disability, against any person in any program or activity conducted, operated, or administered by the state or by any state agency, or that is funded directly by the state, or that receives any financial assistance from the state.

As such, it includes unemployment insurance, disability insurance and workers' compensation. It also defines "sex" and "sexual orientation" as having the same meaning as under the FEHA. The law also expands the definition of discrimination to include a perception that a person has any of these enumerated characteristics or that the person is associated with a person who has, or is perceived to have, any of these characteristics.

For more on domestic partners, see "Domestic Partners and Health Plans" on page 145.

For up-to-date information on this and other employment-related issues, see the California Chamber's ***HR California Extra***. To subscribe to this free publication, visit ***www.hrcaliforniaextra.com***.

1. California Public Contract Code, sec. 10295.3

What Do I Need to Know About Health Care?

A health care plan is an organized way for you to help employees cover their health-related costs. Some employers offer medical, dental, vision, prescription drug, and mental health care plans. This type of benefit is complicated, so you should consult a benefits expert when setting up your plan.

Table 37. Health Care

Question	Response
Do I have to provide this benefit?	No. If you do offer it, you must offer it in accordance with the laws. See "Glossary of Terms, Laws, and Agencies" on page 285 for details about COBRA, HIPAA, and ERISA.
Is this time off paid?	This is a benefit and not time off.
Who's covered?	If you offer a health care plan, you may be subject to ERISA regulations about notifying your employees, etc. Check with your legal counsel; ERISA is very complicated.
Who's eligible?	You decide. Make sure that similarly situated employees are similarly eligible.
How does this start?	You decide. Your insurance carrier will have advice and suggestions.
How long does it last?	N/A
What's the process like?	Your insurance carrier or third party benefits administrator will help you.
What if the employment relationship ends?	If you have 2–19 employees (Cal-COBRA), or more than 20 employees (COBRA) and you offer health care, you are required to give the ex-employee the opportunity to continue coverage by paying their own premiums. See Chapter 8, "Ending the Employment Relationship" for details.
What other benefits are related/can be affected?	During certain leaves, health care benefits must be extended to cover the leave. See "What Do I Need to Know About Family and Medical Leaves?" on page 101 and "What Do I Need to Know About PDL?" on page 97 for details.

Domestic Partners and Health Plans

The California Insurance Equality Act amends the Health and Safety Code and the Insurance Code with regard to domestic partner coverage.

Insurance plans subject to the Insurance Code must comply with this law if the policy is issued, amended, delivered, or renewed on or after January 1, 2005. Health plans subject to the Knox-Keene Health Care Service Plan Act of 1975 must comply with this law for all policies effective January 1, 2005 or thereafter.

The carrier must provide the same coverage to domestic partners as is provided to a spouse. This new law may result in carriers offering employers only plans that provide registered domestic partner and spousal benefits.

The employer still has the option to offer only employee coverage, and no spouse or domestic partner coverage.

Domestic Partners and COBRA

A registered domestic partner is not a qualified beneficiary under COBRA (20 or more employees) because federal law does not treat a domestic partner the same as a spouse. The federal Defense of Marriage Act of 1996 provides that a spouse can only be a person of the opposite sex married as husband or wife. Therefore, domestic partners have no independent rights as qualified beneficiaries.

A former employee's domestic partner may be enrolled as a dependent at open enrollment time, but the duration of that coverage is determined by that of the former employee. However, the child of a domestic partner has COBRA rights independent of the former employee if the child was covered as a dependent under the former employee's plan on the day before the COBRA qualifying event.

> ***Example:*** If an employee in your health plan terminates, the employee is eligible for COBRA, followed by Cal-COBRA, for a total of 36 months. The employee's domestic partner is not eligible for COBRA. If the employee was married, his/her spouse would have an independent right to COBRA.
>
> However, at open enrollment, the employee on COBRA may choose to add his/her domestic partner as a dependent. This does not give the domestic partner any COBRA rights. The domestic partner is entitled to dependent coverage only for the remaining length of time that your former employee is entitled to COBRA coverage. If the former employee and his/her domestic partner end their relationship, the dependent coverage for the domestic partner also ends.

Domestic Partners and Cal-COBRA

In 2005, registered domestic partners became qualified beneficiaries under Cal-COBRA (2–19 employees). Therefore, if a registered domestic partner was a health plan participant on the day before a qualifying event, he or she would be entitled to continuation benefits.

The Cal-COBRA extension of federal COBRA continuation benefits does not apply to a registered domestic partner. A person must have been a COBRA-qualified beneficiary to be entitled to this extension, and COBRA does not cover domestic partners. Once COBRA benefits are exhausted, a domestic partner may be eligible to continue benefits by converting to an individual policy.

What Do I Need to Know About Life Insurance Plans?

Many employers include life insurance among the benefits they offer to their employees. This type of benefit is complicated, so you should consult a benefits expert when setting up your plan.

What Do I Need to Know About a Voluntary Disability Plan?

If you do not want to participate in the SDI program, you can establish your own program with EDD and employee approval. Your plan must offer coverage, benefits, and rights equal to the state program in all aspects, and better in at least one.

Your employees can still opt into the state program. See "What Do I Need to Know About SDI?" on page 122. Check with your legal counsel if you want to set up a voluntary program.

What Do I Need to Know About Providing Bonuses?

See Table 44 in Chapter 5, page 167. This type of benefit is complicated, so you should consult a benefits expert when setting up your plan.

What Do I Need to Know About Retirement or Pension Plans?

Although not required by law, a company-sponsored qualified retirement plan (one that meets IRS specifications) is an excellent benefit that can attract and reward employees and provide you with tax advantages. You can choose from a wide range of options, from complex plans requiring advice from experts, to simple plans that you can establish without any outside consultants. Some examples are Individual Retirement Accounts (IRAs), Simplified Employee Pensions (SEPs), profit-sharing plans [including 401(k)s], and Employee Stock Ownership Plans (ESOPs).

Although there are many different types of retirement plans, they fall into two general categories:

- Defined benefit plans — A predetermined formula determines the benefits received, which are tied to the employee's salary, length of service or both. You bear the responsibility for funding and investment risks; and
- Defined contribution plans — A specified amount is placed in a participant's account. The amount of funds accumulated and the investment gains or losses determine the benefit received at retirement. You bear no responsibility for investment returns, but you must provide a good selection of sound investment options.

Retirement plans are regulated by ERISA. See "Glossary of Terms, Laws, and Agencies" on page 285 for details about ERISA. You should consult with competent legal counsel to make sure you establish and maintain your plans according to this complex and technical area of the law.

Any Other Benefits?

Many small businesses offer their employees other benefits and perquisites, often called perks. A clothing store might offer employees a significant discount on purchases. A restaurant might give employees a free meal for every shift they work. An information technology company might offer memberships to professional organizations, training, and certification to add value to employees and the work they do. Company cars, designated parking spaces, picnics, parties, etc., are all ways for employers to offer competitive compensation packages and motivate employees.

The law doesn't address these creative types of benefits. Remember, though, that if you make a promise (i.e., create a contract), you will be obligated to keep it.

The Hitches, Glitches, and Pitfalls of Providing Benefits

Make sure that you offer benefits evenly. Do not discriminate amongst your employees.

When an employee goes on leave, make sure you know (and the employee knows) which type of leave it is. If you fail to establish that the employee is taking FMLA/CFRA leave, for example, then the leave taken doesn't count toward the enforceable limit.

What Forms and Checklists Do I Use To Provide Benefits?

The following table describes forms associated with leaves of absence and other benefits.

You can find these forms in your online Formspack, described in detail in "Online Forms" on page 4.

Table 38. Forms and Checklists

Form Name	What do I use it for?	When do I use it?	Who fills it out?	Where does it go?
Certification of Physician or Practitioner for Employee Return to Work	To obtain physician or medical practitioner approval for the employee to return to work.	Just before the employee returns to work.	Employee's physician or medical practitioner.	Keep a copy in the employee's confidential medical file, separate from his/her personnel file.
Certification of Physician or Practitioner for PDL or PDL/FMLA	To obtain physician or medical practitioner certification that the employee is disabled due to pregnancy.	At the time of, or just before, PDL leave.	Employee's physician or medical practitioner.	Keep a copy in the employee's confidential medical file, separate from her personnel file.
COBRA Administration Guide **New for 2008**	Use to ensure you use the proper, required forms relating to COBRA (20 or more employees) and Cal-COBRA (2 to 19 employees), as applicable.	Use when an employee is hired and refer back to it when a qualifying event occurs.	No filling out needed.	N/A

Table 38. Forms and Checklists

Form Name	What do I use it for?	When do I use it?	Who fills it out?	Where does it go?
Employee Letter – CFRA Leave Taken after FMLA/PDL	To notify the employee of the type of leave that has been granted.	At the beginning of the leave.	You do.	Send a copy to the employee and keep a copy in the employee's confidential medical file, separate from his/her personnel file.
Employee Letter – FMLA/CFRA	To notify the employee of the type of leave that has been granted.	At the beginning of the leave.	You do.	Send a copy to the employee, and keep a copy in the employee's confidential medical file, separate from his/her personnel file.
Employee Letter-FMLA/CFRA Conditionally Granted **New for 2008**	To notify an employee that their request for FMLA/CFRA leave is conditionally granted.	After an employee requests FMLA/ CFRA leave.	You do.	The employee's personnel file - medical file if the request for leave is for the employee's own medical condi-tion.
Employee Letter - FMLA/CFRA during Workers' Compensation **New for 2008**	Use this letter to respond to notice of an employee's absence due to family and medical leave after a work-related injury.	After an employee's work-related injury.	You do.	In the employee's medical file.

Table 38. Forms and Checklists

Form Name	What do I use it for?	When do I use it?	Who fills it out?	Where does it go?
Employee Letter – PDL/FMLA	To notify the employee of the type of leave that has been granted.	At the beginning of the leave.	You do.	Send a copy to the employee and keep a copy in the employee's confidential medical file, separate from her personnel file.
Employee Letter – PDL Only	To notify the employee of the type of leave that has been granted.	At the beginning of the leave.	You do.	Send a copy to the employee and keep a copy in the employee's confidential medical file, separate from her personnel file.
FMLA/CFRA Application - English **New for 2008**	Give to employees who request or may need a leave of absence under FMLA/CFRA.	Provide this form when an employee has requested a leave of absence or you recognize the need.	The employee.	The employee's personnel file - medical file if the request for leave is for the employee's own medical condition.
FMLA/CFRA Application - Spanish **New for 2008**	Give to employees who request or may need a leave of absence under FMLA/CFRA.	Provide this form when an employee has requested a leave of absence or you recognize the need.	The employee.	The employee's personnel file - medical file if the request for leave is for the employee's own medical condition.

Table 38. Forms and Checklists

Form Name	What do I use it for?	When do I use it?	Who fills it out?	Where does it go?
FMLA-CFRA-PDL Timeline	For information about relationships among various state-mandated leaves of absence and benefits during the time off.	When an employee considers a leave.	No filling out needed.	Your employee would also benefit from this information.
Leave Interaction **New for 2008**	Use this form to determine the relationships among the various state-mandated leaves of absence and benefits during the time off.	When an employee considers a leave.	No filling out needed.	Your employee would also benefit from this information.
Medical Certification – FMLA/CFRA	To obtain physician or medical practitioner certification that the employee is disabled due to "a serious health condition."	At the time of the medical leave.	The patient's health care provider. (The patient could be either the employee or a family member.)	Keep a copy in the employee's confidential medical file, separate from his/her personnel file.
Military Spouse Leave Policy (25 or more employees) **New for 2008**	To notify employees of their rights under the military spouse leave law.	Add to your employee handbook and distribute to employees upon hire.	No filling out needed.	In your employee handbook or with your other leave policies.
Military Spouse Request for Leave (25 or more employees) **New for 2008**	For employees to request military spouse leave in writing.	At the time an employee requests military spouse leave.	The employee.	In the employee's personnel file.

Table 38. Forms and Checklists

Form Name	What do I use it for?	When do I use it?	Who fills it out?	Where does it go?
PDL Timeline	For information about relationships among various state-mandated leaves of absence and benefits during the time off.	When an employee considers a leave.	No filling out needed.	Your employee would also benefit from this information.
Personal Physician or Personal Chiropractor Predesignation Form This form is also a tear-out in the *Workers' Compensation Rights and Benefits* pamphlet (in the *Required Notices Kit* associated with this product).	To notify employees of their right to elect medical treatment by their personal physician or chiropractor.	Give it to the employee at the time of hire.	The employee.	Keep a copy in the employee's personnel file, and send a copy to your contact at your insurer or claims administrator.
Request for Use of Kin Care	To notify the employee of the type of leave that he/she has been granted.	At the beginning of the leave.	The employee.	Keep a copy in the employee's confidential medical file, separate from his/her personnel file.
Request for Use of Kin Care - Spanish **New for 2008**	To notify the employee of the type of leave that he/she has been granted.	At the beginning of the leave.	The employee.	Keep a copy in the employee's confidential medical file, separate from his/her personnel file.

Table 38. Forms and Checklists

Form Name	What do I use it for?	When do I use it?	Who fills it out?	Where does it go?
Temporary Modified Duty Agreement **New for 2008**	To document a temporary modified duty assignment.	When an employee is unable to perform the essential functions of a job without accommodation.	The employee.	Keep a copy in the employee's confidential medical file, separate from his/her personnel file.
Workers' Compensation Insurance Shoppers Checklist **New for 2008**	Use this form to ask potential brokers and carriers important questions as you shop for a workers' compensation policy.	When you are shopping for a workers' compensation insurance policy.	No filling out needed.	In your files.

Where Do I Go for More Information?

CalBizCentral and the federal and state governments have a variety of resources to help you develop written employee policies.

Table 39. Additional Resources

For information on	Check out these resources
General	From CalBizCentral: • ***2008 California Labor Law Digest***; • ***2008 California Labor Law Administration***; • ***2008 Employee Handbook Software***; • ***Required Notices Kit*** • ***http://www.hrcalifornia.com*** • ***http://www.calbizcentral.com***; and • HRH Insurance Services of Northern California, (800) 373-1838.
Paid family leave	***http://www.edd.ca.gov***

Table 39. Additional Resources *(continued)*

For information on	Check out these resources
Military leave	• Veterans' Employment and Training Service "eLaws Advisor" ***http://www.dol.gov/elaws/userra.htm***; • The National Committee for Employer Support of the Guard and Reserve (ESGR) at ***http://www.esgr.org/***; or National Committee for Employer Support of the Guard and Reserve 1555 Wilson Boulevard, Suite 200 Arlington, VA 22209-2405 (800) 336-4590; • Non-technical Resource Guide to the USERRA at ***http://www.dol.gov/vets/whatsnew/uguide.pdf;*** • ***http://www.hrcalifornia.com/cid.cfm?web=26788&cid=userra_notice;*** and • ***http://www.dol.gov/osbp/sbrefa/poster/userra.htm.***
Self-insured employers	• Department of Industrial Relations Office of Self Insurance Plans 2265 Watt Avenue, Suite 1 Sacramento, CA 95825 (916) 483-3392; and • The Department of Industrial Relations website at ***http://www.dir.ca.gov/***.
State disability insurance	• ***http://www.edd.ca.gov/taxrep/taxrte9x.htm***; • ***http://www.edd.ca.gov/employer.htm***; • California Employer's Guide 2008 at ***http://www.edd.ca.gov/taxrep/de44.pdf;*** and
Unemployment Insurance	• The California EDD website at ***http://www.edd.ca.gov/uibdg/uibdgind.htm***; • ***http://www.edd.ca.gov/employer.htm***; and • California Employer's Guide 2008 at ***http://www.edd.ca.gov/taxrep/de44-03.pdf***.

Table 39. Additional Resources *(continued)*

For information on	Check out these resources
Work Sharing	EDD Special Claims Office P.O. Box 269058 Sacramento, CA 95826-9058 (916) 464-3300
Workers' Compensation	• From CalBizCentral: – ***2008 Labor Law Digest***; • The Division of Workers' Compensation within the Department of Industrial Relations will provide assistance and advice; • The Equal Employment Opportunity Commission (EEOC) at ***http://www.eeoc.gov/policy/docs/workcomp.html***; • State Comp Insurance Fund at ***http://www.scif.com***; and • Workers' Compensation Offices 455 Golden Gate Avenue, 9th Floor San Francisco, CA 94102-3660 (415) 703-4600 (800) 736-7401

CalBizCentral also provides many ongoing and comprehensive educational opportunities for small business owners, HR beginners, and experienced HR professionals alike. These include online sexual harassment training, videos, and special HR seminars. For more information, please visit our website at ***http://www.calbizcentral.com***.

Chapter 5

Paying Employees

In California, an exhaustive set of rules governs employee pay. This can be more complicated than it sounds, but it doesn't have to be painful.

In this chapter you can find answers to questions about:

- Work schedules;
- The minimum wage;
- Overtime;
- Payroll deductions; and
- Much more!

Minimum Compliance Elements

1. Hang your *Employer Poster* (available from ***www.calbizcentral.com***), which includes mandatory postings that all employees must be able to see.

2. Require your non-exempt (hourly) employees to keep accurate records of time worked.

3. Calculate overtime for non-exempt employees after eight hours worked in a day (see "What Is Overtime and How Does It Affect Me?" on page 171).

4. Make sure you aren't treating your exempt employees like non-exempt workers — remember, your exempt employees get paid to get the job done, not to work a set number of hours.

5. Get to know the Wage Order for your industry (see the tip on page 159).

The Basics of Paying Employees

Within the protective laws and regulations, it's up to you to determine how and how much to pay your employees. The basic process looks like this:

1. **Classify** — Determine the worker's classification (exempt, non-exempt, independent contractor, full-time, part-time, temporary). See "How Do I Know Which Type of Worker to Hire?" in Chapter 2, page 9.

2. **Work** — Your employee works for a certain wage, either per amount of time (hourly or salary), or per item (piece rate or flat rate). See "What Do I Pay My Workers?" on page 167. The work is done for a defined duration of time according to a work schedule. See the sections starting with "How Do I Set Up Work Schedules?" on page 158.

3. **Calculate** — Calculate the amount he/she has earned, adding up the wages earned (regular and overtime), plus any other compensation earned (such as tips, commissions, or in the case of a final paycheck, accrued vacation, or PTO). This is the gross amount. See the sections starting with "What Do I Pay My Workers?" on page 167.

4. **Deduct** — Then make deductions from that amount for benefits, garnishments, taxes, and the like. This is the net amount. See the sections starting with "What Deductions Must I Make?" on page 175.

5. **Pay** — Create a paycheck for that amount and deliver it to the employee in the appropriate manner at the appropriate time (according to your established workweek and payday schedules), with a statement of how wages and deductions were calculated. See the sections starting with "When Do I Pay My Workers?" on page 181.

6. **Record** — Keep records of everything from basic employee identification information to what deductions you made from employee earnings. See the sections on record keeping, starting with "Do I Need to Report Any Payroll Information?" on page 183.

How Do I Set Up Work Schedules?

You can set up a work schedule that suits your company or a particular job in your company as long as your schedule complies with the day and hour limits and overtime regulations for your industry.

Base your work schedule(s) on workdays and workweeks. You can start the workday and workweek at a specific date and time of your choosing, but from then on you must follow this schedule as a uniform rule.

See "What Are My Scheduling Options?" on page 160 for examples of schedules you can use.

The **California Labor Commissioner** oversees investigations to ensure compliance with, and to resolve disputes arising under, state labor laws and Industrial Welfare Commission (IWC) Wage Orders.

Table 40. Workdays and Workweeks

Workday	Any consecutive 24-hour period starting at the same time each calendar day. If you do not define the workday, the California Labor Commissioner will presume a workday of 12:01 a.m. to midnight.
Workweek	Any seven consecutive 24-hour periods, starting on the same calendar day and at the same time each week. If you do not define the workweek, the California Labor Commissioner will presume a workweek of Sunday through Saturday.

Why Do I Need to Define Workdays and Workweeks?

Despite the freedom to set up your own work schedule, you must make sure to follow regulations that govern day and hour limits, overtime, paydays, and meal and rest breaks.

A **Wage Order** is an IWC regulation that defines minimum wages, hours, and working conditions for non-exempt employees in a specific industry. There are currently 17 Wage Orders, plus a Minimum Wage Order. The purpose of your business determines which Wage Order applies to you.

For help with determining which is the correct wage order for your business, use CalChamber's web-based wizard at ***http://www.hrcalifornia.com/wageorders***.

Table 41. Effects of Workday/Workweek Definitions

Limits	Generally, every employee is entitled to at least one day off in a seven-day workweek or, under some circumstances, the equivalent to one day's rest in seven during each calendar month. You cannot require employees who work under Wage Orders 4 and 13 to work more than 72 hours per week. Other limits are placed on daily and weekly hours of work for certain types of employees such as minors, truck drivers, pharmacists, train crews, and health care employees.
Overtime	The definition of workweek becomes extremely important when calculating overtime under the "seventh-day" rule, because this rule applies only on the last day of your defined workweek, not simply any time an employee works seven days in a row. ***Example:*** In a Sunday through Saturday workweek, the seventh day rule applies only if an employee works each day, Sunday through Saturday. Consequently, even if the employee works each day, Wednesday through Tuesday, Tuesday does not count as the seventh consecutive day in that "workweek." For more information, see "What Is Overtime and How Does It Affect Me?" on page 171.
Paydays	See "When Do I Pay My Workers?" on page 181.
Meals & rest breaks	See "How Do I Handle Time Spent Traveling, on Rest Breaks, or Between Shifts?" on page 164.

What Are My Scheduling Options?

You can choose from a variety of scheduling options for your employees. You may define different workdays or workweeks for different groups of employees as long as all the employees in the group follow the same schedule. Also, make sure to observe rest and meal break requirements, whatever schedule you choose. See "What Are the Meal and Rest Break Requirements?" on page 162.

Table 42. Scheduling Options

Type of schedule	What it means
"Regular" workweek	A seven-day workweek where anything over eight hours in a workday, or 40 hours in a workweek, is considered overtime. See "Why Do I Need to Define Workdays and Workweeks?" on page 159.

Table 42. Scheduling Options *(continued)*

Type of schedule	What it means
Flexible schedule	A workweek schedule of eight hours per day where some employees begin the shift early in the day and others begin their work later in the day.
Split shift	Any two distinct work periods, established by the employer, separated by more than a one-hour meal period. You must pay the employee at least one hour's pay, at no less than minimum wage, for the time between shifts. Any hourly amount the employee earns above minimum wage can be used to partially or fully offset the split shift requirement.
Alternative work-week	Any regularly scheduled workweek requiring an employee to work more than eight hours in a 24-hour period. Common schedules are: • 4/10 — four-day workweek of 10 hours per day; and • 9/80 — two-week schedule of nine-hour days with every other Friday off Employees on an alternative workweek earn overtime differently than those who are subject to overtime after eight hours per day. **Use extreme caution when setting up an alternative workweek.** Consult your industry's Wage Order to learn the specific steps you must follow to create, implement, follow, and repeal an alternative workweek. See ***http://www.hrcalifornia.com/wageorders*** for more information.

Can I Require My Employees to Work Overtime?

With a couple of limited exceptions (see note), employees have no statutory or regulatory basis upon which they may refuse your request that they work overtime. However, you can often find employees who want to work overtime.

A good approach is to first request volunteers among qualified employees, and then require overtime only in the absence of such volunteers. You can enforce overtime requests with disciplinary action if the employee refuses.

For more information, see "What Is Overtime and How Does It Affect Me?" on page 171.

Wage Orders 3, 4, 8, 13, and 16 have special provisions regarding required overtime:

- Wage Order 3 — An employee may work up to a maximum of 72 hours in seven consecutive days, after which the employee shall have a 24-hour period off duty.
- Wage Order 4 — No employee shall be terminated or otherwise disciplined for refusing to work more than 72 hours in any workweek, except in an emergency.
- Wage Order 8 — An employee may work up to a maximum of 72 hours in any workweek, after which the employee shall have a 24-hour period off duty. There are some exceptions, which may be found on the wage order. All employers who permit any employees to work more than 72 hours in a workweek must give each employee a copy of the applicable provision for exemption, in English and in Spanish, and post it at all times in a prominently visible place.
- Wage Order 13 — Any work by an employee in excess of 72 hours in any one workweek shall be on a voluntary basis. No employee shall be discharged or in any other manner discriminated against for refusing to work in excess of 72 hours in any one workweek.
- Wage Order 16 — No employee shall be terminated, disciplined, or otherwise discriminated against for refusing to work more than 72 hours in any workweek, except in an emergency.

What Are the Meal and Rest Break Requirements?

You must provide a half-hour meal period for every work period of more than five hours. However, if six hours of work will complete the day's work, the employee and employer can mutually agree to waive the meal period. The waiver must be written.

Meal periods may be unpaid only if:

- They are at least 30 minutes long;
- The employee is relieved of all duty; and
- The employee is free to leave the premises.

You must provide a second meal period of at least 30 minutes for all workdays on which an employee works more than 10 hours. Refer to the Wage Order for your industry for any exceptions, especially if your workers' shifts are 10-12 hours long.

You must provide rest periods or "breaks" at the rate of 10 consecutive minutes for each four (or major portion thereof) hours worked. The breaks should occur as near as possible to the middle of the work period.

Rest breaks may not be combined with or added on to meal breaks, even at the employee's request. Nor can an employee use them to come in 10 minutes late or leave 10 minutes early.

Since you pay for rest breaks as time worked, you control them. You may require employees to remain on the premises during the 10-minute rest period.

Make sure you comply with these rules, because you can end up paying the employee for any time not provided. See "What Happens If I Fail to Give Non-exempt Employees Meal and Rest Breaks?" on page 188.

Meal periods may be longer than a half-hour at the employer's discretion. Anything longer than a one-hour meal break may raise issues of a split shift. See Table 42 on page 160.

The Industrial Welfare Commission (IWC) is authorized to exempt employees from the required meal period if:

- They work in the wholesale baking industry;
- Are subject to a wage order; and
- Are covered by a collective bargaining agreement that provides for:
  - A 35-hour workweek, consisting of five, seven-hour days;
  - Payment of one and one-half times the regular rate of pay for time worked in excess of seven hours per day; and
  - A rest period of not less than 10 minutes every two hours.

The IWC is also authorized to exempt public sector employees who drive a commercial motor vehicle, from the meal and rest period requirements, if the employee is covered by a collective bargaining agreement.

Employees in the motion picture industry (Wage Order 11) or the broadcasting industry (Wage Order 12) may be exempt from the meal period requirement if they are covered by a valid collective bargaining agreement that provides for meal periods and includes a monetary remedy if an employee does not receive a meal period.

How Do I Handle Time Spent Traveling, on Rest Breaks, or Between Shifts?

There are times when you need to pay a non-exempt employee for time not spent working. If you will pay a special rate for travel time, or other special circumstances, you must establish and communicate the rate to employees in advance of the event. The amount and duration depends on what he/she is doing during that time.

Table 43. Types of Paid Non-Working Time

Type of time	Must be paid if	Amount/duration of pay	Included in overtime calculation?
On-duty meals	You require the employee to remain on the premises.	Hourly wage for the meal time.	Yes.
Time spent between split shifts	The time between shifts is more than one hour.	No less than minimum wage for at least one hour of time between shifts.	No, because the time wasn't actually spent working.
Reporting time Not paid for on-call employees or when disrupted by: • Threats to the employer's property; • Utility failure; and • Acts of God.	You require the employee to report to work at his/her normal work time, and: • Do not put him/her to work; or • Give him/her less than half the hours he/she was scheduled to work.	Hourly wage for at least half of the employee's scheduled hours, which must be paid for no less than two hours, and no more than four.	No.
	You require the employee to report to work a second time in any one workday and give him/her less than 2 hours of work.	Hourly wage for at least 2 hours.	Only the time actually worked.
Call-in	You call the employee in on a day other than normal.	For employees not regularly scheduled to work, employee must be paid at least one-half of his/her usual/scheduled work day.	Only the time actually worked.

Table 43. Types of Paid Non-Working Time *(continued)*

Type of time	Must be paid if	Amount/duration of pay	Included in overtime calculation?
On call (standby)	The time spent on call cannot be used for the employee's benefit. You must also pay for: • Time spent on call-backs; and • Time spent traveling from the point summoned to the work-site and the return trip.	Applicable rate (straight time or overtime).	Yes.
Travel time — general	The employee reports to the regular site and then has to go to another site.	At least minimum wage, for the time between sites	Yes, see "How Do I Calculate Overtime for Non-exempt Employees?" on page 172.
	The employee has to work at another site.	At least minimum wage, for the time in excess of the employee's normal commute.	
	The employee must travel to a distant place, like another city.	At least minimum wage, for the time spent in transit from home/office to the first destination (for example, to the hotel).	
Travel time — mandatory mode of transportation	You require your employees to travel to the worksite on employer-provided transportation.	At least minimum wage for duration of travel.	Yes.
Uniform changing and washing up	You require the employee to do so at work.	Applicable rate (straight time or overtime).	Yes.
Employee meetings	You require attendance.	At least minimum wage	Yes.

Table 43. Types of Paid Non-Working Time *(continued)*

Type of time	Must be paid if	Amount/duration of pay	Included in overtime calculation?
Employer-sponsored: • Training; • Lectures; and • Work courses.	You require attendance or If the training is related to the employee's regular job.	At least minimum wage.	Yes.
Time spent on physical fitness maintenance	You require remedial fitness training for the employee's regular job.	At least minimum wage.	Yes.

How Can I Use Makeup Time?

You have the option of offering makeup time, that is, allowing your non-exempt employees to request time off for a personal obligation and make up the time without receiving overtime pay. You are not obligated to offer this option, but if you offer it, you must abide by these rules:

- You cannot ask or encourage employees to use makeup time;
- The time must be made up within the same workweek;
- The employee is limited to 11 hours per day and 40 hours per week when working makeup time; and
- Before taking off or making up the time, the employee must provide you with a signed, written request for each occasion that makeup time is desired, unless the time off is for a recurring appointment, like a college course.

Make sure to have a time-record system that shows which hours you will pay at an overtime rate and which hours you will pay at a normal rate as makeup time.

Do not confuse makeup time with compensatory time off (CTO), which is illegal for most private employers. For more on CTO, see "What Do I Need to Know About CTO?" in Chapter 4, page 141 and "Can I Offer Compensatory Time Off Instead of Overtime?" on page 174.

The sample *Makeup Time Checklist* and *Makeup Time Request* forms are described in Table 53 on page 191.

What Do I Pay My Workers?

What you pay your worker depends on what type of worker he/she is (see "How Do I Know Which Type of Worker to Hire?" in Chapter 2, page 9) and what type of earnings you designate for the job (Table 44). The state of California has minimum wage and overtime requirements for non-exempt employees, and minimum salary requirements for exempt employees, that you must meet. See "What Is the Minimum Wage?" on page 169 and "What Is the Minimum Salary?" on page 168.

For non-exempt employees, Wage Orders govern pay by industry. Get to know the Wage Order for your industry! You can find this information at ***http://www.hrcalifornia.com/wageorders***. As long as you comply with those regulations you can choose from a variety of compensation scenarios.

Table 44. Types of Earnings

What kind	What it means
Salary (exempt)	Salaried employees receive a fixed amount for each payroll period, whether weekly, bi-weekly, semi-monthly, or monthly.
Salary (non-exempt)	You have to calculate any overtime due to the employee using the regular hourly rate to pay a salaried non-exempt employee who works more than the scheduled hours during the payroll period. To find out how, see "How Does Overtime Affect Salaried Employees?" on page 174.
Hourly (non-exempt)	Workers paid an hourly rate receive a fixed amount for each hour they work.
Piece rate (non-exempt)	A piece rate is based on a figure paid for completing a particular task or making a particular piece of goods. Compensation must add up to at least minimum wage for all hours worked. Piece rate employees are entitled to overtime wages. To determine the regular rate of pay, divide total earnings by total hours (even if more than 40 hours).
Flat rate (non-exempt)	Employee pay is based on the job completed, not the number of hours spent completing it. (Basically, a flat rate is a piece rate where there is only one piece.) Auto mechanics are often paid a flat rate. Compensation must add up to at least minimum wage for all hours worked. Flat rate employees are entitled to overtime wages. To determine the regular rate of pay, divide total earnings by total hours (even if more than 40 hours).

Table 44. Types of Earnings

What kind	What it means
Meals and lodging (non-exempt)	Employer-provided food and lodging counts as wages and can help you meet minimum wage requirements. Meals must be varied and nutritious, and lodging must meet sanitary standards. Employees cannot be required to share beds. Meals or lodging may not be credited against the minimum wage without a voluntary written agreement between the employer and the employee.
Tips and gratuities	Any money left by patrons for an employee is for employees only. You cannot count tips against minimum wage requirements. If tips are paid by credit card, payment can be delayed only until the next payday.
Commissions	Compensation based on a proportional amount of sales of the employer's property or services. Employees' main task must be selling a product or service, not making the product or rendering the service. This amount is part of the worker's regular rate of pay, used to calculate overtime. Divide total earnings by total hours (even if more than 40 hours).
Bonuses	A bonus is money promised to an employee in addition to the salary or hourly rate usually due as compensation. Bonuses must be included in an employee's regular rate of pay for purposes of determining overtime rates. Divide total earnings by total hours (even if more than 40 hours).

What Is the Minimum Salary?

Updated for 2008 To be considered exempt, salaried employees must be paid the minimum salary, which is $2,733.33 per month. This amount is arrived at by multiplying the state minimum wage of $8.00 by 2,080 hours, multiplying by two and dividing by 12 months:

$8.00 x 2,080 = $16,640 x 2 = $33,280/12 = $2,733.33

Salary is limited to cash wages. It may not include payments "in kind" such as the value of meals and lodging.

The minimum wage for computer professionals to be considered exempt is $36 per hour (the rate decreased from 2007). Computer professionals must meet separate exemption requirements (see *Exempt Analysis Worksheet – Computer Professional Exemption* in Table 8 in Chapter 2, page 38).

A licensed physician or surgeon primarily engaged in performing duties that require a license is exempt from overtime if paid $65.59 or more per hour (the rate increased from 2007). This exemption does not apply to employees in medical internships or resident programs, physician employees covered by collective bargaining agreements, or veterinarians.

What Is the Minimum Wage?

Updated for 2008 Effective January 1, California's minimum wage is $8.00 an hour. Even though the federal minimum wage is lower, you must pay at least the state minimum wage.

Not paying the minimum wage can get you in trouble. For more information, see "What Happens If I Fail to Pay the Minimum Wage?" on page 185.

You may be required to pay more than the minimum wage in some cities and counties as a result of local living wage ordinances. You can use the information in Table 54 on page 196 to check if your locality has a living wage ordinance.

A **living wage** is a wage sufficient to provide the necessities and comforts essential to an acceptable standard of living.

Can I Ever Pay Less Than Minimum Wage?

The IWC, which creates and monitors the Wage Orders in California, and the federal FLSA, which is the governing law for most wages and hours issues, both have provisions for paying less than the minimum wage under certain circumstances. For more information about the IWC and the FLSA, see "Glossary of Terms, Laws, and Agencies" on page 285.

Indentured apprentices are workers committed to a particular company for a specified period of time to learn a trade.

Table 45. Exceptions to the Minimum Wage Requirements

Type of employee	Conditions
Learners	Employee must have no previous experience.
Indentured apprentices	Applies only to the first 90 days of work. Must be indentured under the state Division of Apprenticeship Standards.
"Opportunity wage" earners	Applies only to persons under 20 years of age during the first 90 days of work.
People with certain disabilities	Employee productivity must be affected. Requires a license from the state Labor Commissioner to pay less than minimum wage.
Your parent, spouse, or child	No minimum wage laws apply.
Outside sales staff	Must spend more than one-half of work time away from the employer's place of business. No minimum wage laws apply. For more information, see *Exempt Analysis Worksheet – Salesperson Exemption*, described in Table 8 in Chapter 2, page 38.

Must I Reimburse My Employees for Their Expenses?

You must reimburse all employees (exempt and non-exempt) for all the expenses they incur in performing their duties, such as mileage, travel, and dining expenses.

The 2007 mileage reimbursement rate, set by the IRS, is 48.5 cents per mile. At the time of this book's publication, the 2008 rate has not been set by the IRS. Readers will find the updated rate, as soon as it becomes available, at ***www.hrcalifornia.com*** or the ***HR Handbook*** support page at ***www.calbizcentral.com/support***.

What Is Overtime and How Does It Affect Me?

When your non-exempt employees work beyond a "normal" number of hours, you must compensate them at a higher rate. In most cases this means you pay overtime to a non-exempt employee who works more than eight hours a day or 40 hours in a week.

! Remember! Exempt employees do not receive overtime pay.

Employees with an alternative workweek schedule earn overtime differently (see "Alternative Workweek" in Table 42 on page 160).

! Sometimes a collective bargaining agreement can affect overtime rules, so check yours if you have one.

In California, non-exempt employees must be paid overtime at the following rates:

Table 46. Overtime Rates

For these types of hours	Pay the employee's regular rate of pay, multiplied by this factor
Hours beyond 8 in a workday	1.5 (time-and-one-half)
Hours beyond 12 in a workday	2.0 (double-time)
Up to 8 hours on the 7th consecutive day of the workweek	1.5 (time-and-one-half)
Hours beyond 8 on the 7th consecutive day of the workweek	2.0 (double-time)
Hours beyond 40 straight-time hours in a work-week	1.5 (time-and-one-half)

Failing to pay overtime can get you into trouble. For more information, see "What Happens If I Fail to Pay Overtime?" on page 187.

How Do I Calculate Overtime for Non-exempt Employees?

1. Determine the employee's regular rate of pay:
   - For hourly workers, total the amount earned for each hour worked plus any bonuses and commissions, and divide that by the total number of actual hours worked;
   - For piece workers, total the amount earned for units produced and divide that by the total number of actual hours worked, even if it's more than 40; and
   - For non-exempt salaried workers, see "How Does Overtime Affect Salaried Employees?" on page 174.

The **regular rate of pay** equals an employee's actual earnings, which may include an hourly rate, commission, bonuses, piece work, and the value of meals and lodging. See Table 44 on page 167 for examples of different types of compensation.

While you need to include bonuses and commissions in the regular rate of pay, you do not need to include:

- Hours paid but not worked (vacation, reporting time, etc.) (see "How Do I Handle Time Spent Traveling, on Rest Breaks, or Between Shifts?" on page 164);
- Reimbursement of expenses (see "Must I Reimburse My Employees for Their Expenses?" on page 170);
- Gifts or discretionary bonuses (in recognition of services performed during a given period); and
- Benefits payments (profit sharing plan, health care plan, etc.).

See "How Do I Calculate Overtime for Non-exempt Employees with More Than One Rate of Pay?" on page 173 for a sample calculation.

2. Determine how many straight-time hours the employee worked for that workweek. For information on defining your workweek, see "How Do I Set Up Work Schedules?" on page 158.

Straight-time hours are hours that the employees would usually work (the first eight hours of their workday.)

Only hours worked at straight time apply to the weekly 40-hour limit. (This prevents "pyramiding" of overtime, where an employee earns overtime on top of overtime already paid.) Once an employee has been paid overtime for hours over eight in a day, those overtime hours do not count toward the weekly 40-hour limit.

Example: An employee works 10 hours each day Monday through Thursday, and therefore is owed eight hours of straight time and two hours of overtime for each of those days. When that employee comes in on Friday morning, although he/she actually has worked 40 hours already in the workweek, he/she has worked only 32 hours of straight time and does not begin earning weekly overtime until he/she works eight more hours.

3. For any overtime hours, pay the appropriate rate listed in Table 47 on page 173.

How Do I Calculate Overtime for Non-exempt Employees with More Than One Rate of Pay?

Different rates may be paid for different jobs, so long as the work involved is objectively different. In this case, there's a difference between the hourly rate and the regular rate of pay when employee works overtime and earns:

- Time-and-one-half, you must pay him/her the hourly rate for the job he/she is doing, plus one-half of the regular rate of pay; or
- Double-time, you must pay him/her two times the regular rate of pay.

Remember! If your employee works an alternative workweek, different calculations are in order. See "What Are My Scheduling Options?" on page 160.

Table 47. Regular Rate of Pay for Multiple Hourly Rates

An employee normally earns $10 per hour working at trade shows for his/her employer and $8.00 per hour for travel time. In one week, the employee works 40 hours at the trade show and spends 10 hours traveling.	
Total rate 1	$10/hour x 40 hours = $400
Total rate 2	$8.00/hour x 10 hours = $80
Total weekly wages before overtime premiums	$400 + $75 = $475
Regular rate of pay	$480 divided by 50 hours = $9.60
Overtime premium for time-and-one-half	$9.60 divided by 2 = $4.80

- For more than two rates, multiply the additional rates by the number of hours worked at those rates and include them in the total weekly compensation; and
- If the employee earned commissions or bonuses in addition to his/her hourly rates, include those amounts in the total weekly compensation.

How Does Overtime Affect Salaried Employees?

Salaried employees may be either exempt or non-exempt:

- Exempt employees do not receive overtime, but receive a full week's salary for any week in which they perform any work; and
- Non-exempt employees paid salary must be paid at overtime rates when they work overtime.

A full-time (40-hour) salaried non-exempt employee's regular hourly rate is 1/40th of his/her weekly salary. Base the overtime rate on the regular rate of pay, which includes the regular hourly rate plus most commissions, bonuses, or other compensation. See "How Do I Calculate Overtime for Non-exempt Employees?" on page 172.

The definition of "full-time" as 40 hours per week applies only to this particular pay calculation. You can define "full-time" as fewer than 40 hours for all other purposes, such as eligibility for employee benefits.

Can I Offer Compensatory Time Off Instead of Overtime?

If you are a private employer, probably not. There is an extremely limited exception for employers who are not subject to the FLSA. We recommend you consult legal counsel on this subject. Fore more on CTO, see "What Do I Need to Know About CTO?" in Chapter 4, page 141.

Do not confuse CTO with makeup time, which is permitted in California. See "How Can I Use Makeup Time?" on page 166.

In California, a schedule that permits the employee to work extra hours without overtime is allowed under an alternative workweek agreement. For more information about implementing such a schedule, see "What Are My Scheduling Options?" on page 160.

How Do I Calculate a Final Paycheck?

When you're ready to prepare a final paycheck, gather all timecards and documentation regarding the employee's unpaid work period or outstanding advances or expenses. Calculate the paycheck through the final day a work, based on the employee's:

- Regular rate of pay (see "What Do I Pay My Workers?" on page 167);
- Hours worked;
- Earned bonuses or commissions; and
- Accrued vacation.

! If you cannot determine commission wages owed at the time of termination, you must pay the commission owed as soon as the amount is ascertainable.

You can use the *Final Paycheck Worksheet*, described in Table 53 on page 191 to help you.

After determining the amount due to the employee, make proper calculations for any deductions, following the guidelines in "What Deductions Must I Make?" on page 175.

! You cannot deduct from a final paycheck for any property, even if the employee doesn't return the property to you. You can be fined if you do so.

To document that the last paycheck deadline was met as required (see Table 51 on page 181), have employees sign an acknowledgement that they have received the final paycheck. Use this opportunity to verify that the employee received proper payment. You can use the *Final Paycheck Acknowledgement*, described in Table 53 on page 191.

What Deductions Must I Make?

You must make certain deductions from the total compensation of both exempt and non-exempt employees. You are required to take out taxes and wage garnishments, if any. You can also take out money for certain work-related things. In addition, the employee can volunteer to have certain monies deducted. Special rules apply to deductions for salaried employees.

Deductions for the Government

Updated for 2008 You must make certain tax deductions from employee paychecks.

Table 48. Standard Deductions — Taxes

Tax	Deductions
Federal income tax	Use the employee's *W-4 Form - Employee's Withholding Allowance Certificate* (described in Table 8 in Chapter 2, page 38) and the withholding methods described in Publication 15 from the IRS. You can download Publication 15 at the IRS's website: ***http://www.irs.gov***.
State income tax	For information about rates, forms, exemptions, and withholdings, contact EDD or visit their website at ***http://www.edd.ca.gov***.
Social Security (FICA) and medicare	Both you and your employee must pay Social Security and Medicare taxes. The wage base limit has been increased. You must withhold and deposit the employee's withheld taxes and pay a matching amount at the following rates: • Social Security — 6.2% (wage base limit for 2008 is $102,000); and • Medicare — 1.45% (no wage base limit).
State Disability Insurance (SDI)tax and Paid Family Leave (PFL) tax	SDI provides temporary disability benefits for employees who are disabled by a non-work-related illness or injury. You must withhold monies from each paycheck. PFL provides temporary disability benefits for employees who cannot work because of the need to care for a family member or bond with a child. You must withhold monies from each paycheck. The 2008 SDI withholding rate for 2008 is 0.8%, with a taxable wage limit of $86,698 per employee and an annual maximum withholding of $693.58.

Deductions for a Third Party

A public agency or court judgment may require you to withhold money from an employee's paycheck. This is a wage garnishment. Make these deductions after taking out taxes.

The Consumer Credit Protection Act prohibits you from terminating an employee for having his/her wages garnished.

Table 49. Wage Garnishments and Back Taxes

Child support/ alimony	Court orders for child support take precedence over all other garnishments. If the employee has multiple child support garnishments, current support takes priority over past due support. Regardless of the number of garnishments, you cannot deduct more of the employee's disposable income than: • 50 percent if the employee has current spouse/child dependents; or • 60 percent if the employee has no dependents. An additional 5 percent may be garnished for support payments that are more than 12 weeks behind. A law passed in 2006 imposes a penalty on an employer that assists an employee or contractor with child support obligations evade meeting those obligations, including failure to file reports upon hiring. This law imposes liability upon any person or business entity that knowingly assists a child support obligor who has an unpaid child support obligation to escape, evade, or avoid current payment of those unpaid child support obligations. The penalty is three times the value of the assistance to have been provided, up to the total amount of the entire child support obligation due. The penalty will not apply if the unpaid obligation is satisfied. Prohibited actions, when an individual or entity, knows of should have known of the child support obligation, include: • Hiring or employing a child support obligor without timely reporting to the EDD New Employee Registry; • Retaining an independent contractor who is a child support obligor and failing to file a timely report of such engagement with the EDD; or • Paying wages or other forms of compensation, (including cash, barter or trade) that are not reported to the EDD.
Debt repayment	This includes loans, credit collections, and other debts. These are secondary to child support garnishments. Regardless of the number of garnishments, you cannot deduct more than 25% of the employee's disposable income.
Back taxes	The amount deducted depends on how many dependents the employee has. The more dependents, the less the IRS can deduct.

You must notify the appropriate agency if the employee leaves your company.

You must comply with garnishment orders as written until directed otherwise by the issuing agency or the court, stopping the withholdings only when ordered to do so. When you receive the court order:

- Mark the date received on the notice and retain the postmarked envelope in case you need to prove timely compliance;
- Keep a copy of the court order in the employee's personnel file as the legal basis for making the payroll deduction; and
- Advise the employee of the court order and the date you will make the first deduction.

As of January 1, 2005, employers can withhold $1.50 for each payment made, in compliance with an earnings withholding order that enforces payment of support obligations. Prior law permitted withholding $1.00 for each payment.

Deductions for Items That Benefit the Employee

You can make deductions from an employee's paycheck for certain items, such as meals, lodging, or other facilities. These deductions are for the employee's benefit. You can consider it part of his/her wages and include it in your calculations to ensure that you're meeting minimum wage requirements if:

- The employee has entered into a voluntary agreement; and
- The amounts credited do not exceed the limits specified in the applicable Wage Order.

See Table 44 on page 167 for more information.

Deductions for Your Benefit

You cannot deduct from wages for any cash shortages (for example, if a cashier's drawer doesn't match the record), breakage, or loss of equipment.

You may not make deductions for ordinary wear and tear to uniforms and equipment.

You cannot deduct the cost of a uniform from employees' wages. You also cannot require them to purchase the uniform on their own, unless it would be generally worn in an occupation — for example, a nurse's white uniform, or basic wardrobe items, such as white shirts, dark pants, and black shoes and belts (of an unspecified design) for waitstaff.

If you require tools and equipment, you must furnish and maintain them, except for customary hand tools required of employees making at least twice the minimum wage.

Deductions "Paid" to the Employee

The employee can volunteer to have other monies deducted from his/her paycheck for things like:

- Charitable contributions;
- 401(k)/IRA contributions;
- Health insurance plans;
- Loan repayments; and
- Union dues.

Some voluntary deductions can be taken out before taxes, thus reducing the employee's taxable income. For more information go to ***http://www.irs.gov***.

Deductions for Exempt Employees

Exempt employees receive a full week's salary for any week in which they perform any work, except in the following situations:

- If the employee is hired and begins work in the middle of the week;
- If the employee is terminated in the middle of the week; or
- If the employee's absence meets the criteria in Table 50.

In July 2006, the California Division of Labor Standards and Enforcement (DLSE) DLSE amended its Enforcement Policies and Interpretations Manual (section 51.6.15.4) to reflect a California Court of Appeal in a case decided in July 2005. This update authorizes deductions from an exempt employee's accrued vacation or paid time off (PTO) bank for partial-day absences of four or more hours. Different rules apply to partial day absences due to illness.

! If you have a policy permitting partial day deductions from vested benefits, or you wish to implement a policy that complies with current case law, you should consult with your legal counsel before making such deductions.

Table 50. Deductions from an Exempt Employee's Salary

Type of pay	Can I deduct from salary for:	
	Complete day of absence	**Partial day of absence**
Sick pay (bona fide sick leave plan)*		
Sick pay accrued	Yes	Yes, if the employee receives full salary.
No sick pay accrued or all sick pay used	Yes	No
Vacation pay		
Vacation pay accrued	Yes† ! You cannot require employees to use vacation for a partial week's absence for convenience only (for example, for a plant shutdown).	Yes, so long as the employee is exempt, and the salary is equal to a full day using paid, accrued vacation time.
No vacation accrued or all vacation pay used	Yes	No
Paid time off (PTO)		
PTO accrued	Yes‡ ! You cannot require employees to use vacation for a partial week's absence for convenience only (for example, for a plant shutdown).	No
No PTO accrued or all PTO used	Yes, if for personal reasons; or No, if sick.	No

* The sick pay plan must not give the employee a vested right to wages in lieu of sick pay or at termination.

† You must give 90 days or a full fiscal quarter (whichever is greater) notice before requiring exempt employees to take paid time off (vacation or PTO) during a business closure or plant shutdown.

‡ You must give 90 days or a full fiscal quarter (whichever is greater) notice before requiring exempt employees to take paid time off (vacation or PTO) during a business closure or plant shutdown.

When Do I Pay My Workers?

Not paying your workers in a timely manner can get you into trouble (see "What Happens If I Fail to Pay the Wages Due an Employee?" on page 187). You must pay employees according to guidelines that apply to the type of payment.

Table 51. Payday Rules

Type of payment	Must be paid
Regular wages (non-exempt)	At least twice each calendar month on days designated in advance (see "How Do I Notify Employees About Paydays?" on page 183). • Twice-monthly (semi-monthly) – For hours worked between the 1st and the 15th day of the month (no later than the 26th day of the same month) – For hours worked between the 16th and the last day of the month (no later than the 10th day of next month) • Weekly or bi-weekly – Within seven days of the end of the pay period
Regular wages (exempt)	At least once a month by the 26th day of the month.
Overtime	No later than the next work period's payday.
Tips/gratuities paid by patron's credit card	No later than the next scheduled payday following the date the patron authorized the credit card payment.
Expense reimbursements	On any reasonable schedule. Expense reimbursements to terminated employees are not subject to final paycheck deadlines and can be paid at the same time as reimbursements to active employees.
Final paycheck: • Termination	Immediately **You may not** require the employee to wait until the next regular payday. **You may not** withhold a final paycheck
• Voluntary quit (less than 3 calendar days notice)	No later than 72 hours after the employee gives notice. If the employee requests to receive his/her final paycheck by mail and designates a mailing address, the date of mailing is considered the date of payment.
• Voluntary quit (more than 3 calendar days notice)	On the employee's last day of work.

Table 51. Payday Rules *(continued)*

Type of payment	Must be paid
Vehicle sales people commission wages	Once a month.
Farm labor contractor employees	At least once every week on a day designated in advance. Payment must include all wages earned up to and including the fourth day.

Under certain circumstances, you can make exception to the payday requirements.

Table 52. Exceptions to Payday Rules

Type of employee	May be paid	Under these circumstances
Agriculture workers	Once a month	If you lodge and board them
Domestics	Once a month	If you lodge and board them
Striking employees	Next regularly scheduled payday	When they come back to work

What If a Payday Falls on a Sunday or Holiday?

If your business is closed on a payday that falls on a Sunday or a legal holiday, you must pay wages no later than the next business day. Make sure you state your policy in your employee handbook. For more information, see "Payment-related Polices" in Table 12 in Chapter 3, page 65.

What If My Employee Fails to Turn in a Time Card?

Even when a non-exempt employee fails to turn in a record of time worked, you are legally obligated to pay him/her on the established payday.

Since you have no time record to verify actual hours worked, pay all wages that would normally be due for the employee's work period and defer payment of overtime until the next pay period. If for some reason the employee doesn't work a full workweek, causing you to overpay him/her, you can reclaim the overpaid wages. For more information, see "Deductions for Items That Benefit the Employee" on page 178.

Remember! Exempt employees do not turn in time cards for pay purposes.

How Do I Notify Employees About Paydays?

You must post the day, time, and place of the regular payday in a way that your employees can understand. As a convenience, the state provides a small form for this purpose, which CalBizCentral includes as part of the *Employer Poster* (located in the ***Required Notices Kit*** associated with this product).

If you change the payday schedule, notify your employees of the change at least one full payroll cycle in advance.

What Form Can a Paycheck Take?

All paychecks must be payable in cash, on demand, without discount, at a bank that does business in California. The bank's name and address must appear on the paycheck.

At the time the paycheck is issued, and for at least 30 days after, there must be sufficient funds in the payroll account, or credit, for payment. Paying any wage with a check that is backed by insufficient funds is unlawful. See "What Happens If I Issue a Paycheck that Is Returned for Insufficient Funds?" on page 189.

You can also use an electronic transfer system (direct deposit) to transfer wages to a bank, savings and loan, or credit union if the employee chooses to do so. You may not force employees to use a direct deposit system. Even though the money is transferred electronically, you must still provide a written statement of wages and deductions to the employee. See "How Do I Record Deductions from Wages?" on page 184.

You may deposit final wages by direct deposit if the payment complies with existing laws concerning final payment and the payment (direct deposit) has been authorized by the employee. For more information on payday rules, see Table 51 on page 181.

Do I Need to Report Any Payroll Information?

You must provide information to assist district attorneys with the enforcement of garnishments for child support. In an effort to collect child support, federal law requires all employers to report certain information on their newly hired employees to EDD within 20 days of hire. As of January 1, 2001, all businesses and government entities that hire independent contractors must file similar reports. See "What If I Am Using an Independent Contractor?" in Chapter 2, page 31 for more details.

What Sorts of Records Must I Retain?

You must maintain an accurate record of employees' hours of work and compensation. The basic record keeping obligation includes the employee's:

- Name;
- Home address;
- Date of birth (if under 18);
- Occupation/job title; and
- Total wages and other compensation paid during each payroll period.

and for non-exempt employees:

- Clock time when each work period and off-duty meal period begins and ends;
- Total hours worked in each payroll period and applicable rates of pay; and
- Number of piece rate units earned, if applicable, and any piece rate paid.

How Do I Record Deductions from Wages?

You must keep an indelible record of payments and deductions for each employee for at least three years. The employee, upon reasonable request, can inspect and/or copy these records.

Indelible records are records that cannot be erased or deleted.

At the time wages are paid, you must provide each employee an itemized statement, in writing, that contains the following information:

- Gross wages earned;
- All hourly rates in effect during the pay period and the corresponding number of hours worked at each hourly rate (non-exempt employees);
- Piece rate units and piece rate, if applicable;
- All deductions, including:
  - Taxes;
  - Disability insurance; and
  - Health and welfare payments.

- Net wages earned;
- Employer's name and address.
- Inclusive dates of the pay period;
- Employee's name; and
- Employee's Social Security number.

New for 2008 As of January 1, 2008, only the last four digits of the employee's Social Security number may appear on the itemized statement.

Prior legislation provided for the use of an employee identification number in lieu of a social security number, but the number had to be an existing number. Legislation enacted in 2005 permits the use of the last four digits of the employee's social security number or an employee identification number other than a social security number.

! Deductions ordered by the employee may be combined and shown as one item.

You must comply within 21 calendar days to a request by an employee or ex-employee to review or receive copies of the payments and deductions listed above. You may charge the individual for the actual cost of reproducing the requested information.

The penalty (for actual damages) for failure to comply may be up to $4,000 plus costs and attorney's fees for the employee. The Labor Commissioner may also impose a penalty of up to $750.

For more information, see "What Happens If I Fail to Provide a Statement of Wage Deductions?" on page 189.

The Hitches, Glitches, and Pitfalls of Paying Employees

Employee pay is serious business. Penalties are steep for cheating your employees and government agencies out of money that is due to them.

What Happens If I Fail to Pay the Minimum Wage?

The California Labor Commissioner can:

- Assess fines
  - First offense — $100 per employee per pay period
  - Subsequent offenses — $250 per employee per pay period; and

- File charges with the district attorney.

A **misdemeanor** is a criminal offense that's less serious than a felony.

If you are found guilty of a misdemeanor you will have to:

- Pay the difference between the minimum wage and the wage paid during the period of violation; and
- Pay the court costs.

You may also have to:

- Pay a fine of $100 or more;
- Go to jail for 30 days; or
- Both!

If you fail to pay an exempt employee the minimum salary, the employee's exempt status can change, and force you to pay for overtime worked.

What Happens If I Fail to Pay Overtime?

The California Labor Commissioner can assess civil penalties against you, or any other person acting on your behalf.

- First offense — $50 fine per underpaid employee plus the amount of underpaid wages; and
- Subsequent offenses — $100 fine per underpaid employee plus the amount of underpaid wages.

The term "other person acting on behalf of the employer" means that payroll personnel, other employees who perform payroll functions (for example, human resources), and contracted payroll services could potentially be liable to pay fines out of their own pockets for miscalculating overtime under California law. However, the Labor Commissioner has stated that individual employees will not be fined, unless they are the individuals who formulate policies that lead to non-payment of required overtime.

What Happens If I Fail to Pay the Wages Due an Employee?

This is a misdemeanor, and can bring about court cases and court costs. The Labor Commissioner can assess fines of up to $200 per employee per pay period plus 25% of the wages not paid to each employee each pay period. All awards made by the Labor Commissioner accrue interest on all due and unpaid wages.

When employees file complaints with the Labor Commissioner to recover unpaid wages, the Labor Commissioner will:

- Investigate these complaints;
- Hold hearings and take action to recover wages; and
- Assess penalties and make demands for compensation.

Within 30 days after a complaint has been filed, the Labor Commissioner will notify the parties whether or not a hearing will be held.

In the event of a dispute over wages, you must pay, without condition, all of the undisputed wages. If you do not pay the disputed wages within 10 days after the dispute is resolved by the Labor Commissioner, you will have to pay triple the amount due to the employee.

If you are subject to the federal FLSA, employees may initiate claims with the United States Department of Labor (DOL). Employers should contact labor counsel if a DOL investigation commences.

For details about the FLSA and the DOL, see "Glossary of Terms, Laws, and Agencies" on page 285.

What Happens If I Fail to Give Non-exempt Employees Meal and Rest Breaks?

For each workday you fail to provide an employee (or if the employee fails to take) a meal period, you must pay the employee one additional hour of pay at his/her regular rate.

For each workday you fail to provide an employee (or the employee fails to take) a rest period, you must pay the employee one additional hour of pay at his/her regular rate.

! You are only liable for one hour of pay, even if the employee fails to take both rest periods. However, if the employee does not receive a meal break and one or more rest breaks, you owe two hours of pay at the regular rate of pay. Failure to pay the wages due may result in a waiting time penalty of one day of wages for every day that the wages are unpaid, for up to 30 calendar days.

You must pay the employee for the additional hour even if the employee was scheduled to miss the meal or rest period. Penalty pay for missed meal or rest breaks can raise your payroll costs by as much as 25%.

New for 2008 The California Supreme Court ruled that a three-year statute of limitations, not one year, applies to the "one additional hour of pay" employers are required to pay employees when meal and/or rest breaks are not provided. The court also found that employees and employers can add wage claims not presented in an administrative hearing when a trial court hears the case.[2]

What Can Go Wrong with an Alternative Workweek Schedule?

The Labor Commissioner can invalidate an alternative workweek schedule for a number of reasons, including improper implementation, improper payment of overtime, and changing the schedule without the required procedure, among others. In addition, employees on public works and those in agricultural occupations under Wage Order 14 may not work alternative workweeks. Employees covered by collective

2. Murphy v. Kenneth Cole Productions, Inc. (2007) 40 Cal. 4th 1094

bargaining agreements that pay premium rates for overtime hours and at least 30% more than the state minimum wage are not required to comply with the alternative workweek regulations.

What Happens If I Fail to Provide a Statement of Wage Deductions?

If you don't provide the paycheck information, the employee can recover:

- $50 per employee for the initial violation; and
- $100 per employee for subsequent violations, up to $4,000.

If you do not provide the statements in writing, or fail to keep the records for three years, you must pay a civil penalty of:

- $250 per employee for the first violation; and
- $1,000 per employee for each subsequent violation.

If you make a clerical error or inadvertent mistake on the first violation, the Labor Commissioner has discretionary power not to penalize you.

What Happens If I Issue a Paycheck that Is Returned for Insufficient Funds?

Penalties for issuing insufficient checks have increased to:

- $100 per employee for an initial failure to pay each employee; and
- $200 for each subsequent failure to pay for each employee, plus 25% of the amount unlawfully withheld.

What Happens If I Don't Issue a Final Paycheck in a Timely Manner?

You are liable for a penalty of one day's wages for each day the check is late, up to a maximum of 30 days. Any penalty awarded by the Labor Commissioner is paid to the employee who was not paid on time.

Could I Be Liable for a Civil Claim?

Employees who believe they have not been paid correctly may file a wage claim with the state Labor Commissioner or pursue a civil claim. When a claim is filed with the Labor Commissioner and a decision rendered, either party can file an appeal to the trial court. If the party seeking the review is not successful, the court could award the non-appealing party money damages for court costs and attorney's fees. The party that appealed would have to pay these costs.

Prior court decisions held that the trial court award had to exceed the award by the Labor Commissioner in order for the appealing party to be successful, and thus avoid paying court costs and attorney's fees. Legislation effective January 1, 2004 overturns case law and considers an employee to be successful if he/she recovers a judgment in any amount greater than zero.

The Labor Code Private Attorneys General Act of 2004 permits employees to bring a civil action for labor code violations.

The Act was amended in 2004, retroactive to January 1, 2004, to require the employee to comply with specific procedural and notice requirements before filing a civil suit; employers also have an opportunity to "cure" violations before the lawsuit proceeds.

The law includes civil penalties of:

- $100 per aggrieved employee per pay period for the initial violation; and
- $200 per aggrieved employee per pay period for subsequent violations.

Twenty-five percent of the penalties goes to the employee(s). If the employee prevails in the civil action, he/she is also entitled to an award of reasonable attorney's fees and costs.

What Forms and Checklists Do I Use to Help Me Pay Employees?

The following table describes forms and checklists associated with paying employees.

You can find these forms in your online Formspack, described in detail in"Online Forms" on page 4.

Table 53. Forms and Checklists

Form name	What do I use it for?	When do I use it?	Who fills it out?	Where does it go?
Absence Request - English **New for 2008**	Give this form to employees when requesting future time off or reporting previous time off. This form also gives your employees the opportunity to indicate a Family Medical Leave absence, although it is not required.	When an employee is requesting time off or reporting time off taken.	The employee	In the employee's personnel file and a copy should go to payroll.
Absence Request - Spanish **New for 2008**	Give this form to employees when requesting future time off or reporting previous time off. This form also gives your employees the opportunity to indicate a Family Medical Leave absence, although it is not required.	When an employee is requesting time off or reporting time off taken.	The employee.	In the employee's personnel file and a copy should go to payroll.

Table 53. Forms and Checklists *(continued)*

Form name	What do I use it for?	When do I use it?	Who fills it out?	Where does it go?
Final Paycheck Acknowledgement	Recommended for ALL types of separation.	When the final paycheck is issued to the employee.	Employee signs the form.	Keep it in your personnel records.
Final Paycheck Worksheet	Recommended for ALL types of separation	When preparing the employee's final paycheck. (For more information about how to calculate an employee's final paycheck, see "How Do I Calculate a Final Paycheck?" on page 175.)	You do.	Keep the worksheet in your personnel records.
Makeup Time Checklist	To help you figure out if, when, and how to offer the time.	When you are planning your pay policies	You do.	Keep the checklist in your own employee pay records.
Makeup Time Request	To document requests for the time.	When an employee requests the time.	The employee.	Keep it in the employee's personnel file.
Makeup Time Request - Spanish **New for 2008**	To document requests for the time.	When an employee requests the time.	The employee.	Keep it in the employee's personnel file.

Table 53. Forms and Checklists *(continued)*

Form name	What do I use it for?	When do I use it?	Who fills it out?	Where does it go?
Meal and Rest Periods Policy **New for 2008**	Use this policy to remind employees of the legally required meal and rest breaks to ensure employees understand that your obligation to provide such breaks is met.	Not required by law, but should be part of your employee hand-book or distrib-uted to employees upon hire.	No filling out needed.	Employees keep their own copies. You should keep a copy as part of your employee handbook or personnel poli-cies file.
Meal Break Waiver - English **New for 2008**	Written docu-mentation of a worker's waiver of the 30 minute meal break.	When you have a nonexempt worker who will work a shift of six hours or less and both you and the worker wish to waive the required 30-minute meal break, use this form.	You and the employee.	In the employee's file; a copy to payroll.
Meal Break Waiver - Spanish **New for 2008**	Written docu-mentation of a worker's waiver of the 30 minute meal break.	When you have a nonexempt worker who will work a shift of six hours or less and both you and the worker wish to waive the required 30-minute meal break, use this form.	You and the employee.	In the employee's file; a copy to payroll.

Table 53. Forms and Checklists *(continued)*

Form name	What do I use it for?	When do I use it?	Who fills it out?	Where does it go?
Meal Break Waiver - On Duty **New for 2008**	Written documentation of an on duty meal break.	When you have a non-exempt worker whose work prevents them from being able to take a meal break and both you and the worker wish to waive the required 30-minute meal break, use this form. WARNING - On-duty meal breaks are enforceable in very limited circumstances, please consult with legal counsel before using this form.	You and the employee.	In the employee's file; a copy to payroll.
Meal Break Waiver - Second Meal **New for 2008**	Written documentation of a second meal break waiver.	When you have a nonexempt worker whose shift will be more than 10 hours but less than 12 hours, the worker has not waived his first meal break, and both you and the worker wish to waive the second required 30-minute meal break, use this form.	You and the employee.	In the employee's file; a copy to payroll.

Table 53. Forms and Checklists *(continued)*

Form name	What do I use it for?	When do I use it?	Who fills it out?	Where does it go?
Overtime Request - English **New for 2008**	To document in writing employee requests to work overtime hours.	Provide these forms to supervisors, managers and employees and train all employees in the use of this form whenever overtime work is needed or performed.	You and the employee.	In the employee's file; a copy to payroll.
Overtime Request - Spanish **New for 2008**	To document in writing employee requests to work overtime hours.	Provide these forms to supervisors, managers and employees and train all employees in the use of this form whenever overtime work is needed or performed.	You and the employee.	In the employee's file; a copy to payroll.

Where Do I Go for More Information?

CalBizCentral and the federal and state governments provide a variety of resources to help you learn the ins and outs of wages and hours.

Table 54. Additional Resources

For information on	Check out these resources
General	From CalBizCentral: • The ***2008 California Labor Law Digest***, the most comprehensive, California-specific resource to help employers comply with complex federal and state labor laws and regulations; • ***2008 California Labor Law Administration***; • ***2008 Employee Handbook Software***; • ***http://www.hrcalifornia.com***; and • ***http://www.calbizcentral.com***.
Child support wage garnishments	• State Department of Social Services, Office of Child Support (916) 654-1532 at ***http://www.childsup.cahwnet.gov/pub/brochures/pub160.pdf;*** and • Franchise Tax Board at ***http://www.ftb.ca.gov/aboutFTB/manuals/arm/cpm/2430.html#2430.02%20Issuance%20of%20EWOTs***
Living wage	• Living Wage Resource Center at ***http://www.livingwagecampaign.org***; and • Communities with Living Wage Ordinances at ***http://www.epionline.org/lw_proposal.cfm?state=CA***

CalBizCentral also provides many ongoing and comprehensive educational opportunities for small business owners, HR beginners, and experienced HR professionals alike. These include online sexual harassment training, videos, and special HR seminars. For more information, please visit our website at ***http://www.calbizcentral.com***.

Chapter 6

Ensuring Workplace Safety

You have an obligation to provide a safe working environment for all your workers. Employees who can concentrate on their jobs without constant fear of work-related injury will be more productive and less inclined to complain to Cal/OSHA. By keeping safety a top priority, this doesn't have to be difficult.

The law requires you to protect your employees reasonably from:

- Work-related illness and injuries; and
- Workplace violence.

In this chapter, you can find answers to questions about:

- Preventing injuries;
- Workplace violence;
- OSHA inspections;
- Ergonomics; and
- Much more!

Minimum Compliance Elements

1. Hang your *Employer Poster* (available from ***www.calbizcentral.com***), which includes the mandatory Cal/OSHA postings.

2. Have an Injury and Illness Prevention Program (IIPP) (see "Injury and Illness Prevention Program" on page 199), and make sure your employees know about the workplace safety practices it covers (see "The Basics of Ensuring Workplace Safety" on page 198).

The Basics of Ensuring Workplace Safety

Every employer must follow the regulations created by OSHA and Cal/OSHA (see "Glossary of Terms, Laws, and Agencies" on page 285) that set standards for workplace safety. The general standard that every company must comply with requires you to establish an overall plan [an Injury and Illness Prevention Program (IIPP)] for keeping your workforce free from work-related injuries and illnesses. The individual standards require more detailed plans (like the Emergency Action Plan) that describe how you will help your employees stay safe on the job.

Knowing which safety standards apply to your company, and communicating them clearly to your employees, is essential for avoiding inspections and, more importantly, preserving the welfare and safety of your workplace and employees.

You can get copies of the exact standards from the Department of Occupational Safety and Health (DOSH). See "Where Do I Go for More Information?" on page 226.

How Do I Know Which Standards Apply to Me?

The Cal/OSHA standards you have to comply with vary on the size of your company and whether your company is deemed high—or low—hazard.

Five basic standards apply to just about every company:

- IIPP (see page 199);
- Emergency Action Plan (see page 201);
- Fire Prevention Plan (see page 202);
- Hazard Communication Program (HAZCOM) (see page 204); and
- Repetitive Motion Injuries (Ergonomics) (see page 205).

Even in cases where your company is exempt from complying with part or all of a standard, consider establishing a plan or program for handling potential situations, especially if the information can be added to your employee handbook or employee manual. See "The Basics of Developing Policies" in Chapter 3, page 54 for more information.

Injury and Illness Prevention Program

Every company in California must create an IIPP, which essentially contains a generalized plan for keeping its workforce free from work-related injuries and illnesses. For companies with more than 10 employees, the plan must be in writing.

The Formspack that comes with this book contains an approved *Injury and Illness Prevention Program*. The following table provides information about developing an IIPP.

Table 55. IIPP

Question	Response
Do I need to comply with this standard?	Yes, every employer must have a program. You are exempt from the record keeping requirements if you: • Have 10 or fewer employees; • Have 20 or fewer employees and are in a designated low-hazard industry; or • Are a local government entity, seasonal employer, or a licensed contractor. See "How Do I Know If I Have to Report an Incident?" on page 212 for more information about record keeping requirements.
Do I have to create a written program?	Yes, if you have more than 10 employees. You can use the *Injury and Illness Prevention Program*, described in Table 64 on page 219, to help you get started. Your plan must specify: • Management approval of the plan and the person(s) responsible for implementing it; • A company safety policy statement; • A system to identify workplace hazards; • A plan for periodic scheduled inspections; • A plan for investigating injuries; • A plan for safety training; • How you will communicate with employees about safety; and • The record keeping and posting requirements and any exceptions to these.

Table 55. IIPP *(continued)*

Question	Response
Do I have to provide training?	Yes. Training is required when you: • Implement your IIPP; • Assign a new employee to a position; • Transfer an existing employee to a new position; and • Make changes to workplace conditions. Provide refresher training as necessary. You can use the *Individual Training Certificate*, *Individual Employee Training Documentation – Initial Safety Training*, and *Training Sign-in Sheet*, described in Table 64 on page 219, to document training sessions.
Do I have to provide PPE? **PPE**, or Personal Protective Equipment, includes items such as gloves, masks, and special clothing used to protect against hazardous, toxic, or infectious material.	Only if other standards (like those governing chemical use or certain types of machinery) require you to supply equipment to protect your employees.
Do I have to perform inspections?	Yes. You can choose the frequency, depending on how hazardous your work environment is.
Do I have to record and/ or report anything?	Yes. Any injury that requires medical treatment beyond first aid, and all occupational illnesses, must be investigated, recorded, and reported. You can use the *Accident, Injury and Illness Investigation Form*, described in Table 64 on page 219, to help you document the incident. For more information on knowing what to record and when, see "How Do I Report and Record Work-Related Injuries and Illnesses?" on page 211.

Emergency Action Plan

The Emergency Action Plan standard requires you to have a plan for handling emergencies, including evacuating employees, providing emergency medical attention, and reporting emergencies to employees and community agencies.

Table 56. Emergency Action Plan

Question	Response
Do I need to comply with this standard?	Yes, every employer must have a program. You are exempt from the record keeping requirements if you: • Have 10 or fewer employees; • Have 20 or fewer employees and are in a designated low-hazard industry; and • Are a local government entity, seasonal employer, or a licensed contractor. See "How Do I Know If I Have to Report an Incident?" on page 212 for more information about record keeping requirements.
Do I have to create a written program?	Yes. You can use the *Emergency Action Plan,* described in Table 64 on page 219, to help you document your program. Your plan must specify: • Person(s) responsible for implementing the plan or portions of the plan; • How to communicate emergencies to employees; • Fire and emergency evacuation policies; and • Personnel assigned to provide first aid and emergency medical attention.
Do I have to provide training?	Yes. Train employees when you establish or change your plan, and when you hire new employees. Conduct emergency training and drills periodically. You can use the *Individual Training Certificate, Individual Employee Training Documentation – Initial Safety Training*, and *Training Sign-in Sheet*, described in Table 64 on page 219, to document training sessions.
Do I have to provide PPE?	Yes. You must comply with blood borne pathogens exposure regulations, exposure prevention requirements for any employee who provides emergency first aid, and provide any other equipment employees need to handle emergencies. See "Where Do I Go for More Information?" on page 226 for links to helpful websites.

Table 56. Emergency Action Plan *(continued)*

Question	Response
Do I have to perform inspections?	No, but you should cover this as part of your periodic IIPP inspections.
Do I have to record and/or report anything?	Not for the Emergency Action Plan, but record keeping is required for your IIPP. Follow those requirements in case of an incident.

Fire Prevention Plan

The Fire Prevention Plan standard requires you to know what fire hazards your employees are exposed to and to have a plan for handling fires. For companies with more than 10 employees, the plan must be in writing.

Table 57. Fire Prevention Plan

Question	Response
Do I need to comply with this standard?	Yes, every employer must have a plan.
Do I have to create a written program?	Yes, if you have more than 10 employees. You can use the *Fire Prevention Plan*, described in Table 64 on page 219, to help you document your program. Your plan must specify: • Person(s) responsible for implementing the fire prevention program; • Known fire hazards in the area; • Your fire prevention practices; • What fire control measures you have in place (i.e. sprinkler systems); • The frequencies of inspection and maintenance of fire control devices; • Alarm systems; and • Special employee responsibilities.
Do I have to provide training?	Yes. Train employees on fire prevention and safe work practices, either as part of your IIPP training, or as a separate fire prevention program. You can use the *Individual Training Certificate*, *Individual Employee Training Documentation – Initial Safety Training*, and *Training Sign-in Sheet*, described in Table 64 on page 219, to document training sessions.
Do I have to provide PPE?	No PPE is required, but standard fire protection equipment, such as fire extinguishers, sprinkler systems, and alarms, is required.

Table 57. Fire Prevention Plan *(continued)*

Question	Response
Do I have to perform inspections?	Yes. Use the *Fire Prevention Checklist*, described in Table 64 on page 219, to help you determine what and when you should inspect.
Do I have to record and/or report anything?	Yes. Record employee training in fire prevention, and document periodic inspections and fire protection equipment maintenance.

Work Surfaces, Control Devices, and Emergency Equipment

The Work Surfaces, Control Devices, and Emergency Equipment standards cover employee-occupied areas, and set minimum safety limits for lighting, flooring, housekeeping, entrances, and exits.

Table 58. Work Surfaces, Control Devices, and Emergency Equipment

Question	Response
Do I need to comply with this standard?	Yes, every employer must comply with the standards. Use the *Inspection Checklist for Work Spaces and Surfaces*, described in Table 64 on page 219, to help you comply.
Do I have to create a written program?	No. Include general information about potential hazards in your written IIPP.
Do I have to provide training?	Only if engineered controls, such as guard rails, are used. Include it as part of your IIPP training.
Do I have to provide PPE?	Not unless another standard also applies, such as working with chemicals, projectiles, or machinery.
Do I have to perform inspections?	Not required. Most situations are covered by IIPP inspections.
Do I have to record and/or report anything?	Yes. Record employee training, and document any inspections.

HAZCOM

The Hazard Communication Program (HAZCOM) standard requires all employers to communicate workplace hazards to employees, particularly when employees handle, or may be exposed to, hazardous substances during normal work or foreseeable emergencies.

Table 59. HAZCOM

Question	Response
Do I need to comply with this standard?	Everyone must comply, except for in a few, limited situations. See "Where Do I Go for More Information?" on page 226 for a link to the federal SIC website.
Do I have to create a written program?	Yes. Use the *Hazard Communication Program* form, described in Table 64 on page 219, to help you document the program, and the *Hazard Communication Information Summary*, also described in Table 10, to inventory hazardous substances in the workplace. You are also required to obtain MSDSs from manufacturers for all labeled containers and items on your inventory of hazardous substances. These sheets must be those provided by suppliers. **MSDSs** — Material Safety Data Sheets — Information provided by the manufacturer of a product that describes the product's chemical properties, potential hazards, and instruction in safe handling.
Do I have to provide training?	Yes. Train all new employees, and provide refresher training when you receive new information on hazards and standards. In addition, provide Proposition 65 warnings in the training. You can use the *Individual Training Certificate* and *Training Sign-in Sheet*, described in Table 64 on page 219, to document training sessions. **Proposition 65** requires that employers with 10 or more employees warn any person prior to their exposure to a chemical known to the state of California to cause cancer, birth defects, or other reproductive harm.
Do I have to provide PPE?	Not unless another standard also applies, such as working with chemicals, projectiles, or machinery.
Do I have to perform inspections?	Inspections are optional as long as you properly maintain all standard documents, such as MSDSs, labels, and warnings.
Do I have to record and/or report anything?	Yes. You must develop and maintain an inventory of all hazardous substances, and document employee training and compliance with the standard.

Repetitive Motion Injuries (Ergonomics)

The Repetitive Motion Injuries Standard, commonly referred to as the Ergonomics standard, requires employers to address workplace injuries due to repetitive motion. Repetitive motion hazards are work tasks that require repeated actions with the additional stress of improper ergonomics or work-station design.

Ergonomics is the scientific study of the relationship between people and their work environments.

Table 60. Ergonomics

Question	Response
Do I need to comply with this standard?	Technically, all employers must do what they can to prevent repetitive motion injuries (RMIs). The formal requirements of the standard only apply when: • More than one employee has suffered an RMI; • The RMIs are musculoskeletal injuries diagnosed by a licensed physician; • The RMIs were predominantly caused by a repetitive job, process, or operation; • The employees were performing a job, process, or operation of identical work activity; and • The reports of the two RMIs occurred within 12 months of each other.
Do I have to create a written program?	No. However, a written procedure can assist you in properly implementing the standard. You can use the *Hazard Prevention Data Sheet – Ergonomics Safety* form, described in Table 64 on page 219, as a guide. Your written program should describe: • How the standard applies and step-by-step instructions for compliance; • Any interim actions to prevent RMIs; • How to verify the diagnosis of an RMI; • How to conduct worksite evaluations; and • How to implement controls of RMI hazards.

Table 60. Ergonomics *(continued)*

Question	Response
Do I have to provide training?	Yes, you must provide initial training; however, refresher training is not required. The standard itself specifies training program content and implementation. See the *Hazard Prevention Data Sheet - Ergonomics Safety* form, described in Table 64 on page 219, for an example of the required training elements.
Do I have to provide PPE?	Only as a supplement to engineering controls (workstation redesign, adjustable fixtures, etc.) and administrative controls (job rotation and work pacing).
Do I have to perform inspections?	You need to evaluate a representative number of jobs, processes, or operations for proper ergonomic design and to determine if they involve certain motions, positions, or other bodily movements that are hazardous to muscles and joints.
Do I have to record and/or report anything?	You must keep records of all worksite evaluations conducted, control measures taken, training provided, and Cal/OSHA *Log 300* reporting completed.

Are There Any Other Standards I Need to Consider?

Other specific Cal/OSHA standards may apply to your company, especially if you work in a designated high-hazard industry. The following table will help you determine which standards may apply.

Table 61. Other Standards

If employees	This standard applies
May be exposed to an airborne contaminant.	Permissible Exposure Limits
Use or are exposed to a certain level or concentration of hazardous chemicals, such as lead, benzene, formaldehyde, and other carcinogens.	Chemical Protection Standards
Use any respirator, except for voluntary filtering dust masks.	Respiratory Protection
Are exposed to hazardous substances in a laboratory operation, except for test kits, and manufacturing and process simulations.	Exposure to Hazardous Substances in Laboratories
Are assigned to provide an emergency medical response, or may potentially be exposed to blood borne pathogens.	Blood Borne Pathogens

Table 61. Other Standards *(continued)*

If employees	This standard applies
Are required to work in a facility that contains a confined space, such as a tunnel, underground storage tank, or utility vault, that presents or contains a hazard.	Permit Required Confined Space Entry
May be exposed to hazardous machinery motion during normal operations or servicing.	Lockout/Tagout and Machinery Guarding
Operate a forklift or industrial truck, or if onsite materials are handled in volume.	Forklifts and Material Handling
Are exposed to noise averages over 85 dBA during a work shift.	Occupational Exposure to Noise
Are exposed to certain highly dangerous chemicals at or above the specified threshold quantities.	Process Safety Management (PSM) of Acutely Hazardous Materials (also known as the "Access Standard")
Work outdoors and/or are exposed to extreme heat and the possibility of heat illness.	Final regulations are available at: ***http://www.dir.ca.gov/DOSH/HeatIllnessInfo.html***.

For additional information on high-hazard industries, visit the Department of Industrial Relation (DIR) Model IIPP website at ***http://www.dir.ca.gov/dosh_publications/iiphihzemp.html***.

Why Do I Need to Have All These Plans?

If you don't have a plan, Cal/OSHA can cite you for violating the applicable standard. In addition, documenting your plans for compliance can help you prove your intentions of complying in the case that you are cited, which can help reduce the citation.

Sharing the information in these standards with your employees also helps you provide the knowledge they need to avoid or handle potential dangers. For example, let them know what the best escape route is in case of a fire, where you store the first aid kit, what health dangers they might be exposed to at work, and how they can communicate their safety concerns to you.

How Do I Create a Written Program?

When you create a written program, either for your IIPP or for any other standard, base it on processes and policies you have in place for your company. The following table guides you through the process of developing a written program.

Table 62. Written Program

Research/ Prepare	**1.** Gather any existing documents you have that can help you fill in the information (such as a fire escape plan, local emergency contact information, MSDSs, or workplace violence policies). **2.** Find out if your company is considered to be in a high-hazard industry by the Department of Industrial Relations (DIR). For general guidelines on high hazard employers, see the DIR's Model IIPP website at ***http://www.dir.ca.gov/dosh/dosh_publications/iiphihzemp.html***. **3.** Find out if Cal/OSHA considers your workplace to be at-risk for workplace violence. For workplace violence guidelines, visit the DIR's Workplace Security website at ***http://www.dir.ca.gov/dosh/dosh_publications/worksecurity.html***. **4.** Identify what processes or policies are lacking or missing, and what else you need to implement. **5.** Create two levels of information: general and detailed. The general information will go in your IIPP and your employee handbook, and the detailed information will go in the appropriate document for each specific standard.
Compile	**1.** Use the *Injury and Illness Prevention Program*, described in Table 64 on page 219 to create your IIPP, and to figure out what information you need to supply. Keep in mind that your IIPP doesn't need to cover every detail; the IIPP is only an outline of your entire compliance plan. **2.** Use the detailed information to complete the written programs for all other standards. **3.** Consider adding text for standards that don't require written programs to your employee handbook or safety manual. For an example of a safety policy, see the sample *Employee Handbook* in your online Formspack.
Maintain	The easiest way to help your company avoid violations, injuries, and claims is to keep your compliance information up-to-date, and to communicate changes to your employees. See "How Should I Cover Safety Training?" on page 209 for more information.

How Should I Cover Safety Training?

Most Cal/OSHA standards require training, which is an effective way for you to keep employees informed of your policies and procedures. The regulations do not specify the type of training or the frequency. The following table shows you the essentials of developing a training program.

Table 63. Safety Training

Question	Response
What	**1.** Determine which standards require you to train your employees. You can also refer to the *Training Requirements* form, described in Table 64 on page 219, for information on training requirements for all Cal/OSHA standards. Keep in mind that often, even when a standard doesn't require training, the IIPP does. **2.** Compile all the subjects into a list to determine if you can combine subjects to cover multiple standards. You can use this list as a foundation for selecting your method of training.
Who	Designate an internal or external resource who is qualified to provide training, based on the requirements of the standard. Remember that you are also responsible for providing training to independent contractors.
When	Provide the training: • To all new employees, and existing employees who transfer to new positions; • After an incident or change of process (e.g., when you install new equipment or move to a new site); and • As an annual refresher.
How	The method you use to provide training is up to you, depending on how complex the training needs to be, the number of employees you need to train, and your budget. Keep in mind that supervisors may need separate training. In addition, always document the training employees receive to show your compliance with the IIPP, and that you are serious about safety.

How Do I Properly Provide PPE to My Employees?

Providing PPE (e.g., gloves, lead aprons, hard hats, and keyboard wrist rests) for your employees, if required, helps prevent injuries and illnesses. Use the following guidelines to help you determine what your employees need to work safely.

1. Evaluate your workplace for the need for PPE; consider all the jobs, processes, and operations (day-to-day and emergency) employees will perform. Some examples of evaluation questions might be:
   - Do your employees handle, or are they exposed to, chemicals or blood borne pathogens?
   - Do your employees perform tasks that require the same bodily motions to be repeated?
   - Do your employees work in areas with falling items, flying projectiles, or heavy machinery?
   - Do your employees lift heavy or cumbersome objects, or work in areas that require forceful exertion to perform tasks?
2. Document the situations that require your employees to use PPE, and identify what PPE items you will supply.

You cannot charge employees for the use and cost of PPE.

3. Provide and maintain PPE for all employees exposed to hazards.
4. Perform periodic inspections:
   - Make sure the PPE is in good working order, and is readily accessible; and
   - Verify that employees are using PPE properly and consistently.

How Do I Report and Record Work-Related Injuries and Illnesses?

Recording and reporting are two separate processes required by Cal/OSHA's *Log 300* regulation, although you don't always have to do both.

The ***Log 300*** regulation requires employers to record and report work-related fatalities, injuries, and illnesses.

- **Reporting** includes notifying Cal/OSHA of a serious work-related injury or death. See "What Qualifies As a "Serious" Injury?" on page 211 for more information. All employers must report fatal or serious incidents within eight hours of the incident or fatality. Report fatal or serious incidents to the Cal/OSHA district office nearest to your business. To find the nearest Cal/OSHA district office, go to ***http://www.dir.ca.gov/DOSH/DistrictOffices.htm***.
- **Recording** involves creating and maintaining records of work-related injuries, both to keep documents as references, and to prepare in case an inspection requires you to present your records. You are exempt from recording if you have 10 or fewer employees or if your company is classified in a specific low hazard Standard Industry Code (SIC) category. SICs classify businesses by their primary activity, and are used for a variety of statistical purposes.

  To find out if you have to record incidents using the *Log 300* forms, go to ***http://www.hrcalifornia.com/log300*** and click the Log 300 Exempt Wizard link.

What Qualifies As a "Serious" Injury?

A work-related incident that results in the:

- Death of an employee;
- Hospitalization of an employee for more than 24 hours for treatment other than observation; or
- Loss or serious disfigurement of any body part.

How Do I Know If I Have to Report an Incident?

You are required to submit incident reports in two situations:

- When an employee is seriously or fatally injured; or
- When you receive an annual survey form from the Bureau of Labor Statistics, or a specific request from Cal/OSHA.

California law mandates a fine of $5,000 for employers who do not report a serious injury or death. Individual employees serving in supervisory, management or like roles, may be individually liable for up to one year in jail and/or a $15,000 fine. Corporations face fines up to $150,000.

How Long Do I Need to Keep These Records?

You must save the *Log 300* forms for five years following the end of the calendar year the records cover.

During the storage period, you must update the *Log 300* forms to include newly discovered recordable injuries or illnesses and to show changes that have occurred in the classification of previously recorded injuries and illnesses.

The *Log 300* forms are available to CalChamber members at ***www.hrcalifornia.com/log300***.

Why Do I Need to Perform Inspections?

Many benefits can come from performing your own inspections of your site and equipment, your employees' safety practices, and safety documents, including:

- Internal inspections are the best defense against and preparation for inspections by other agencies;
- Many OSHA standards require you to document periodic inspections for compliance;
- During an inspection, you may identify a potential hazard, find a broken safety guard, or determine that your employees need refresher safety training; and
- Inspections keep you familiarized with your site, processes, and operations, so you can evaluate your workplace's efficiency and productivity.

What Is the Cal/OSHA Inspection Process Like?

Cal/OSHA inspections follow a process governed by the Labor Code and the Cal/OSHA Policy and Procedure Manual:

1. **Surprise!** No advance notice is given, except:

    - When apparent imminent danger requires prompt correction;
    - To ensure availability of essential personnel or access to the site, equipment, or process; and
    - When the Cal/OSHA chief or his/her designee decides that giving advance notice would help achieve a thorough inspection.

2. **Opening conference** — The Cal/OSHA inspector presents credentials and provides the reason for the inspection to someone with the authority to consent to the inspection.

    You can ask for a postponement of the inspection, but only for a good reason, such as:

    - All essential personnel are not available; or
    - The inspector's stated reason for the inspection or credentials lack credibility.

    The inspector has the authority to obtain a search warrant if you refuse the inspection.

3. **Document request** — The inspector usually requests the following documents to review:

    - Cal/OSHA *Log 300* forms for the current year and *Log 200* forms (the previous record keeping regulation) for the five previous years;
    - Your written IIPP;
    - Any written programs required by a standard to which your business is subject;
    - Codes of safe practice at a construction site; and
    - A copy of any permit issued by Cal/OSHA.

4. **Walk-through** — The inspector conducts a walk-through of the premises subject to the inspection, accompanied by key personnel from your company.

    This can be a wall-to-wall inspection or involve only the limited area defined by the inspector's represented reasons for the inspection (such as an employee complaint about the warehouse). It is good practice to restrict the inspector's access to the areas specifically designated for inspection.

During a wall-to-wall inspection the inspector may stop to examine machinery, interview employees, and observe working situations. Your personnel accompanying the inspector may be asked to explain an operation or answer questions.

5. **Exit and closing conferences** — When the inspection is over, the inspector:
   - Summarizes the results of the inspection;
   - Makes any pertinent observations;
   - Discusses findings and conclusions; and
   - Requests information, documents, or further inspections.

If no citations are issued, this is considered an exit conference and nothing else follows. If the inspection results in a citation or another action (such as a Special Order), the exit conference is followed by a formal closing conference scheduled after the issuance of citations that comes approximately one month later.

The Hitches, Glitches, and Pitfalls of Ensuring Workplace Safety

Safety in the workplace is a very serious topic. You're up against inspections, citations, and compliance schedules. There is a limited appeals process, but your best bet is simply to maintain a safe workplace.

When Does Cal/OSHA Do Inspections?

The Cal/OSHA inspection program targets workplaces where there is a likelihood of health and safety hazards and/or violations of standards. Due to constitutional limitations on government searches and seizures, the agency must have reasonable cause to conduct an inspection. However, the courts have granted Cal/OSHA broad discretion in determining what is reasonable cause. Cal/OSHA inspects when:

- An employer reports a fatality or serious injury or illness;
- An employee complains;
- The issuance of a permit requires a follow-up inspection;

- The Cal/OSHA general administrative plan calls for inspections for a certain type of employer (the targeted group shifts periodically based on injury/illness statistics for that industrial classification); and
- An industry has been selected as part of the TICP.

The **TICP**, or Targeted Inspection and Consultation Program, is a Cal/OSHA program that identifies certain high-hazard employers, and requires they pay a fee to fund a special inspection unit.

How Can I Prepare for an Inspection?

You should develop policies for handling an inspection, designate key personnel to participate, train them in procedures to follow, and advise them on handling potential issues that may emerge as the inspection progresses. Your policy can be formal or informal but should cover the key phases of an inspection. See "What Is the Cal/OSHA Inspection Process Like?" on page 213.

To find resources that can help you develop these procedures, check out "Where Do I Go for More Information?" on page 226.

What Happens If the Inspector Finds a Violation?

- You could receive a citation with civil penalties based on the violation's severity, extent, likelihood, and the size of your business. These penalties are:
  - Non-serious or minor violations — up to $7,000;
  - Repeat or willful violations — from $5,000 to $70,000;
  - Serious violations — up to $25,000;
  - Failure to correct or abate a violation — up to $15,000 for each day the failure continues; and
  - Substantial if you fail to report a fatal or serious incident. See the note on page 212 for details.
- You could receive a Special Order to remedy any unsafe condition, device, or other workplace hazard to employee safety and health that is not covered by any existing standard. In a sense this creates a special standard for you;

- If the violation is a general or regulatory offense, and does not have an immediate relationship to employee safety and health, you may receive a Notice to Comply;
- You could receive an Information Memorandum to direct your attention to a workplace condition that has the potential of becoming a hazard to the safety or health of employees;
- In situations where an unsafe workplace condition, covered by an existing standard, requires specific instruction, you may receive an Order to Take Special Action; and
- When any condition, equipment, or practice poses an imminent hazard to employees that could cause death or serious physical harm immediately or before you can eliminate the hazard, Cal/OSHA issues an Order Prohibiting Use ("Yellow Tagging").

Whatever the result of your violation, you must:

- Post the citation, order, or notice of violation in a place where employees working nearby can easily read it; and
- Correct (abate) the problem within a prescribed amount of time and notify Cal/OSHA of abatement.

Make sure to review the content of the citation or order for accuracy in terms of its statement of the violated standard's requirements and your observations of the inspection and understanding of the inspector's findings. If you object to the citation, and have enough evidence, you can appeal. See "What Can I Do If I Disagree with the Results of an Inspection or with a Citation?" on page 216 for more information.

What Can I Do If I Disagree with the Results of an Inspection or with a Citation?

Within 15 working days of receipt of a citation or order, you can appeal to the Occupational Safety and Health Appeals Board.

How Does the Appeals Process Work?

1. Because the time allotted to appeal is so short (15 days), you should start the decision-making process immediately upon receipt.

   You should identify issues that you can appeal, and consider:

   - The size of the penalty, and the cost and time allowed for abatement compared to appeal;
   - The potential for a repeat citation; and
   - Your likelihood of success, given the strength of your defenses.

2. Communicate your desire to appeal to the Board by hand delivery, mail, fax, or telephone.

   The Board provides you an appeal form and other information on the appeal process. If you return the form to the Board within 10 working days, the appeal is considered perfected.

   The appeal is in progress. The Board assignment of a docket may take up to 6 months. When docketed, the Board will send a copy of the form back to you with a docket number and Board stamp affixed.

You must post a copy of the docketed appeal form at or near the site of the already posted citation. The posting must remain in place until the commencement of the appeal hearing or receipt of an order disposing of the appeal.

3. Since notification of docketing can be a lengthy process, begin preparing your defense for the hearing while the incident/inspection/facts are current and fresh.

   Hearings are typically held no more than six months from the docketing of the appeal. You can investigate Cal/OSHA's information by filing a discovery letter on the agency, with copies sent to the Board and any other interested party. You can subpoena witnesses or physical evidence.

   You cannot communicate with the Board unless all parties to the appeal are notified. You may serve a document on another party by personal delivery, first-class mail, overnight delivery, or fax. You can do this by a declaration, a written statement, or by a letter of transmittal.

4. You can request an informal conference.

   This meeting between you, your representatives, Cal/OSHA's district manager, and the inspector responsible for the citation allows you to discuss any evidence in an attempt to resolve any disputes and avoid the need for an appeal.

District managers must hold the conference no more than 10 working days after issuance of citations. If you have already filed an appeal, the conference can occur any time up to the date of the hearing.

You must notify employees of the conference, its date, and location, usually by posting this information near the already posted citation and a copy of the conference confirmation issued by Cal/OSHA.

At this stage the district manager, based on new evidence or interpretation, can withdraw or amend citations including the existence of the violations, proposed penalties, and abatement methods and schedules.

5. If you don't reach a settlement, you will make your defense in an official hearing before an Administrative Law Judge (ALJ).

   At least 30 days prior to a hearing, the Board will send the parties a notice of hearing, advising them of the location, date, and time. A hearing is postponed only if an emergency arises, or if a party or witness has a preexisting scheduling conflict. If either party fails to appear at the hearing, the Board will notice an intent to dismiss. To reinstate the matter, the absent party must establish just cause within 10 days for the failure to appear.

You must notify employees of the pending hearing, usually by posting this information near the already posted citation.

6. At the close of the hearing, all the proceedings are considered submitted for decision. Within 30 days the ALJ summarizes the evidence received, makes findings, and files a proposed decision along with his/her reasons for the decision.

   The Board may confirm, adopt, modify, or set aside the proposed decision. The Board then sends copies of the decision to each party. If no one files a petition for consideration, the decision is final and cannot be reviewed by any court or agency.

7. Either party has 30 days to file a petition for reconsideration. The petition must set forth, specifically and in full detail, every issue to be considered by the Board. Anything not raised in the petition is waived and cannot be re-examined. If the Board does not act upon a petition within 45 days, it is considered denied.

   Upon reconsideration, the Board can make another decision or let the original one stand. If no one requests a judicial review, the decision is final.

8. Any party that disagrees with a decision after reconsideration or the denial of a petition must apply to the Superior Court for a writ of mandate within 30 days of the Board's decision or denial.

What Forms and Checklists Do I Use for Ensuring Workplace Safety?

The following table describes forms and checklists associated with workplace safety.

You can find these forms in your online Formspack, described in detail in "Online Forms" on page 4.

Table 64. Forms and Checklists

Form Name	What do I use it for?	When do I use it?	Who fills it out?	Where does it go?
Accident, Injury and Illness Investigation Form	To help you document information about a workplace incident that involves an accident, injury, or both.	As soon as possible after an incident has occurred.	You do.	If you don't have to report the incident, keep the document for at least one year (longer if you are documenting compliance). If you are required to record the incident on the *Log 300* form, keep the document for five years.
Code for Safe Practices for Construction Workplaces **New for 2008**	The sample code in this form was developed by the California Department of Occupational Safety and Health. It is a suggested code, is general in nature and is intended as a basis for preparation of a code that fits the specific contractor's operations more exactly.	Use this form to assist your company in preparing a code of safe practices.	No filling out needed.	N/A

Table 64. Forms and Checklists *(continued)*

Form Name	What do I use it for?	When do I use it?	Who fills it out?	Where does it go?
Ergonomics Checklist - Computer and Keyboard Issues **New for 2008**	As an inspection tool to help you identify potential ergonomic problems related to computers and keyboards.	Annually and as needed.	You do.	N/A
Ergonomics Checklist - Hand Tool Use **New for 2008**	As an inspection tool to help you identify potential ergonomic problems related to hand tool use.	Annually and as needed	You do.	N/A
Ergonomics Checklist - Manual Handling **New for 2008**	As an inspection tool to help you identify potential ergonomic problems related to manual handling.	Annually and as needed.	You do.	N/A
Ergonomics Checklist - Task-Work Methods **New for 2008**	As an inspection tool to help you identify potential ergonomic problems related to task/work methods.	Annually and as needed.	You do.	N/A
Ergonomics Checklist - Workstation Layout **New for 2008**	As an inspection tool to help you identify potential ergonomic problems related to workstation layout.	Annually and as needed.	You do.	N/A

Table 64. Forms and Checklists *(continued)*

Form Name	What do I use it for?	When do I use it?	Who fills it out?	Where does it go?
Emergency Action Plan	To help you create a written plan for handling emergency situations, and to satisfy Cal/OSHA compliance.	Before your business opens, or as soon after as possible.	You do	Make the information in your plan available to your employees, through training and in your employee handbook or safety manual. Keep and maintain the document as long as the company operates.
Hazard Assessment and Correction Record	To document hazard identification and correction, and to assure compliance with applicable Cal/OSHA standards.	When an unsafe working condition has been brought to your attention.	You do.	In your files.
Hazard Prevention Data Sheet – Ergonomics Safety	To help you identify and prevent repetitive motion injuries, and to satisfy Cal/OSHA standard compliance.	Before your business opens, or as soon after as possible.	No filling out needed; this form is for reference only.	Make the information in your plan available to your employees, through training and in your employee handbook or safety manual. Keep and maintain the document as long as the company operates.

Table 64. Forms and Checklists *(continued)*

Form Name	What do I use it for?	When do I use it?	Who fills it out?	Where does it go?
Heat Illness Prevention Plan (Outdoor Employees) **New for 2008**	To develop your company's plan and procedures for complying with Cal/OSHA regulations on heat illness prevention for outdoor workers.	Before your business opens, or as soon after as possible.	You do.	Make the information in your plan available to your employees, through training and in your employee handbook or safety manual. Keep and maintain the document as long as the company operates.
Fire Prevention Checklist	To determine which fire hazards are present in your workplace, so you can create and maintain a written plan for preventing and handling workplace fires.	Before your business opens, or as soon after as possible.	You do.	Use the checklist as an inspection tool. Keep and maintain the document as long as the company operates.
Fire Prevention Plan	To help you create a written plan for preventing and handling workplace fires, and to satisfy Cal/OSHA standard compliance.	Before your business opens, or as soon after as possible.	You do.	Make the information in your plan available to your employees, through training and in your employee handbook or safety manual. Keep and maintain the document as long as the company operates.

Table 64. Forms and Checklists *(continued)*

Form Name	What do I use it for?	When do I use it?	Who fills it out?	Where does it go?
Hazard Communication Information Summary	To document the inventory of hazards in your workplace, and to satisfy Cal/OSHA standard compliance.	Before your business opens, or as soon after as possible.	You do.	Make the information in your plan available to your employees, through training and in your employee handbook or safety manual. Keep and maintain the document as long as the company operates.
Hazard Communication Program	To document training provided to an employee, and to satisfy Cal/OSHA standard compliance.	Before your business opens, or as soon after as possible.	You do.	Make the information in your plan available to your employees, through training and in your employee handbook or safety manual. Keep and maintain the document as long as the company operates.
Individual Employee Training Documentation – Initial Safety Training	To document the first training provided to an employee.	When you hire someone, reassign someone, or identify a previously unknown hazard.	You do.	Keep the certificate in the employee's personnel file. Provide a copy of the certificate to the employee if requested.

Table 64. Forms and Checklists *(continued)*

Form Name	What do I use it for?	When do I use it?	Who fills it out?	Where does it go?
Individual Training Certificate	To document training provided to an employee, and to satisfy Cal/OSHA standard compliance.	When the employee successfully completes the training.	The employee does.	Keep the certificate in the employee's personnel file. Provide a copy of the certificate to the employee if requested.
Injury and Illness Prevention Program	To outline your plan for compliance with all OSHA standards, including a detailed plan for: • Handling emergency situations; • Preventing and handling workplace fires; • Addressing ergonomic issues; and • Documenting information about workplace hazards.	Before your business opens, or as soon after as possible.	You do.	Make the information in your plan available to your employees, through training and in your employee handbook or safety manual. Keep and maintain the document as long as the company operates.
Inspection Checklist for Work Spaces and Surfaces	To help you identify and prevent work space and surface hazards in your workplace, and to satisfy Cal/OSHA standard compliance.	During periodic inspections, and after incidents or a change in process.	You do.	Keep the checklist as a record of periodic inspections for five years after you fill it out.

Table 64. Forms and Checklists *(continued)*

Form Name	What do I use it for?	When do I use it?	Who fills it out?	Where does it go?
Safety Program Self Audit Checklist **New for 2008**	To help ensure that your workplace safety program complies with state requirements and is well tailored to reducing risks and claims in your workplace.	Before your business opens, or as soon after as possible.	You do.	Keep and maintain the document as long as the company operates.
Training Requirements	To determine which standards require you to provide safety training for your employees.	Use the form for reference when you're planning your safety training program.	No filling out needed.	Incorporate the information in the document into your training program.
Training Sign-in Sheet	To record and track employee attendance at training courses.	Before or after the completion of the training course.	You prepare the form, and employees sign their names.	Keep the documents as proof that an employee attended mandatory training for five years after the training.
Training Sign-In Sheet - Spanish **New for 2008**	To record and track employee attendance at training courses.	Before or after the completion of the training course.	You prepare the form, and employees sign their names.	Keep the documents as proof that an employee attended mandatory training for five years after the training.
Worker Training and Instruction Record **New for 2008**	To document and track all training provided to an employee.	Whenever an employee attends or completes training.	You do.	Maintain in your training files and a copy in the employee's personnel file.

Where Do I Go for More Information?

CalBizCentral and the federal and state governments have a variety of resources to help you ensure safety in your workplace.

Table 65. Additional Resources

For information on	Check out these resources
General	From CalBizCentral: • ***http://www.calbizcentral.com***; and • ***http://www.hrcalifornia.com***.
Workers' compensation	From CalBizCentral: • ***2008 Labor Law Digest***.
State government	• California Department of Industrial Relations at ***http://www.dir.ca.gov***; • California Division of Occupational Safety and Health at ***http://www.dir.ca.gov/DOSH/dosh1.html***; • California's Occupational Safety and Health Standards Board at ***http://www.dir.ca.gov/oshsb/oshsb.html***; • Model Injury and Illness Prevention Program for High Hazard Employers at ***http://www.dir.ca.gov/dosh/dosh_publications/iiphihzemp.html***; • Cal/OSHA guidelines for Workplace Security at ***http://www.dir.ca.gov/dosh/dosh_publications/worksecurity.html***; • User's Guide to Cal/OSHA at ***http://www.dir.ca.gov/dosh/dosh%5Fpublications/osha%5Fuserguide.pdf***; and • For contact information for various Cal/OSHA offices, see the *Cal/OSHA Poster* (located in the **Required Notices Kit** associated with this product).
Federal government	OSHA's SIC manual at ***http://www.osha.gov/oshstats/sicser.html***

CalBizCentral also provides many ongoing and comprehensive educational opportunities for small business owners, HR beginners, and experienced HR professionals alike. These include online sexual harassment training, videos, and special HR seminars. For more information, please visit our website at ***http://www.calbizcentral.com***.

Chapter 7

Preventing Discrimination and Harassment

Discrimination and harassment can trouble any workplace. With proper preparation, your workplace can remain healthy, and you can remain lawsuit-free.

In this chapter, you can find answers to questions about:

- Sexual harassment;
- The Americans with Disabilities Act;
- Protected classes; and
- Much more!

Minimum Compliance Elements

1. Hang your *Employer Poster* (available from ***www.calbizcentral.com***), which includes mandatory postings that all employees must be able to see.
2. Pass out the mandatory *Sexual Harassment Information Sheets* (located in the ***Required Notices Kit*** available from ***www.calbizcentral.com***), forbidding unlawful harassment at your company.
3. Have a written policy forbidding discrimination and harassment in your workplace, and enforce it consistently for all employees (see "Establish Policies" on page 240).
4. Take every discrimination or harassment complaint seriously — establish a complaint procedure, tell your employees about it, and follow it faithfully if you learn of suspicious behavior (see "How Should I Handle a Discrimination/ Harassment Complaint?" on page 248).
5. Hold a mandatory training session where all your employees and managers can learn about discrimination and harassment (see "Provide Training" on page 241).

6. Accommodate employees with disabilities, so they can work equally with their non-disabled colleagues (see "What Is Reasonable Accommodation?" on page 235).

The Basics of Preventing Discrimination and Harassment in the Workplace

One successful discrimination or harassment lawsuit could bankrupt your company. Courts have awarded penalties in excess of one million dollars to employees who have been subject to harassment or discrimination. And even if a complaint never reaches the courts, discrimination and harassment claims can be very costly in terms of employee morale and diverted resources. You can begin to protect yourself by understanding discrimination and harassment, and taking steps to avoid situations that would inspire claims, and by knowing how to handle complaints when they do arise.

What Is Discrimination?

Discrimination, legally speaking, covers only actions taken against people because of their membership, perceived membership, or associated membership in certain protected classes. See "What Characteristics/Activities Are Protected from Discrimination?" on page 230.

Discrimination means treating those people differently, and disadvantageously, compared with other people not in the same class. Remember, though, that everyone is part of a protected class. Everyone has a race and a marital status, is perceived as one gender or another, and associates with people in protected classes.

Discrimination can occur in two different ways:

- **Disparate (unequal) treatment** — When an employee or applicant is treated differently, specifically because of his/her protected class status; or
- **Disparate (unequal) impact** — An employment practice that appears neutral on its face but is discriminatory against protected classes in practice (for example, height and weight requirements may unequally impact women and minorities).

You have committed a discriminatory employment practice if you, among other things:

- Base any employment decision (e.g., hiring, benefits, promotion, discipline, etc.) in whole or in part on an individual's protected class status;

- Rely on stereotypes about the competence, appearance, health, interest, or qualifications of individuals in protected classes;
- Engage in any employment practice that has an adverse impact on the hiring, training, classification, promotion, or retention opportunities of individuals in a protected class;
- Engage in, or permit your employees to engage in, harassment of any member of any protected class;
- Act on the perception or assumption of a disability without evaluating the individual's fitness for the job;
- Retaliate against an employee, applicant, or independent contractor for opposing sexual harassment or other unlawful discrimination, or for filing a complaint, testifying, assisting, or participating in an investigation, proceeding or hearing, etc.;
- Refuse to honor an otherwise eligible employee's request for pregnancy disability leave or for leave under CFRA or FMLA (see "Glossary of Terms, Laws, and Agencies" on page 285 for more details);
- Refuse to reasonably accommodate disabilities, religious requirements, etc.; and
- Inquire on a written job application (except in limited circumstances) whether a job applicant has ever been arrested.

What Characteristics/Activities Are Protected from Discrimination?

You may not discriminate against a person on the basis of:

Table 66. Protected Classes and Activities

Characteristic	Discrimination
Age	If you have five or more employees, be careful how you treat those who are over 40 years old. Among other things, you may not: • Use age as a consideration for employment decisions, unless it is a bona fide occupational qualification (BFOQ); • Discriminate against someone who has opposed, filed a charge against, testified, or participated in an investigation of unlawful employment practice under the ADEA (see "Glossary of Terms, Laws, and Agencies" on page 285 for more information on the ADEA); • Place an employment notice or advertisement indicating a preference, limitation, or specification based on age, unless it is a BFOQ; • Terminate employees based on salary if there is a disproportionate impact on older workers; • Force an employee to retire because he/she has reached a certain age; or • Discriminate on the basis of age with regard to the terms, conditions, or privileges of employment; for example, denying an employee over 40 the educational opportunities that you give to younger employees.
AIDS/HIV+ status	These conditions are considered protected disabilities. If you have five or more employees, you may not: • Use blood tests as a condition of employment or to determine insurability; or • Terminate, deny insurance coverage, or refuse to hire individuals exposed to the AIDS virus. ! There may be limited exceptions in the medical field.

Table 66. Protected Classes and Activities *(continued)*

Characteristic	Discrimination
Disability	The ADA (federal law) covers employers with 15 or more employees; the FEHA (state law) covers employers with five or more employees. See "Glossary of Terms, Laws, and Agencies" on page 285, for more information on these laws. You may not discriminate against a disabled person or someone you perceive to be disabled. In California, a **disability** is a physical or mental impairment that limits one or more of the major life activities. Disability discrimination is very complicated. See "How Is Disability Discrimination Special?" on page 234.
Domestic partner status	State law prohibits discrimination and/or harassment based on several protected classes. Recent legislation adds registered domestic partners to this list of protected classes, by giving domestic partners the same rights as spouses. Conversely, you could not discriminate against someone based on marital status, in favor of another person who is in a registered domestic partner relationship.
Gender	If you have five or more employees, you cannot discriminate or allow harassment on the basis of gender. Gender is defined as an employee's or applicant's actual sex or the employer's perception of the employee's/applicant's sex. This includes your perception of the employee's/applicant's identity, appearance, or behavior, whether or not that identity, appearance, or behavior is different from that traditionally associated with the employee's/applicant's sex at birth.
Genetic characteristics	This means any inherited characteristic or scientifically or medically identifiable gene or chromosome or combination or alteration thereof that is known to be a cause, or increase the risk, of a disease or disorder in a person or his/her offspring. You may not subject any person to a test for the presence of a genetic characteristic.
Height/weight	You cannot establish height and weight standards unless you can show that such a restriction relates directly to, and is an essential function of, the job.

Table 66. Protected Classes and Activities *(continued)*

Characteristic	Discrimination
Language	You cannot deny someone an employment opportunity because that person's accent makes him/her unable to communicate well in English, unless you can show that the ability to communicate effectively in English is necessary to the job. If you have five or more employees, you cannot enact an English-only policy unless the language restriction is justified by a business necessity, and you have notified your employees of the circumstances when the language restriction must be observed.
Lawful, off-duty conduct	If you have even one employee, you cannot discriminate against applicants and employees for lawful conduct they engage in during non-working hours away from the company premises. Examples of lawful conduct are: • Exercising free speech rights; • Engaging in political activity; • Reporting information to the government; • Moonlighting (working a second job for a different employer); and • Engaging in conduct you feel to be morally in conflict with your business.
Marital status	This is an individual's state of marriage, non-marriage, divorce or dissolution, separation, widowhood, annulment, or other marital status. If you have even one employee, you may not condition benefits or employment decisions upon whether the employee is considered a "principal wage earner" or "head of household." You also cannot use job responsibilities such as travel or customer entertainment as justification for discrimination. You may not impose a "no employment of spouses" rule, but you can establish a policy that outlines how you can situate spouses within the company. See "Employment of Relatives" in Table 12 in Chapter 3, page 65 for more details.

Table 66. Protected Classes and Activities *(continued)*

Characteristic	Discrimination
Medical condition	This includes any health impairment related to, or associated with, a diagnosis of cancer, or a record or history of cancer, as well as an individual's genetic characteristics. See "Genetic characteristics" in this table on page 231. If you have even one employee, you cannot: • Base employment decisions on an employee or applicant's medical condition; or • Request any sort of medical examination until after you have made an offer of employment.
National origin/ ancestry	The broad definition means the country from which the applicant or employee, or his/her ancestors, came. If you have even one employee, you cannot base employment decisions on an employee or applicant's national origin.
Pregnancy	If you have even one employee, you cannot discriminate in any way against an employee due to that employee's pregnancy or potential to become pregnant.
Race/color	If you have even one employee, you cannot base employment decisions on an employee or applicant's race.
Religion	This is broadly defined to include all aspects of religious belief, observance, and practice, including the absence of religion, agnosticism. You must also accommodate the known religious creed (such as allowing the person time off for religious observance) of an applicant or employee unless you can demonstrate that such accommodation imposes undue hardship. Religious corporations and associations are generally exempt from laws that govern this class.
Sex	If you have even one employee, you cannot base employment decisions on an employee or applicant's sex or gender. If you do more than $500,000 worth of business a year, or if you are a school or educational institution, you may not pay men and women differing wages for the same work.
Sexual orientation	This is defined as heterosexuality, homosexuality, and bisexuality. Employers of four or fewer employees and religious non-profit organizations are exempt from laws that govern this class.
Union membership	Employees have the right to organize and form unions, with which you must bargain.

Table 66. Protected Classes and Activities *(continued)*

Characteristic	Discrimination
Veteran status	You cannot base employment decisions on an employee or applicant's status as a veteran. Military personnel also enjoy limited protection from termination for a period of time after returning to work. See "Time off for Protected Activities" in Table 12 in Chapter 3, page 65.
Whistleblowers	If you have even one employee, you cannot: • Retaliate against an employee who discloses information to a government or law enforcement agency, if your employee has reasonable cause to believe that the information discloses a violation of state or federal statute, or a violation of, or noncompliance with, a state or federal rule or regulation; • Retaliate against an employee who refuses to participate in an activity that would result in a violation of law; or • Retaliate against an employee if the employee's action occurred when he/she worked for a former employer. Fines for retaliation are up to $10,000 for each violation. The Attorney General of California is required to establish a whistle-blower hotline to receive calls from individuals with knowledge about possible violations of state or federal statutes. You must display a posting that details employees' rights and responsi-bilities under the whistleblower laws and includes the telephone number of the whistleblower hotline. The posting is included on the *Employer Poster* (located in the ***Required Notices Kit*** associated with this product).
Workers' compensation claim	If you have even one employee, you cannot discharge, threaten, or discriminate in any way against an employee because he/she has received an award from, has filed, or even intends to file a workers' compensation claim.

How Is Disability Discrimination Special?

Disability discrimination law protects qualified individuals with disabilities from disparate treatment by employers. A qualified individual with a disability is a person who meets legitimate skill, experience, education, or other requirements, and can perform the essential functions of the position with or without reasonable accommodation. An individual is not unqualified simply because he or she is unable to perform marginal or incidental job functions.

Disabilities come in all varieties. A person is considered disabled if he/she:

- Has a physical or mental impairment that limits one or more of the major life activities;
- Has a record of such an impairment;
- Is regarded as having such an impairment;
- Is regarded by the employer as having some condition that has no present disabling effect but may become a physical disability; or
- Has any health impairment that requires special education or related services.

Major life activities include caring for oneself, sleeping, learning, walking, interacting with others, working, and other physical, mental, and social activities.

California law has broader scope than federal law. The federal definition of disability requires that an individual be "substantially limited" in a major life activity. The California definition only requires the individual be "limited."

You cannot ask questions that would be likely to lead to information about a disability unless the questions are job-related and consistent with business necessity.

You cannot request a medical examination until after you've made an offer of employment.

Drug or alcohol abuse is not a disability. However, a person in successful recovery can be considered disabled.

A blanket prohibition on the reemployment of workers terminated for violating company drug/alcohol policy may violate the ADA. The ADA protects job applicants who have recovered from drug and alcohol dependencies. This protection extends to former employees who were terminated for alcohol or drug abuse. Consult with your legal counsel before refusing to rehire someone you terminated for violating such a policy.

What Is Reasonable Accommodation?

A "reasonable accommodation" is any modification or adjustment in a job, an employment practice, or the work environment that allows a qualified individual with a disability to enjoy an equal employment opportunity.

Examples of reasonable accommodations include, but are not limited to:

- Modifying a work schedule;
- Providing an interpreter;
- Making facilities accessible; and
- Acquiring accessibility equipment.

The reasonable accommodation obligation is an ongoing duty, and may arise any time a person's disability or job changes. You must engage in a timely, good faith, interactive process to determine and provide effective, reasonable accommodations. You should document this process.

When you don't know how to accommodate the disability, you can ask an employee for reasonable documentation about his/her disability, its functional limitations that require reasonable accommodation, and how the disability might be accommodated.

Documentation of a disability:

- Describes:
  - The nature, severity, and duration of the employee's impairment;
  - The activity or activities that the impairment limits; and
  - The extent to which the impairment limits the employee's ability to perform the activity or activities.
- Substantiates why the requested reasonable accommodation is needed.

What Are Essential Functions?

You do not have to alter the essential functions of a job — that is not reasonable accommodation.

Essential functions are fundamental job duties of the position or the reason the job exists.

You need to establish the essential functions of a job, both to determine whether an individual with a disability (with or without reasonable accommodation) is able to perform the job, and as a defense against any subsequent claim of discrimination. When determining essential functions:

- Document all important job functions;
- Be accurate and realistic;

- Stay current;
- Be flexible; and
- Review job descriptions with the employee in that job.

You are not required to reasonably accommodate a qualified individual with a disability if you can prove that the accommodation would cause undue hardship. The Equal Employment Opportunity Commission (EEOC) and the California Fair Employment and Housing Commission (FEHC) determine undue hardship on a case-by-case basis, taking into consideration the size of your business and the availability of tax incentives and assistance from the government.

The concept of **undue hardship** includes any accommodation that is unduly costly, extensive, or substantial, or an accommodation that would fundamentally alter the nature of the operation of your business.

You do not need to hire or retain a person who poses a direct threat to the health and safety of coworkers. The risk must be current, not speculative, not remote, not lessened by accommodation, and based on reasonable medical judgment or other objective evidence.

Legislation effective in 2004 requires state employees who supervise other workers to receive additional training related to persons with disabilities. Each supervisory employee, at the time he/she is initially appointed to a supervisory position, must have a minimum of 80 hours of training. The training must be completed within the term of the probationary period or within 12 months of the appointment to supervisor.

What Is Harassment?

Harassment is a pattern of unwelcome behavior. If an individual indicates that advances, attentions, remarks, or visual displays are unwanted and should stop, yet the behavior continues, that's harassment.

All workers in any size company are shielded from harassment. It is your duty as an employer to create a hostility-free work environment for all your workers, whatever their gender, age, race, or other protected class status might be.

Any workplace relationship can contain harassment: employee to independent contractor or vendor to employee, and vice versa; employee to employee; supervisor to employee, etc.

Harassment includes:

- Verbal harassment — epithets, continued requests for dates, derogatory comments, slurs, obscenities, explicit/racial jokes, graphic commentary about someone's body, verbal abuse, questions about personal practices, use of patronizing terms or remarks, threats and demands to submit to sexual advances;
- Physical harassment — assault, unwanted touching, grabbing, brushing against, or interfering with movement;
- Visual harassment — offensive cartoons, posters, drawings, gestures, or staring; and
- Any form of retaliation for reporting or threatening to report harassment.

Though most harassment is a pattern of conduct, a single incident may be harassment under California law, if the conduct is sufficiently severe.

Harassment can be:

- An employment condition (submission to harassing conduct is made a term of employment);
- An employment consequence (submission to or rejection of harassing conduct is used as basis for employment decisions); or
- An offensive job interference (harassing conduct unreasonably interferes with an employee's work performance or creates an intimidating, hostile, or offensive work environment).

If you fail to take action to stop harassment, you will be liable for damages if an employee files a complaint. Harassed employees do not need to share their complaints with a manager, they can go straight to the DFEH and file a claim against your company and against any supervisors who engaged in harassing behavior. See "What Are the Penalties for Discrimination/Harassment?" on page 256.

Legislation effective in 2004 overturns previous state case law and imposes liability on employers for harassment by a non-employee. You are liable for acts of sexual harassment by a third party if you, your agents, or supervisors knew or should have known of the conduct and failed to take immediate and appropriate action.

What Characteristics/Activities Are Protected from Harassment?

All the people protected from discrimination are protected from harassment, regardless of company size. See "What Characteristics/Activities Are Protected from Discrimination?" on page 230.

Sexual harassment is the most common type of workplace harassment. There are two types of sexual harassment:

- "Quid pro quo," which conditions job continuance, benefits, promotions, etc., on receipt of sexual favors; and
- "Hostile environment," where the pattern of unwelcome sexual comments, touching, or visual displays of a supervisor or coworker creates an environment that inhibits the employee's ability to work.

California courts use a "reasonable woman" standard as a means to determine if a particular situation is harassment. Though any person of any gender can be subject to unlawful harassment, courts ask whether a reasonable woman would consider the conduct sufficiently severe or pervasive to create a hostile or abusive working environment.

In 2004, the prohibition against sexual discrimination was expanded by the addition of "gender" to the definition of sex. You must permit employees to appear or dress consistently with the employee's gender identity. The sexual harassment policy in the sample *Employee Handbook* has been changed to reflect this new legislation.

What Is Affirmative Action?

Affirmative action is meant to be a temporary effort designed to redress past wrongs. This remedial concept imposes on employers the duty to take positive steps to identify discrimination based on protected class status and to improve work opportunities for persons belonging to protected groups who have been historically deprived of job opportunities.

Affirmative action involves making a specific effort to recruit individuals on the basis of membership in a protected class, and taking positive actions to ensure that such individuals, when employed, have an equal opportunity for benefits and promotions.

There is controversy over California's Proposition 209, but any company that has contracts with the federal government is required to have an affirmative action plan. Other companies may have voluntary plans. Check with your legal counsel.

Proposition 209 bars state and local governments from granting preferential treatment on the basis of race, sex, ethnicity, or national origin.

How Can I Avoid a Discrimination/Harassment Claim?

The first step in avoidance is awareness. If you're aware of the possibility of discrimination and harassment claims, both can be avoided.

Fair dealing, candid communications, objective evaluation of persons and situations, and an ongoing regard for the personal dignity of each employee are the best strategies for avoiding any appearance of discrimination.

Prepare yourself and your company for the possibility of a claim:

- Develop a policy, see page 240;
- Follow the provided guidelines, see page 241;
- Train your supervisors and staff, see page 241; and
- Use the *Manager's Checklist to Avoid Discrimination* (see Table 68 on page 258).

Establish Policies

You are required to have written policies that explain your commitment to protecting your employees from discrimination and harassment. Your employee handbook should include your discrimination and harassment policies. Sample language for these important policies is available in the sample *Employee Handbook* (in the online Formspack included with this product) and in the *Sexual Harassment Information Sheets* (in the ***Required Notices Kit*** associated with this product).

Your policies need to describe the kinds of conduct that your company and the law forbid. Outline the discipline plan. Point out that retaliation will not be tolerated, and harassers may be personally liable as well. See "The Basics of Developing Policies" in Chapter 3, page 54 for tips on writing sound policies.

The fact that you have policies and procedures is not enough to insulate you from litigation. The law requires you to provide information for all employees, contractors, etc., about your discrimination and harassment policies. Follow through with your policies, and update them as often as needed. You also must have an effective internal complaint procedure, and an investigation procedure. See "How Should I Handle a Discrimination/Harassment Complaint?" in Chapter 7, page 248 for details.

Follow Guidelines

Any act or omission that has the appearance of unfairness may initially be viewed as discrimination. Follow these guidelines:

- Apply all rules and standards equally to everyone;
- Give consistent signals and honest appraisals. Mixed signals breed complaints;
- Don't delay decisions. Delay may greatly enhance the appearance of acceptance or unfairness;
- Assume everyone wants to advance within the organization. Supervisors may overlook some candidates because they assume certain employees have no interest in advancement or better salaries because of attitudes they appear to display or assumptions about family obligations. All employees should be considered for advancement;
- Avoid making decisions based on subjective "feelings" about people — rely on objective facts;
- Explain decisions to affected employees. Someone who knows he/she was being considered for a promotion deserves an explanation of why he/she was passed over;
- Make sure communication channels are open;
- Give clear instructions and warnings. Don't ever think that employees "should have known" what was expected;
- Always hear an employee's side of the story before taking action against him/her. Conduct a full investigation;
- Keep complete and accurate records and documentation of all incidents. This includes testimony of witnesses, employer response, charges filed, etc. Date and sign all documents;
- Reasonably accommodate disabilities, religious differences, etc.; and
- Consider setting someone in charge of measuring how well you're doing. Self-analysis now can head off litigation later.

Provide Training

Training can save you time, money, and stress. If training can prevent you the hassle of one angry employee and one lawsuit, it's worth it. Diversity training, harassment prevention training, and discrimination prevention training should occur at least once a year.

Take all steps necessary: affirmatively raise the subject, express strong disapproval, develop appropriate sanctions, inform employees of their right to raise complaints and the methods of raising complaints, and develop methods to sensitize all concerned.

Training is the best way for you to communicate your expectations to your employees. You should probably train supervisors and subordinates separately. They need to know different things, and you may not be able to have a productive discussion with one when the other is present.

You can bring in a professional trainer or lead the training sessions yourself. There are videos, worksheets, and many other teaching materials available. See "You can find these forms in your online Formspack, described in detail in "Online Forms" on page 4." on page 260.

Final Training Regulations

New for 2008 California's sexual harassment training regulations were finalized in 2007. This section provides an in-depth overview and answers to frequently asked questions.

Do the regulations apply to my company?

You must provide sexual harassment to all supervisors if your company has 50 or more employees - anywhere, not just in California. The state of California or a political subdivision thereof (local agencies, counties, public school districts, etc.) is also an employer under these regulations.

What is a supervisor or supervisory employee?

An employee who works in California means any individual having the authority, in the interest of the employer, to hire, transfer, suspend, lay off, recall, promote, discharge, assign, reward, or discipline other employees, or the responsibility to direct them, or to adjust their grievances, or effectively to recommend such action to the employer. The exercise of that authority is not of a merely routine or clerical nature, but requires the use of independent judgment.

How do I determine if I have "50 or more" employees?

Employees include full-time, part-time, and temporary workers or contractors for each working day in any twenty consecutive weeks in the current calendar year or preceding calendar year. The 50 individuals do not need to work at the same location or within the state of California.

I hire independent contractors as well as employees, do they count towards the 50 employee minimum?

Yes, a contractor who performed services for your company for each working day in 20 consecutive weeks in the current or preceding calendar year counts towards the 50 employee minimum.

How long must the supervisor training last?

The training must take the supervisor no less than two hours to complete. The training need not be for two consecutive hours, the minimum duration of a training segment is no less than one half hour for classroom training or webinars. E-learning courses may include features allowing the supervisor to pause the training so long as the e-learning program cannot be completed in less than two hours.

What is classroom training?

Also referred to as "in-person" training, classroom training is instruction whose content is created by a trainer and provided to supervisors by a trainer, in a setting removed from the supervisor's daily duties.

What is webinar training?

An Internet based seminar whose content is created and taught by a trainer and transmitted over the Internet or an intranet in real time. Employers using a webinar for training must document that each supervisor who was not physically present in the same room as the trainer actually attended the training and actively participated in it.

What is E-learning training?

E-learning is individualized, interactive, computer-based training created by a trainer and an instructional designer. Supervisors must have the opportunity to ask a trainer questions and get a response within two business days after the question is asked.

Can we provide training other than classroom, webinar or e-learning?

The regulations authorize other effective interactive training including audio, video, or other computer technology only in conjunction with classroom, webinar or e-learning training.

What is a trainer?

A trainer, or educator, is qualified to provide sexual harassment training for supervisors who has the training and experience about the following:

- What unlawful harassment, discrimination, and retaliation are as defined by California and federal law.
- What steps to take when harassing behavior occurs in the workplace.
- How to report harassment complaints.
- How to respond to a harassment complaint.
- The employer's obligation to conduct a workplace investigation of a harassment complaint.
- What constitutes retaliation and how to prevent it.
- Essential components of an anti-harassment policy.
- The effect of harassment on harassed employees, co-workers, harassers, and employers.

How can I tell if someone is a qualified trainer?

The regulations specify three categories of qualified trainers:

- Attorneys admitted to the bar of any state for two or more years whose practice includes employment law under the California Fair Employment and Housing Act (FEHA) and/or Title VII of the federal Civil Rights Act of 1964; or
- Human Resource Professionals or Harassment Prevention Consultants with a minimum of two years with practical experience in one or more of the following:
  - Designing or conducting discrimination, retaliation, and sexual harassment prevention training; or
  - Responding to sexual harassment complaints or other discrimination complaints; or
  - Conducting investigations of sexual harassment complaints; or

  - Advising employers or employees regarding discrimination, retaliation and sexual harassment prevention.
- Professors or instructors in law schools, colleges, or universities who have a post-graduate degree or California teaching credential and either 20 instruction hours or two or more years experience teaching about employment law under FEHA or Title VII at a law school, college, or university.

What is an instructional designer?

Instructional designers have expertise in current instructional practices and develops the training content based upon material provided by a trainer.

How often do my supervisors need to be trained?

You must provide a minimum of two hours of training once every two years. You can track compliance in either of the following methods or a combination of the two:

- **Individual Tracking** — Each supervisory employee must be trained no later than the 2 year anniversary date of his or her prior training. For example, a supervisor who took sexual harassment training on July 1, 2005, must complete her training in 2007 no later than July 1, 2007.
- **Training Year Tracking** — Employers may designate a "training year" when all sexual harassment training is completed. All supervisors must complete their training by the end of the designated training year. For example, if supervisors were initially trained in 2005, you may designate 2007 as your training year and those supervisors trained in 2005 must complete their training by the end of 2007.

When do my new supervisors need to be trained?

A newly hired supervisor or an individual who has promoted to a supervisor role must be trained within six months of hire/promotion and every two years after that using either the individual or training year tracking method. If using the training year tracking method, newly hired or promoted supervisors who receive training within six months of hire/promotion and that training falls in a different training year, the employer may include them in the next group training year, even if that occurs sooner than two years. For example, if all supervisors were trained in 2005 and 2007 is the "training year" a new supervisor trained in 2006 would need to be trained in 2007 with the employer's other supervisors to keep them on track, or the new supervisor would have to be trained no later than the two year anniversary date of her original training.

I hired a new supervisor who was trained by their previous employer, do I still need to train them within six months of hire?

The burden of proving that any training received by an employee is compliant is on the current employer, so you must be able to demonstrate that the training the new employee received was sufficient under these regulations. If you are able to do so, you can wait until the employee's two year training anniversary, based on the training date with the prior employer. However you must still give the employee a copy of your anti-harassment policy and acknowledge receipt thereof within six months of hire/ promotion to the supervisory position. CalChamber recommends providing your own sexual harassment training to new supervisors and ensuring they are on the same tracking method as the rest of your supervisors.

What sort of documentation must I keep relating to this training?

You must maintain documentation for a minimum of two years of the name of the supervisory employee trained, the date of the training, and the name of the training provider.

I started a new business in 2006 with more than 50 employees, when do I need to provide training?

Businesses created after January 1, 2006 having more than 50 employees as defined above must provide sexual harassment supervisor training within six month of their establishment and every two years thereafter using one of the above tracking methods. Businesses created before January 1, 2006 that expand beyond 50 employees must provide sexual harassment supervisor training within 6 months after they become eligible under these regulations and every two years thereafter.

What if I do not provide this training to my supervisory employees?

The Fair Employment and Housing Commission may issue an order that compliance with these regulations occur within 60 days of the order.

What if my supervisors were trained in 2007 before these regulations were final?

An employer that has made a substantial good faith effort to comply with the sexual harassment supervisor training requirements before the effective date of the regulations will be deemed in compliance.

What does the training have to include?

For any training method, the instruction must include:

- Questions that assess learning;
- Skill-building activities that assess the supervisor's application and understanding of content learned; and
- Numerous hypothetical scenarios about harassment, each with one or more discussion questions so supervisors remain in the training.

The content that must be included, at a minimum, is:

- A definition of unlawful sexual harassment under FEHA and Title VII;
- FEHA and Title VII statutory provisions and case law principles concerning the prohibition against and the prevention of unlawful harassment, discrimination, and retaliation in employment;
- The types of conduct that constitute sexual harassment;
- Remedies available for sexual harassment;
- Strategies to prevent sexual harassment in the workplace;
- Practical examples and hypotheticals based on workplace situations and other situations that illustrate sexual harassment, discrimination, and retaliation using training modalities such as role plays, case studies, and group discussions;
- The limited confidentiality of the complaint process;
- Resources for victims of sexual harassment, such as to whom they should report alleged harassment;
- The employer's obligation to conduct an effective workplace investigation of a harassment complaint;
- Training on what to do if the supervisor is personally accused of harassment;
- The essential elements of an anti-harassment policy and how to use it if a harassment complaint is filed;
- Either the employer's policy or a sample policy must be provided to supervisors as part of the training;

Regardless of whether the employer's policy is used as part of the training, the employer must give each supervisor a copy of its anti-harassment policy and require each supervisor to read and acknowledge receipt thereof.

The Hitches, Glitches, and Pitfalls of Preventing Discrimination/Harassment

Because discrimination and harassment claims are so serious, you need to know what to do ahead of time. This way, if a complaint arises, proper handling may prevent it from becoming a lawsuit.

How Should I Handle a Discrimination/Harassment Complaint?

You should take all complaints of discrimination or harassment very seriously. When an employee makes a complaint, you must be prepared to conduct an investigation. A proper investigation:

- Reassures employees that complaints will be heard and resolved within the company;
- Minimizes the chance of disciplining or terminating an employee for something he/she did not do; and
- Makes it less likely that an outside agency and/or attorney will become involved.

When an employee complains, use the *Harassment Investigation Checklist*, described in Table 68 on page 258, and follow this basic process:

1. Interview the complainant and document the complaint (see page 249).
2. Determine if a formal investigation is necessary (see page 250).
3. Decide on interim actions (see page 250).
4. Conduct a formal investigation (see page 251).
5. Take quick corrective action (see page 255).

1 — Interview the Complainant and Document the Complaint

After finding out the general nature of the complaint, make sure the employee feels comfortable that you can be objective in addressing it or that you will identify an investigator who can. Then:

- Arrange for a private, comfortable setting;
- Provide ample time and opportunity to gather the facts. Make sure the employee knows he/she can take as much time as needed, and can come back if he/she recalls other facts later;
- Encourage him/her to speak freely and make all complaints known;
- Restate your policies against both harassment and retaliation for having brought up a complaint, and ask him/her to report any retaliation to you immediately;
- Tell him/her your procedure for resolving complaints;
- Instruct him/her to keep information about the complaint as confidential as possible;
- Tell him/her that you will only disclose information on a need-to-know basis;
- Ask for any suggestions for a resolution to the problem. Stress that you may not be able to follow these suggestions, but you will take them into consideration;
- Ask if he/she has anyone else they would like you to speak with to back up the allegations; and
- Review the interview notes and prepare a formal statement. Although the complainant is not required to, request that he or she sign the statement.

A Note About Notes

! Accurate, consistent note-taking is critical.

When you take notes on the complaint:

- Document the date and beginning and ending time of the interview;
- Record only the facts and descriptions of what occurred during the interview, not your interpretations of the interview, employee, or situation;
- Keep these notes in a separate place from notes regarding other business issues, and don't record them in a bound notebook or format that might contain information outside of the particular complaint; and
- Keep notes about different employees on separate pieces of paper.

2 — Determine If a Formal Investigation is Necessary

Certain situations automatically trigger your duty to investigate:

- A formal complaint of harassment, written or oral;
- A subtle complaint that a coworker makes the concerned employee uncomfortable;
- A charge from the EEOC or DFEH, or a civil lawsuit;
- An observation of harassment; and
- An anonymous note stating that harassment is occurring.

In other situations, you may need to determine if you need additional information to resolve an employee's concerns. Consider whether:

- The problem has a simple, straightforward solution, or if the problem is more complex;
- It involves more people than just this complainant;
- It stems from a single incident or a pattern of conduct;
- You need more facts than the employee can provide; and
- You need the help of other experts (legal counsel, security personnel, risk management professionals).

If you need more information, conduct a formal investigation.

3 — Decide on Interim Actions

You may need to take some action during the investigation in order to protect:

- The health and safety of employees; and
- The integrity of the company's policies or guidelines.

Leave of Absence

If you suspect an employee of ongoing harmful behavior, you may place the individual on leave pending the completion of an investigation. Give the employee a leave of absence notice that states:

- His/her name;
- The estimated time required for the investigation;
- Who to contact if he/she has any questions or concerns;
- Any expectations you may have, such as:
  - Full cooperation and complete honesty during the investigation;
  - All information and documentation relevant to the investigation; and
  - Confidentiality.
- How you will handle his/her return to work.

4 — Conduct a Formal Investigation

Carefully plan how to conduct the investigation. A poorly planned investigation may expose both the company and the investigator to liability.

Select the Investigator

Select someone who employees view as:

- Fair;
- Objective;
- Reasonable; and
- Able to make difficult decisions.

If the complaint progresses to legal action, the investigator may be called as a witness, so if you want your attorney to defend you in the event of litigation, find someone else to conduct the investigation.

Make sure that the complainant feels comfortable with the investigator. If you choose a third-party investigator, he/she must be a private investigator or attorney licensed to practice in California.

Gather Support Documents

Identify all documents relevant to an investigation. They may:

- Provide background information to help verify facts;
- Identify people to interview; and
- Identify which questions to ask.

Throughout the investigation, ask repeatedly for any documentation that might be helpful.

Interview Appropriate People

Interview the following people in this order:

1. The complainant — For guidance on conducting this interview, see "1 — Interview the Complainant and Document the Complaint" on page 249.
2. The alleged harasser — Keep in mind that everyone is innocent until proven guilty.
   - State that you are investigating a complaint of workplace misconduct;
   - Review the allegations in their entirety, and give him/her the opportunity to respond generally. This allows you to get his/her emotional response to the allegations;
   - Give him/her an opportunity to tell his/her side of the story;
   - Ask questions that provide chronological answers. You can use the *Harassment Investigation Interview Guidelines*, described in Table 68 on page 258, to help you form questions;
   - Remind him/her of the company policy against retaliation, and make sure he/she understands that this applies to retaliation against him/her as well as retaliation against the complainant;
   - Tell him/her that he/she must not discuss the investigation with other employees; and
   - Prepare a written statement for the harasser to sign.
3. Any witnesses — Since being interviewed as part of an investigation can be quite stressful for an interviewee, make an effort to put him/her at ease.
   - Stress that you have not reached a conclusion;

- Tell him/her to keep the information discussed confidential and that you will only share the information he/she provides with people who have a need to know;
- Reiterate the company policy against retaliation against him/her as well as the alleged harasser or the complainant; and
- Use the *Harassment Investigation Interview Guidelines*, described in Table 68 on page 258, to structure your interview, go through events chronologically, and ask for any information he/she has to confirm or refute what you have been told;
- Ask if he/she is aware of any other workplace misconduct; and
- Ask if he/she knows whether the complainant has any bias against the alleged harasser, and vice versa.

! Divulge only enough information as is necessary to learn what information this witness has to offer.

Examine Facts and Assess Credibility

You must determine whether the information you've gathered is credible before relying on it for a conclusion. You need to make credibility assessments while conducting interviews. Ask yourself:

- Did the person raise the complaint in a timely manner? If not, why? Why did he/she raise the complaint now?
- Did similar things happen in the past that did not result in a complaint? If so, why?
- Did any person you interviewed say something that you found later to be untrue?
- Did anyone change his/her story or withdraw an allegation?
- Is the complainant's story consistent and plausible? Does it make sense? Does it correspond with the information learned from other witnesses?
- Is there any evidence at all to corroborate the complaint?
- What motivation would the complainant have to fabricate facts?
- Are there any indications of bias, hostility, or self-interest? Part of this involves observing:
  - Body language;
  - Tone of voice;
  - Eye contact;

- Reactions to questions; and
- Word selection — for example, "girl" vs. "woman."

Do not be afraid to make credibility decisions. However, be sure you can back them up with a reasonable explanation. For additional questions to consider, see the *Credibility Assessment Guidelines for Harassment Investigations*, described in Table 68 on page 258.

Come to a Conclusion

After analyzing the facts and assessing credibility, you will conclude one of the following:

- Company policy was violated; or
- Company policy was not violated.

You should not state that the law has been violated. Only competent legal counsel should make legal conclusions. You only determine whether or not company policy has been violated.

Document Findings and Conclusions

Write an investigation summary that includes:

- The sequence and process followed for the investigation;
- The key facts relied on to make the final decision, such as interviews and any relevant support documentation;
- The criteria used to assess credibility;
- The bottom-line factual conclusions, for example, "the alleged harasser did touch [name of complainant], and this touch was unwanted and offensive to the reasonable woman"; and
- Any complaints that were not resolved in the investigation, and why they were not resolved.

Keep this summary and other relevant documentation, interview notes, etc. in a file labeled as "Need-to-Know, Confidential." Limit access to this file to only those with a legitimate business need-to-know. Even the complainant and the alleged harasser do not need access to this file in the normal course of business.

Communicate results

Notify the alleged harasser of the results. Discuss:

- The complaint(s) raised;
- The steps you took to investigate;
- How you reached the conclusion;
- Any complaints that were not resolved and why;
- The actions you are taking as a result of the investigation; and
- Whom to contact if he/she has questions or information in the future.

Notify the complainant of the results. Discuss:

- The conclusion you reached;
- How you reached the conclusion;
- What actions you are taking that affect him/her;
- What he/she should do if he/she experiences any retaliation; and
- That you expect him/her to keep all aspects of the investigation confidential.

! While you should not divulge the nature of the disciplinary action against the alleged harasser, you may want to indicate that you are taking action.

5 — Take Quick, Corrective Action

You need to move quickly in determining what action to take. Consider the following:

- Do any federal, state, or local laws require you to take certain actions?
- What has the company done in the past for similar violations of policy?
- How serious was the discrimination/harassment?
- Has the employee violated any other policies in the past?
- How long has the employee been employed with your company, and what is his/her performance history?

After weighing these factors, determine the amount of discipline this situation warrants. Some of your options include:

- No action;
- Verbal discussion/counseling;

- Written warning;
- Training;
- Transfer;
- Suspension; or
- Termination.

You can use the *Harassment Discipline Checklist*, described in Table 68 on page 258, to help you make sure you cover all the issues. Terminating a harasser is acceptable when, after an investigation, you have reasonable grounds for believing that the employee engaged in sexual harassment.

Be careful not to give information about allegations, investigations, or resulting discipline, to anyone but those with a legitimate business need to know.

What Are the Penalties for Discrimination/Harassment?

The amount of liability you can incur varies on the type and severity of the claim, repeat offenses, and if you can provide a relevant defense. The penalties include posting notices, reinstatement, payment of back wages, and payment of damages and attorneys' fees. Damages can total enormous sums of money. Courts have levied small businesses with damages large enough to destroy the business. Typically, fines are based on a business's assets.

Liability

Under California law, liability for a claim of discrimination belongs solely to you, the employer. Liability for a claim of harassment can sometimes be shared with the harasser.

Liability is legal responsibility. In most court situations, the liable party is the one who has to pay.

Table 67. Liability

For	Employer liable?	Supervisor liable?	Employee liable?
Discrimination	Yes	No	NA
Harassment of an employee by a supervisor	Yes, whether you knew about the harassment or not	Yes	NA
Harassment between coworkers	Yes, if you knew and failed to take action	No	Yes

What Can I Do to Defend Myself Against a Claim?

The best defense is to avoid claims altogether. For more information, see "How Can I Avoid a Discrimination/Harassment Claim?" on page 240.

Discrimination Claims

You can defend yourself against a claim of discrimination by demonstrating that you have a proper defense, such as:

- **Bona fide occupational qualification (BFOQ)** — pertains to cases where you can prove that a position's requirement of religion, sex, or national origin, etc., is an essential function of the job and is reasonably necessary for your normal business operations. An example of this qualification is a position for a male dancer, or a "Big and Tall" model;
- **Business necessity** — pertains to cases where apparently neutral practices have an adverse impact on a protected class, such as a vigorous physical fitness exam for a firefighter, and the adverse impact on women. You must be able to prove that you have an overriding, legitimate business purpose necessary to the safe and effective operation of the business, and that no alternative practice could equally accomplish the task;
- **Job-relatedness** — pertains to cases where successfully performing the job in question depends on a particular criterion or qualification. For example, a secretary could be required to pass typing and spelling tests to earn a job or promotion;

- **Security regulations** — pertains to cases where your employment practice complies with applicable federal or state security regulations; and
- **Non-discrimination or affirmative action plans** — pertains to cases where your employment practice complies with a bona fide affirmative action or non-discrimination plan, or with a state or federal court's or administrative agency's order.

Harassment Claims

Defending yourself against a claim of harassment is almost impossible. Avoiding harassment claims is your best hope. For more information, see "How Can I Avoid a Discrimination/Harassment Claim?" on page 240.

What Forms and Checklists Do I Use to Help Me Prevent Discrimination and Harassment?

The following table describes forms and checklists associated with discrimination and harassment.

Table 68. Forms and Checklists

Form Name	What do I use it for?	When do I use it?	Who fills it out?	Where does it go?
Credibility Assessment Guidelines for Harassment Investigations	Not required. This form will help you evaluate the people involved in your investigation.	Before and after an investigation interview.	No filling out is needed.	Just read it as a guideline.
Harassment Complaint Procedure - English **New for 2008**	To explain your company's harassment complaint procedure.	Distribute the procedure along with your non-harassment policy to new employees and perhaps annually to all employees.	No filling out is needed.	Give a copy to all employees or incorporate in your employee handbook that is distributed to all employees.

Table 68. Forms and Checklists *(continued)*

Form Name	What do I use it for?	When do I use it?	Who fills it out?	Where does it go?
Harassment Complaint Procedure - Spanish **New for 2008**	To explain your company's harassment complaint procedure.	Distribute the procedure along with your non-harassment policy to new employees and perhaps annually to all employees.	No filling out is needed.	Give a copy to all employees or incorporate in your employee handbook that is distributed to all employees.
Harassment Discipline Checklist	Not required. This form will help you decide how to discipline a harasser.	Before and after an investigation.	No filling out is needed.	Just read it as a guideline.
Harassment Investigation Interview Guidelines	Not required. This form will help you conduct a legal, useful investigation interview.	When preparing for an investigation interview.	No filling out is needed.	Just read it as a guideline.
Manager's Checklist to Avoid Discrimination	Not required. This form will help your managers and supervisors avoid discriminatory behavior.	In any situation where a discrimination complaint could be filed.	No filling out is needed.	Just read it as a guideline and give it to your managers.

Table 68. Forms and Checklists *(continued)*

Form Name	What do I use it for?	When do I use it?	Who fills it out?	Where does it go?
Sexual Harassment Information Sheets	Required. This form describes the problem and the penalties of sexual harassment, as well as what an employee with a complaint should do.	Whenever you hire a new employee, or engage an independent contractor, etc.	No filling out is needed.	Give it to your workers and make sure they understand its contents.
Harassment Investigation Checklist	Not required. This form will help you run your investigation smoothly and legally.	When considering an investigation interview.	No filling out is needed.	Just read it as a guideline.

You can find these forms in your online Formspack, described in detail in "Online Forms" on page 4.

Where Do I Go for More Information?

CalBizCentral and the federal and state governments have a variety of resources to help you prevent discrimination and harassment.

Table 69. Additional Resources

For information on	Check out these resources
General	From CalBizCentral: • The ***2008 California Labor Law Digest***, the most comprehensive, California-specific resource to help employers comply with complex federal and state labor laws and regulations; • *Sexual Harassment Information Sheets*, sold separately or as part of CalBizCentral's ***Required Notices Kit***; • ***Sexual Harassment in California***; • ***http://www.calbizcentral.com***; and • ***http://www.hrcalifornia.com***.
EEOC	• Equal Employment Opportunity Commission 350 Embarcadero, Suite 500 San Francisco, CA 94105 (415) 625-5600 or 1-800-669-4000; • Compliance Manual "Threshold Issues" section at ***http://www.eeoc.gov/policy/docs/threshold.html***; and • The EEOC's enforcement guidance on employer liability for unlawful harassment by supervisors at ***http://www.eeoc.gov/policy/docs/harassment.html.***
DFEH	Department of Fair Employment and Housing Sacramento District Office 2000 O Street, Suite 120 Sacramento, CA 95814-5212 (916) 445-5523 or (800) 884-1684 ***http://www.dfeh.ca.gov/default.asp***
FEHC	Fair Employment and Housing Commission 350 The Embarcadero, Suite 500 San Francisco, CA 94105 (415) 625-5600 or 1-800-669-4000 ***http://www.eeoc.gov/offices.html***

CalBizCentral also provides many ongoing and comprehensive educational opportunities for small business owners, HR beginners, and experienced HR professionals alike. These include online sexual harassment training, videos, and special HR seminars. For more information, please visit our website at ***www.calbizcentral.com***.

Chapter 8

Ending the Employment Relationship

Ending an employment relationship, called "termination," or "separation," involves more than your employee leaving your working environment, and can be very complex. You need to manage your potential for liability, fill out paperwork, and properly calculate and deliver the employee's final paycheck.

You can protect yourself from headaches or even lawsuits with good preparation, and by using a consistent approach in the separation process.

In this chapter, you can find answers to questions about:

- Legal termination procedures;
- Layoffs;
- "Just cause"; and
- Much more!

Minimum Compliance Elements

1. Hang your *Employer Poster* (available from ***www.calbizcentral.com***).
2. Use the *Termination Checklist* to make sure you fill out all the required paperwork for every employee who leaves your company (see Table 73 on page 277 for a description of this form).
3. Use the *Checklist for a Termination Decision* to alert you to possible negative repercussions that could follow a termination decision (see Table 73 on page 277 for a description of this form).
4. Provide the employee's final paycheck in the correct amount and within the required time period (see "What Is the Basic Process for Ending the Employment Relationship?" on page 267).

The Basics of Ending the Employment Relationship

Use the following guidelines to help you through the separation process:

1. Determine the type of separation:
   - Voluntary quit;
   - Discharge (involuntary termination);
   - Layoff;
   - Change in status;
   - Job abandonment; or
   - Refusal to accept work.

   For detailed definitions and examples of each type, see "What Are the Different Types of Separation?" on page 264.

2. Assemble all of the relevant documentation.

   This includes the employee's personnel file, disciplinary notices, and forms required at separation. See ""What Forms and Checklists Do I Use to End the Employment Relationship?" on page 277.

3. Assess the risk of your situation.

   Different rules about UI benefits and wrongful termination lawsuits apply to different situations and different types of separations. See "The Hitches, Glitches, and Pitfalls of Ending the Employment Relationship" on page 272.

4. Have an established procedure and follow it consistently.

   Basic information about what you should do for all types of separation is covered in "The Basics of Ending the Employment Relationship" on page 264. For specific information on what steps to take in each type of separation, see "What Other Steps Do I Need to Take to Cover Specific Situations?" on page 269.

What Are the Different Types of Separation?

There are several distinct types of separation. Different laws and guidelines apply to each. This section provides required processes and best practices to guide you through each of these separation events. The following table provides definitions for each of the separation types.

Table 70. Separation Types

Separation Type	Definition
Voluntary quit	When an employee quits, either with or without notice, the separation is called a "voluntary quit." When someone quits, see "The Basics of Ending the Employment Relationship" on page 264 and "Voluntary Quit" on page 269.
Discharge (involuntary termination)	California is an at-will employment state, so you can discharge any employees at any time as long as they are not under contract, and as long as it is not for a discriminatory reason. To avoid possible wrongful termination lawsuits, however, you should follow the parameters of your company policy or union agreement. Before you fire someone, see "The Basics of Ending the Employment Relationship" on page 264 and "Discharge (Involuntary Termination)" on page 270.
Layoff	A "layoff" occurs when available work ends, either temporarily or permanently, through no fault of the employee. Before you lay off employees, see "What Is the Basic Process for Ending the Employment Relationship?" on page 267 and "Layoff" on page 270. ! There are new notice requirements for employers with 75 or more employees. Read carefully!
Change in status	You and your employee may decide to alter the employee-employer relationship in a number of significant ways. The "change in status" may be from an employee to an independent contractor; it may be a demotion; it may be that an employee on leave is fired or resigns, or that the employee will work fewer hours. Before you change an employee's status, see "What Is the Basic Process for Ending the Employment Relationship?" on page 267 and "Change in Employment Status" on page 270.

Table 70. Separation Types *(continued)*

Separation Type	Definition
Job abandonment	"Job abandonment" means that the employee is missing in action. You can set a policy that limits the number of days an employee can be gone without contacting you before you consider the job abandoned. You are not required to terminate an employee who does not show up for the days defined in your policy. But if you have an established and objective policy and you deviate from it, you could be challenged in cases where you apply it. If you do terminate the employee and he/she later presents a reasonable excuse for the disappearance, you can choose to hire the person again, see "How Do I Hire an Employee?" in Chapter 2, page 8 for more details. When someone abandons his/her job, see "What Is the Basic Process for Ending the Employment Relationship?" on page 267 and "Job Abandonment" on page 271.
Refusal to accept available work	"Refusal to accept available work" means that the employee has refused to perform work that is: • Appropriate to the individual's health, safety, morals, and physical condition; • Consistent with the individual's prior experience and earnings; and • A reasonable distance from the individual's residence. When the employee refuses appropriate, available work, you have the option to terminate. You do not have to terminate an employee who refuses to accept work. You can choose to offer other work or to put the employee on a temporary leave of absence. If you have an established and objective policy and you deviate from it, you could be challenged in cases where you apply it. This type of separation is likely to occur when something about the work changes, for example, your management changes, you reassign an employee to a new work unit, you begin a new project, etc. When an employee refuses available work, see "What Is the Basic Process for Ending the Employment Relationship?" on page 267 and "Refusal to Accept Available Work" on page 271.

What Is the Basic Process for Ending the Employment Relationship?

There are many different ways to end an employee-employer relationship, but all types require you to perform essentially the same group of tasks. Table 71 on page 267 describes the guidelines to follow for all types of separation. For information about what else you'll need to do for a particular type of separation, see "What Other Steps Do I Need to Take to Cover Specific Situations?" on page 269.

See "How Do I Protect Myself Against Wrongful Termination Lawsuits?" on page 272 for information on how to protect your company against potential lawsuits.

Table 71. Basics of Ending Employment Relationship

Before	• Using the information in Table 70 on page 265, determine what type of separation applies to the situation. • For a list of the important legal issues to consider when terminating an employee, review the *Checklist for a Termination Decision*, described in Table 73 on page 277. • Depending on the type of separation, either the employee or the employer provides written notice. Use the *Notice to Employee as to Change in Relationship*, described in Table 73 on page 277, to document the separation event. • For a list of the forms you must fill out or provide to the departing employee, review the *Termination Checklist*, described in Table 73 on page 277.

Table 71. Basics of Ending Employment Relationship *(continued)*

During	**1.** Gather the employee's personnel records and relevant documentation. **2.** Provide the EDD's *For Your Benefit, California's Program for the Unemployed* pamphlet, described in Table 73 on page 277 and located in CalChamber's ***Required Notices Kit*** available from ***www.calbizcentral.com***. **3.** If the employee receives health benefits, fill out and provide the appropriate health insurance and COBRA forms, described in Table 73 on page 277. See COBRA and Cal-COBRA in the "Glossary of Terms, Laws, and Agencies" on page 285, for more details. **4.** Prepare the employee's final paycheck, including all wages and accrued, unpaid vacation. You can use the *Final Paycheck Worksheet*, described in Table 73 on page 277 to help you prepare the paycheck. **5.** Provide the final paycheck to the employee in the appropriate manner within the required time period, based on the type of separation. In most circumstances you must provide the final paycheck on the employee's last day of work. See "How Do I Calculate a Final Paycheck?" in Chapter 5, page 175 for more details. **6. Optional:** have the employee sign the *Final Paycheck Acknowledgement*, described in Table 53 in Chapter 5, page 191, to document that the last paycheck deadline was met as required. It also gives you an opportunity to clarify with the employee that proper payment was received. **7. Optional:** conduct an exit interview on the employee's final day of employment or allow him/her to take the *Exit Interview* form (described in Table 73 on page 277) home and return it by mail. The exit interview gives you a chance to learn the employee's thoughts about employment with your company, and to document any employee claims.

Table 71. Basics of Ending Employment Relationship *(continued)*

After	The employee may be eligible for UI benefits. **1.** The employee schedules an interview with EDD to apply for benefits. **2.** The EDD mails a notice to you, advising you whether the claimant is eligible and whether your account will be charged for benefits paid to the former employee. Respond to correspondence from EDD promptly; EDD is serious about its deadlines. **3.** You can use the *Responding to a Claim for Unemployment Insurance* form, described in Table 73 on page 277, to determine how to respond to the EDD notice that a claim has been filed. **4.** To appeal a claim, see "What Do I Need to Know About UI?" in Chapter 4, page 125. Follow your company's policy on references for former employees. Be careful what you tell remaining employees about the termination. A privacy and/or defamation lawsuit could result from the sharing of too much information with other employees. If you need to communicate the reason for the termination to other employees, consult with your legal counsel first.

What Other Steps Do I Need to Take to Cover Specific Situations?

For specific types of employment separation, you may need to complete additional tasks to ensure that you protect yourself from potential lawsuits.

Voluntary Quit

Follow the basic process described in Table 71 on page 267.

You may wish to confirm the voluntary quit by asking for a letter of resignation. Or, you may use the *Notice to Employee as to Change in Relationship*, described in Table 73 on page 277, as it contains all the important information.

Be sure to provide the final paycheck:

- Within 72 hours of his/her final employment date (if you were given less than 72 hours notice); or
- On his/her last day of work (if you were given more than 72 hours notice).

For a definition of voluntary quit, see Table 70 on page 265.

Discharge (Involuntary Termination)

Follow the basic process described in Table 71 on page 267.

Review the questions in the *Checklist for a Termination Decision*, described in Table 73 on page 277.

You are required to provide written notice for involuntary termination. Use the *Notice to Employee as to Change in Relationship*, described in Table 73 on page 277.

Layoff

Follow the basic process described in Table 71 on page 267.

Document the layoff with a *Notice to Employee as to Change in Relationship*, described in Table 73 on page 277. Provide the employee with any information about severance packages you are offering.

If you have 75 or more employees and the layoff will affect 50 or more of them, you must provide advance notice of the layoff. Consult legal counsel before taking any action.

If you need to lay off an employee who is on a certain statutory leave (PDL, family and medical leave, workers' compensation leave, or disability leave), the employee has the same rights and seniority that he/she would have had he/she been at work.

You may want to consider alternatives to layoffs, including job sharing. See "Where Do I Go for More Information?" on page 284 for helpful agencies and websites.

For a definition of layoff, see Table 70 on page 265.

Change in Employment Status

Follow the basic process described in Table 71 on page 267.

Review the *Employee Orientation* checklist, described in Table 8 in Chapter 2, page 38, if the employee is getting a new status.

Fill out the necessary forms:

- A *Notice to Employee as to Change in Relationship*, described in Table 73 on page 277;
- Any required reporting forms associated with the new status [for example, *Report of New Employee(s) (Form DE 34)* and *Report of Independent Contractor(s) (Form DE 542)*, described in Table 8 in Chapter 2, page 38];
- Any financial paperwork affected by the new status (for example, the *W-4 Form – Employee's Withholding Allowance Certificate*, described in Table 8 in Chapter 2, page 38); and
- Any benefits paperwork associated with the new status (health care, retirement, time off).

Provide an orientation session explaining the details (timesheets, paycheck deductions) that result from the change in relationship.

For a definition of change in employment status, see Table 70 on page 265.

Job Abandonment

Follow the basic process described in Table 71 on page 267.

Prepare the final paycheck immediately upon determining that the job has been abandoned.

You are not required by law to mail or otherwise deliver the final wages. You should make the check available to that employee at the place wages normally are paid. You should, however, notify the employee that he/she has been terminated, and that he/she should pick up the paycheck.

For a definition of job abandonment, see Table 70 on page 265.

Refusal to Accept Available Work

Follow the basic process described in Table 71 on page 267.

Consider the questions in the *Checklist for a Termination Decision*, described in Table 73 on page 277. It will alert you to possible negative repercussions that could follow a termination.

If the former employee makes a UI claim, use the *Responding to a Claim for Unemployment Insurance* form, described in Table 73 on page 277.

For a definition of refusal to accept available work, see Table 70 on page 265.

The Hitches, Glitches, and Pitfalls of Ending the Employment Relationship

The increase of wrongful termination lawsuits in the past few decades has made the idea of terminating an employee a frightening one. When faced with an unexpected lawsuit, there's not much that you can do. If you have prepared for the possibility of a wrongful termination lawsuit, then you'll have much less to worry about. This section provides helpful information about:

- "How Do I Protect Myself Against Wrongful Termination Lawsuits?" on page 272;
- "What Are the Most Common Kinds of Wrongful Termination Lawsuits?" on page 275; and
- "How Should I Handle Employee References?" on page 276.

How Do I Protect Myself Against Wrongful Termination Lawsuits?

Avoiding a wrongful termination lawsuit begins long before you actually terminate an employee. An error or miscommunication in any part of the employment process, from job applications to interviews to employee handbooks to performance reviews, can open you up to a wrongful termination lawsuit. You must take early action to protect yourself against legal action.

Document! Document! Document!

Nothing creates a strong defense against an angry ex-employee like a personnel file documenting that you consistently followed your established disciplinary process, gave the employee honest performance evaluations, tracked any behavior/work problems, attempted to accommodate the employee's needs/complaints, and precisely followed your termination policy and process. It is a good idea to keep copies of:

- A signed *Acknowledgement of Receipt of Notification of COBRA Rights*, described in Table 73 on page 277;
- A signed *Confirmation of Receipt*, described in Table 13 in Chapter 3, page 89;
- A signed *Notice to Employee as to Change in Relationship*, described in Table 73 on page 277;
- Job description(s);

- Performance reviews;
- Records of pay changes and promotions/demotions;
- Records of disciplinary actions/warnings; and
- Written complaints, both by and about the employee (for example, harassment or discrimination charges) and records of each complaint's investigation and resolution.

Establish Company Policies Ahead of Time

An employee handbook sets forth your rules and expectations and creates a fair and simple way to resolve disputes. Once you set forth policy, you need to follow that policy until you discontinue or change it. If you need to discontinue a policy or implement a new or updated policy, make sure you communicate the new information to employees and document the distribution of the updated handbook.

For more information on creating employee policies, see "The Basics of Developing Policies" in Chapter 3, page 54.

Be careful when you write your policies that you don't "paint yourself into a corner."

> ***Example:*** You may have a disciplinary process that allows for a verbal warning, written warning, and suspension before terminating an employee. If you terminate an employee without following your own policy, you may face a claim for a breach of contract.

To avoid this situation, you should describe the disciplinary process, but reserve the right to follow whatever course of discipline is warranted in a particular situation. See "Disciplinary Process" in Table 12 in Chapter 3, page 65 for specific guidelines, and see "The Basics of Developing Policies" in Chapter 3, page 54 for tips on writing sound and sensible policies.

Watch Your Language

In all communication with employees be careful to avoid language that could limit your right to terminate an individual employee.

California is an at-will state, but certain language or conduct may create an employment contract, written, oral, or implied, that may override the legal presumption that employment is at-will. See "Don't Create a Contract" in Chapter 2, page 36 for details.

Train Supervisors and Managers

No matter how much you know about avoiding a wrongful termination lawsuit, if your managers do not follow your guidelines, you will be the one to pay the price. Take the time and resources to ensure that your managers and supervisors follow the policies set forth in the employee handbook and know how to:

- Avoid creating oral or implied employment contracts;
- Prevent and deal with harassment or discrimination in the workplace;
- Handle problem employees; and
- Implement the company's discipline policy.

Be Aware of Public Policies

State and federal laws include many exceptions to the doctrine of at-will employment, primarily to create protections from discrimination against people who belong to protected classes. For more information, see "What Is Discrimination?" in Chapter 7, page 228. When faced with the prospect of terminating an employee in a protected class, be sure you have all the documentation you will need to show that the termination was for legitimate and not discriminatory reasons.

Be Aware of Protected Activities

In addition to protecting certain characteristics, state law also protects certain activities. For example, you may not terminate someone for:

- Performing service — serving jury duty, performing military service, acting as a volunteer firefighter;
- Asserting legal rights — refusing to commit an illegal act, "whistle blowing" if he/she believes the company is violating the law, exercising a statutory obligation to report apparent victims of abuse or neglect, refusing to participate in abortions;
- Maintaining privacy — keeping private any arrest records that do not lead to convictions, refusing to authorize disclosure of medical information, disclosing or refusing to disclose wages; and
- Engaging in lawful behavior — participating in political activity, enrolling in an adult literacy program, taking time off for a child's school or day care activities, refusing to patronize the employer.

Follow a Standardized Method of Separation

To make sure that all employees get treated the same way upon separation, create a standard separation process, and do not deviate from the established method. There is no specific law that requires you to terminate an employee in person, so if you terminate someone by phone or letter, have a standard "script" or form letter that the terminating manager can use.

The sample *Checklist for a Termination Decision*, described in Table 73 on page 277, can help you decide whether to go forward with the termination and how to proceed. The sample *Termination Checklist*, described in Table 73 on page 277, can help you make sure you've done everything you need to during the separation event. For specific guidelines for different types of separation, see Table 71 on page 267.

What Are the Most Common Kinds of Wrongful Termination Lawsuits?

In every employment relationship there is an implied covenant of good faith and fair dealing. If an ex-employee feels he/she has been treated unfairly, he/she may file a wrongful termination suit against you.

Good faith and fair dealing means that you should make decisions on a fair basis, and you should treat employees who are similarly situated in the same manner.

There are several types of lawsuits that ex-employees may file against you. Some of the most common are listed in Table 3.

Table 72. Types of Lawsuits

Discrimination	The employee claims the separation was based on his/her possession of certain characteristics rather than for legitimate reasons. For examples of these characteristics, see "What Is Discrimination?" in Chapter 7, page 228.
Wrongful termination in violation of public policy	The employee must show that the public policy involved is derived from an administrative regulation state or federal statute and is fundamental and of benefit to the general public, rather than just to the employee or employer. You, in turn, must show that your decision to terminate the employee is based on legitimate business reasons. A well-documented separation process can help you defend against this type of lawsuit. See "How Do I Protect Myself Against Wrongful Termination Lawsuits?" on page 272.

Table 72. Types of Lawsuits *(continued)*

Breach of contract	Quite simply this means the employee claims that you did not fulfill an understood contract. This includes written, oral, and implied contracts. The employee must prove that the contract exists and that he/she was terminated in violation of that contract. Your best defense against this type of suit is to not create a contract in the first place! A copy of the *Confirmation of Receipt* signed by the employee can defeat his/her claim that there was an implied/oral contract. And a clause in a written contract that allows for termination at-will can protect you from wrongful termination claims.
Fraud based on misrepresentation at hiring	If you make promises at the time of hiring that you fail to keep, you may be liable for fraud when the employee is later terminated. ***Example:*** If at the time of hiring you promise regular pay raises that you never deliver, you have committed fraud. Be careful of the promises you make when recruiting for a position. See "3 — Advertise and/or Recruit for the Position" in Chapter 2, page 12 for more details.
Constructive discharge	In this type of suit, the employee claims that you made working conditions so intolerable that a reasonable person would be compelled to resign, effectively terminating him/her and breaching your implied covenant of good faith and fair dealing. This most often happens when the employee claims that he or she was harassed at work, and that you did nothing. An open door policy may be your best protection against constructive discharge claims. Make sure you document and address employee concerns in an appropriate manner.

An **open door policy** encourages employees to bring employment issues to the attention of the employer, rather than going outside the company.

How Should I Handle Employee References?

There are risks involved in providing references for former employees. You need to be able to protect yourself from liability that stems from:

- Failing to provide enough information to protect future employers and coworkers — for example, not revealing an employee's record of sexual assault in the workplace;

- Invading the former employee's privacy — for example, disclosing an employee's sexual orientation;
- Defaming the former employee — for example, alleging that the former employee is a "womanizer"; and
- Exposing discriminatory motives for termination — for example, talking about how your former female employee just "didn't fit in" in your male-dominated work environment.

You should develop a company policy for handling employee references and follow it consistently. See "Employee References" in Chapter 3, page 87 for more details.

What Forms and Checklists Do I Use to End the Employment Relationship?

The following tables describe required and recommended forms and checklists associated with the termination process.

You can find these forms in your online Formspack, described in detail in "Online Forms" on page 4.

Table 73. Required Forms and Checklists

Notification/ Form	What do I use it for?	When do I use it?	Who fills it out?	Where does it go?
Acknowledgement of Receipt of Notification of COBRA Rights	Required for **all** types of separation if your insurance plan has 20 or more participants.	Within 14 days of the time you are notified of a qualifying event.	Employee signs the notice.	Send via certified mail to the employee and spouse.
Affidavit to Collect Compensation of Deceased **New for 2008**	Provide this form to the surviving spouse, registered domestic partner, guardian or a conservator of an estate (Affiant) in order to allow collection of the Decedent's salary or other compensation.	After the death of an employee.	The surviving spouse, registered domestic partner, guardian or conservator an an estate.	Maintain in deceased employee's personnel file.

Table 73. Required Forms and Checklists *(continued)*

Notification/ Form	What do I use it for?	When do I use it?	Who fills it out?	Where does it go?
Authorization to Release Personnel Records **New for 2008**	To authorize your company to release various information regarding an employee or former employee's employment.	Upon termination.	An employee or former employee should sign this form.	Maintain in an employee's personnel file.
Cal-COBRA – Notice to Carrier	Required for **all** types of separation if your insurance plan has 2–19 participants.	Within 31 days of the time of the qualifying events of either separation or reduction in hours.	You do.	Send the original form to your insurance carrier within 31 days of the qualifying event. Keep a copy of the form in your personnel records.

Table 73. Required Forms and Checklists *(continued)*

Notification/ Form	What do I use it for?	When do I use it?	Who fills it out?	Where does it go?
Cal-COBRA – Notice to Employee	Required if you are changing health plans and have former employees protected by Cal-COBRA.	At least 30 days before a change in group plans.	You do.	Send the original form to each individual who has elected Cal-COBRA. Also, be sure to send information about the new group benefit plan(s), premiums, enrollment forms, instructions, and anything else necessary to allow the individuals to continue coverage. Keep a copy of the form in your personnel records.
Certificate of Group Health Plan Coverage This form is also known as the "HIPAA Certificate."	Required for **all** types of separation if you have an insurance plan.	Within 14 days if the employee is eligible for COBRA, or otherwise within "reasonable" time.	You do.	Send the original certificate to the employee by first class or registered mail. Dependents may need their own certificates. Keep a copy of the certificate in your personnel records.

Table 73. Required Forms and Checklists *(continued)*

Notification/ Form	What do I use it for?	When do I use it?	Who fills it out?	Where does it go?
COBRA Continuation Coverage Election Notice (California Employees)	Required for **all** types of separation if you are an employer with 20 or more employees who provides an employee health plan and self-administers COBRA.	Within 44 days of a qualifying event.	Employee fills it out.	Send via certified mail to the California employee and spouse.
COBRA Continuation Coverage Election Notice (Outside California)	Required for **all** types of separation if you are an employer with 20 or more employees, some of whom are outside California, who provides an employee health plan and self-administers COBRA.	Within 44 days of a qualifying event.	Employee fills it out.	Send via certified mail to the employee and spouse.
COBRA – Notice to Plan Administrator	Required for **all** California employers with 20 or more employees who outsource COBRA administration.	Within 30 days of a qualifying event.	You do.	Send to the plan administrator.
Employer Proof of Identity and Disbursement of Final Pay **New for 2008**	Complete this form upon receipt of the Affidavit to Collect Compensation of Deceased – Not To Exceed $5000 Net.	After the death of an employee when their survivor(s) request the employee's final pay.	You fill it out and the Affiant signs it.	Place a copy of this completed form in the Decedent's file and provide a copy to the Affiant.

Table 73. Required Forms and Checklists *(continued)*

Notification/ Form	What do I use it for?	When do I use it?	Who fills it out?	Where does it go?
Final Paycheck Acknowledgment - English **New for 2008**	To have an employee certify receipt of final paycheck.	Upon termination.	You fill it out and the employee signs it.	In the employee's personnel file.
Final Paycheck Acknowledgment - Spanish **New for 2008**	To have an employee certify receipt of final paycheck.	Upon termination.	You fill it out and the employee signs it.	In the employee's personnel file.
For Your Benefit, California's Program for the Unemployed	Required for **all** types of separation.	Immediately	No filling out is needed.	Give a copy to the employee. Use the *Termination Checklist* to document his/her receipt.
HIPP Notice (English)	Required for **all** types of separation.	Immediately	No filling out is needed.	Give a copy to the employee. Use the *Termination Checklist* to document his/her receipt.

Table 73. Required Forms and Checklists *(continued)*

<table>
<tr><th>Notification/ Form</th><th>What do I use it for?</th><th>When do I use it?</th><th>Who fills it out?</th><th>Where does it go?</th></tr>
<tr><td>HIPP Notice (Spanish)</td><td>Required for all types of separation.</td><td>Immediately</td><td>No filling out is needed.</td><td>Give a copy to the employee. Use the Termination Checklist to document his/her receipt.</td></tr>
<tr><td>Notice to Employee as to Change in Relationship</td><td>Required for:
• Discharge;
• Layoff; and
• Leave of absence.

Recommended for all types of separation.

Written notice must be provided by:
• Letter;
• Employer's own form; or
• The form in your online Formspack.</td><td>In your preparations to terminate an employee.</td><td>You do.

You should request the employee's signature, but it is not required by law.

The notice must include:
• Employer name;
• Employee name;
• Employee Social Security number;
• Indication that the action was a discharge, layoff, leave of absence, or a change in status; and
• The date of the action.</td><td>Give a copy to the employee.

Keep a copy in the employee's personnel records.</td></tr>
</table>

Table 74. Recommended Forms and Checklists

Notification/ Form	What do I use it for?	When do I use it?	Who fills it out?	Where does it go?
Appealing a UI Claim to an Administrative Law Judge	To help you prepare an appeal to a judge for a UI claim you are protesting.	During the appeal process.	You do.	Keep a copy in the employee's personnel file.
Appealing a UI Claim to the UI Appeals Board	To help you present your final case to the UI Appeals Board.	At the final stage of the appeal process after your appeal has been rejected by an ALJ.	You do.	Keep a copy in the employee's personnel file.
Checklist for a Termination Decision	Recommended for **all** types of separation.	Before deciding to terminate an employee	You consider the questions	N/A
Exit Interview	Recommended for **all** types of separation.	On the final day of the employment, or ask the employee to return a paper form by mail.	Employee fills it out, unless the interview is conducted orally; in that case, you may fill in the employee's answers.	Keep the exit interview in your personnel records.
Responding to a Claim for Unemployment Insurance	Recommended for **all** types of separation.	After the separation process.	You do.	Keep the checklists in your personnel records.
Termination Checklist	Recommended for **all** types of separation.	During the separation.	You do.	Keep the checklist in your personnel records.

Where Do I Go for More Information?

CalBizCentral and the federal and state governments have a variety of resources to help prepare you for the separation process.

Table 75. Additional Resources

For information on	Check out these resources
General	From CalBizCentral: • The ***2008 California Labor Law Digest***, the most comprehensive, California-specific resource to help employers comply with complex federal and state labor laws and regulations; • ***Recruiting, Performance & Termination in California***; • ***http://www.calbizcentral.com***; and • ***http://www.hrcalifornia.com***.
State government	California's Employment Development Department: ***http://www.edd.ca.gov***

Glossary of Terms, Laws, and Agencies

4/10 workweek

A weekly schedule that allows the employee to work four 10-hour days each week.

9/80 workweek

A two-week schedule that allows an employee to work nine days and 80 hours — five days in one calendar week and four days the following week.

accrue

To accumulate or have due after a period of time.

ADA

Americans with Disabilities Act of 1990. Administered by the federal EEOC, prohibits employers of 15 or more employees in the private sector, and state and local governments from discriminating against qualified individuals with disabilities. It requires employers to provide reasonable accommodation for individuals with disabilities, unless the accommodating measures would cause undue hardship. *See also* **reasonable accommodation**.

ADEA

Age Discrimination in Employment Act of 1967. Prohibits employers with 20 or more employees from discriminating against individuals 40 years of age and older.

administrative control

Procedural improvements intended to reduce the duration, frequency, and severity of work-related injuries and illnesses. Examples include job rotation, work pacing, and work breaks.

adverse action

An employment decision that has a negative impact on hiring, promotion, termination, benefits, or compensation.

affirmative action

An active effort to improve the employment or educational opportunities of members of protected classes.

ALJ

Administrative Law Judge. A judge appointed by an administrative agency for the purpose of conducting hearings and rendering decisions under the agency's unique jurisdiction. Typically, an ALJ's decisions are reviewed by the agency and by the courts.

alternative workweek

Any regularly scheduled workweek requiring an employee to work more than eight hours in a 24-hour period.

arbitration

A non-court procedure for resolving disputes using one or more neutral third parties as decision makers.

at-will employment

A legal concept, mandated by California law, assuring both employer and employee that either party can terminate the relationship at any time and for any reason or no reason.

BFOQ

Bona fide occupational qualification. Qualifications and characteristics reasonably necessary to perform duties, tasks, or processes required to conduct normal business operations.

California Labor Commissioner

Sets and enforces regulations for employee wages, paycheck deductions, breaks, vacation, jury/witness duty, or temporary military leave, the workweek, minors, employee access to personnel files, "lawful conduct" discrimination, exempt status, and independent contractor status. The Commissioner also assesses fines and files charges with the District Attorney on behalf of underpaid employees, and investigates, holds hearings, takes action to recover wages, assesses penalties, and makes demands for compensation.

Cal-COBRA

California Continuation of Benefits Replacement Act. Requires insurance carriers and HMOs to provide COBRA-like coverage for employees of smaller employers (2–19 employees) not subject to COBRA.

Cal/OSHA

California Occupational Safety and Health Administration. Enforces California laws and regulations pertaining to workplace safety and health and provides assistance to employers and workers about workplace safety and health issues.

CFRA

California Family Rights Act. Provides employees 12 weeks of leave for bonding with a newborn or adopted child, caring for a family member with a serious health condition, and/or caring for the employee's own serious health condition. This law applies to companies with 50 or more employees.

COBRA

Consolidated Omnibus Budget Reconciliation Act of 1985. Requires employers with 20 or more employees to offer all employees covered by health care the option of continuing to be covered by the company's group health insurance plan at the worker's own expense for a specific period (often 18 months) after employment ends.

commission

A fee paid to an agent or employee for transacting a piece of business or performing a service.

concurrent leave

Two different types of leave (for example PDL an FMLA) that are used up simultaneously. Table 19 in Chapter 4, page 109 provides an overview of the ways PDL, FMLA/CFRA, workers' compensation, and disability leaves interact concurrently.

conflict of interest

A conflict between the private interests and the official responsibilities of a person in a position of trust.

constructive discharge

A wrongful termination claim that the working conditions were so intolerable that a reasonable person would be forced to resign.

Civil Rights Act of 1991

Amended Title VII, creating, among other things, the right to jury trials, and allowing those claiming intentional discrimination or harassment based on sex, race, religion, national origin, or color under Title VII, or disability under the ADA or Rehabilitation Act, to obtain compensatory and punitive damages measured by the size of the employer's workforce, up to a maximum of $300,000.

CTD

Cumulative trauma disorder. *See also* RMI.

CTO

Compensatory time off. Gives a non-exempt employee time off for extra hours worked instead of paying overtime. It is also commonly referred to as "comp time" and is almost always illegal for private employers.

DFEH

California Department of Fair Employment and Housing. Enforces California's non-discrimination laws. DFEH has jurisdiction over private and public employment, housing, public accommodations, and public services. DFEH receives and investigates discrimination complaints, and provides technical assistance to employers regarding their responsibilities under the law.

DIR

California Department of Industrial Relations. Seeks to improve working conditions for California's wage earners and to advance opportunities for profitable employment in California. DIR has these major areas of responsibility: labor law, workplace safety and health, apprenticeship training, workers' compensation, statistics and research, mediation, and conciliation.

disability

In California, a physical or mental impairment that limits one or more of the major life activities.

disability insurance

A voluntary plan, for employers who do not want to participate in SDI, that provides short-term benefits for employees who are disabled by a non-work-related illness or injury.

DLSE

California Division of Labor Standards Enforcement. Investigates wage claims and discrimination complaints and enforces California's labor laws and IWC Wage Orders.

DOL

U.S. Department of Labor. Administers a variety of federal labor laws including those that guarantee workers' rights to safe and healthful working conditions, a minimum hourly wage and overtime pay, freedom from employment discrimination, unemployment insurance, and other income support.

domestic partner

Either one of an unmarried heterosexual or homosexual cohabiting couple, especially when considered as to eligibility for spousal benefits.

DOSH

Division of Occupational Safety and Health. Enforces California's occupational and public safety laws, and provides information and consultative assistance to employers, workers, and the public about workplace and public safety matters.

double-time

Two times an employee's regular rate of pay. *See also* overtime.

EDD

California Employment Development Department. Part of the California Health and Human Services Agency, helps California employers meet their labor needs, job seekers obtain employment, and the disadvantaged and welfare-to-work recipients to become self-sufficient. It supports state activities and benefit programs by collecting and administering employment-related taxes (UI, SDI, Employment Training Tax, and Personal Income Tax).

EEOC

Equal Employment Opportunity Commission. A federal agency that interprets discrimination law, collects employment data, and handles employee complaints.

employee benefit plans

Welfare and pension plans voluntarily established and maintained by an employer, an employee organization, or jointly by one or more such employers and an employee organization. Governed by ERISA.

employment at-will

See at-will employment.

engineered controls

Protective devices designed to reduce or eliminate the risk of workplace injury. Examples include machine guards, adjustable fixtures, and tool redesign.

English-only policy

Prohibits the use of other languages in the workplace. It is illegal in California unless certain conditions are met, including business necessity and employee notice.

ergonomics

The scientific study of the relationship between people and their work environments. The goal of the field is to minimize workplace injuries and illnesses through improved workplace design.

ERISA

Employee Retirement Income Security Act. Regulates employee benefit plans and the numerous persons (for example, employers and unions) involved in establishing and maintaining these plans. ERISA sets uniform minimum standards to assure that employee benefit plans are established and maintained in a fair and financially sound manner. In addition, employers have an obligation to provide promised benefits and satisfy ERISA's requirements for managing and administering private pension and welfare plans.

essential functions

Fundamental job requirements of the position, or the reason the job exists.

exempt

An employee who is not subject to any of the laws pertaining to overtime, meal periods, and rest periods.

FCRA

Fair Credit Reporting Act. Requires specific disclosures in a specific format, in addition to any waiver that might be on an application, before checking the applicant's credit, and restricts an employer's ability to use credit reports for employment purposes.

FEHA

California Fair Employment and Housing Act. Prohibits discrimination/harassment on the basis of race/color, religious creed, national origin/ancestry, physical disability, mental disability, medical condition (including no genetic testing), marital status, sex, age, and sexual orientation. This law provides more protection than the ADA.

FEHC

California Fair Employment and Housing Commission. Hears complaints brought before it by the DFEH, and has the power to levy fines and assessments for damages.

flat rate

Pay based on a job completed, not the number of hours spent completing it.

flexible schedule

An eight-hour work schedule where some employees begin the shift early in the day and others begin their work later in the day.

FLSA

Fair Labor Standards Act. Regulates minimum wages, overtime, and working conditions for all employees of businesses that engage in interstate commerce and have an annual gross volume of sales of not less than $500,000, or an individual employee who is involved in interstate commerce, contracts to do work for a firm engaged in interstate commerce, or travels across state lines in the course of employment.

FMLA

Family and Medical Leave Act. Provides up to 12 weeks of job-protected, unpaid leave during a pre-defined 12-month period for employees who work for a public agency, a local education agency, or an employer in the private sector who has 50 or more employees each working day during at least 20 calendar weeks in the current or preceding calendar year.

full-time

An employee who works the number of hours designated by the employer as "full-time."

garnishments

Money withheld by court order from an employee's check to pay for debt, back taxes, or child support.

good faith and fair dealing

Employment decisions that are made fairly, treating similarly situated employees in the same manner.

harassment

Behavior toward a person that a reasonable person would find unwelcome or hostile.

HAZCOM

Hazard Communication Program. Requires all employers to communicate workplace hazards to employees, particularly when employees handle or may be exposed to hazardous substances during normal work or foreseeable emergencies.

HIPAA

Health Insurance Portability and Accountability Act. Limits the extent to which a new employer's health plan can establish barriers, such as pre-existing conditions, that will delay or prevent new employees from becoming fully covered under a new plan. The law was designed to limit or eliminate what Congress called "job lock," which occurs when employees are unable to change jobs because of inability to financially withstand the typical pre-existing condition limitations in a new employer's medical plan.

HIPP

Health Insurance Premium Payment program. A California program that requires all employers to provide departing employees with notice of a state program that pays COBRA payments under certain circumstances.

HMO

Health maintenance organization. An organization that provides comprehensive health care to voluntarily enrolled individuals and families in a particular geographic area by member physicians with limited referral to outside specialists, and that is financed by fixed periodic payments determined in advance.

hostile work environment

An unproductive work environment caused by unwelcome sexual comments, touches, or visual displays.

IIPP

Injury and Illness Prevention Program. A company's general plan for keeping its workforce free from work-related injuries and illness, mandated by California law.

independent contractor

A person or company that supplies goods or services to an individual or business. The independent contractor should not have any of the characteristics of an employee.

INS

U.S. Immigration and Naturalization Service. The INS has been renamed to the U.S. Citizenship and Immigration Services (USCIS). The USCIS is an agency of the Department of Homeland Security (DHS), which enforces the laws regulating the admission of foreign-born persons to the U.S., and administers various immigration benefits, including work visas and the naturalization of qualified applicants for U.S. citizenship. The USCIS investigates violations of IRCA.

IRS

Internal Revenue Service. The nation's tax collection agency, which administers the Internal Revenue Code enacted by Congress.

IRCA

Immigration Reform and Control Act. A federal law requiring employers to verify all employees' legal eligibility to live and work in the U.S.

IWC

Industrial Welfare Commission. A California agency that monitors the hours and conditions of employment; investigates employee health, safety, and welfare; and determines the Wage Orders.

just cause

A fair and honest cause or reason, acted on in good faith by the employer.

kin care

Care of a sick child, parent, spouse, registered domestic partner, or child of a registered domestic partner.

Labor Commissioner

See California Labor Commissioner.

layoff

To cease to employ a worker, often temporarily, because of economic reasons.

living wage

A wage sufficient to provide the necessities and comforts essential to an acceptable standard of living. Generally mandated by local ordinances.

Log 300

A series of record keeping forms for recording workplace injuries and illnesses. Part of a Cal/OSHA record-keeping requirement.

major life activities

Caring for oneself, sleeping, learning, walking, interacting with others, working, and other physical, mental, and social activities. Used to determine whether a worker is disabled.

makeup time

Allows non-exempt employees to request time off for a personal obligation and make up the time within the same workweek without receiving overtime pay.

mass layoff

The laying off of 50 or more employees, under WARN.

medical certification

A statement from an employee's health care provider as to the necessity of time off from work. Usually required by an employer when an employee is off for a reason protected by law.

minimum salary

The smallest amount a salaried exempt employee can make, in order to be considered exempt. On January 1, 2008 the amount increased to $2,774 per month.

minimum wage

The smallest hourly wage a non-exempt employee can make. Currently $8.00 per hour. *See also* **regular rate of pay**.

minor

Any person under the age of 18 who is required to attend school, or any person under the age of six.

misdemeanor

A criminal offense that is more serious than an infraction, but less serious than a felony. A misdemeanor is punishable by fine, incarceration in county jail, or a combination of both.

MSD

Musculoskeletal disorder. See **RMI**.

MSDS

Material Safety Data Sheet. An information sheet provided by the manufacturer of a product that describes the product's chemical properties, potential hazards, and instruction in safe handling.

negligence

A lack of prudent care (neglect).

non-compete agreements

An agreement between an employer and an employee, which says that, when an employee leaves the company, the employee will not work for a competitor for a certain amount of time. With few exceptions, non-compete agreements are illegal in California under most circumstances.

non-exempt

An employee who is subject to the laws pertaining to overtime, minimum wage, meal periods, and rest periods.

occupational wage order

Same as Wage Order. Contain the instructions for payment of wages to non-exempt employees as well as specific rights and responsibilities of the employee and the employer. There are currently 17 Wage Orders, organized according to industry and occupation, plus a Minimum Wage Order. The purpose of your business determines which Wage Order applies to you. *See* ***Wage Orders***.

open door policy

A policy encouraging employees to bring employment issues to the attention of the employer, rather than going outside the company.

OSHA

Occupational Safety and Health Administration. The federal agency that ensures safe and healthful workplaces by issuing standards, performing inspections, and levying penalties for violations.

overtime

Hours worked beyond a "normal" amount of hours for a day or week. For non-exempt employees with a regular workweek, normal is eight hours per day. For employees with an alternative workweek, normal could be nine or 10 hours. For more information on alternative workweeks, see Chapter 5, "Paying Employees." *See also* pyramiding of overtime.

part-time

An employee who works less than the number of hours that qualify him/her as a full-time employee, according to your policy.

PDA

Pregnancy Discrimination Act of 1978. An amendment to Title VII, requires that employers treat a pregnant employee the same as any other employee, and that when a female employee becomes unable to work due to pregnancy, childbirth, or related medical conditions, the employer treat her disability the same as any other disability.

pension plan

Provides retirement income or defers income until termination of covered employment or beyond. Governed by ERISA.

PFL

Paid Family Leave. A wage replacement program funded through employee contributions and administered by the Employment Development Department for employees unable to work when they are needed to care for a family member.

piece rate

An amount paid for completing a particular task or making a particular piece of goods.

plant closing

The shutting down of a facility or laying off 50 or more employees. *See also* WARN, *mass layoff.*

PPE

Personal protective equipment. Items such as gloves, masks, and special clothing used to protect against hazardous, toxic, or infectious material.

Proposition 65

Requires that employers with 10 or more employees warn any person (employees and others who may enter a laboratory) prior to their exposure to a chemical known to the state of California to cause cancer, birth defects, or other reproductive harm.

Proposition 209 (1996)

Bars California's state and local governments from granting preferential treatment to any individual or group on the basis of race, sex, ethnicity, or national origin in the operation of government hiring contracting, and education. This state measure does not affect the affirmative action programs required by the federal government.

PTO

Paid time off. An informal term referring to an employer-defined combination of sick pay, holiday pay, and/or vacation.

pyramiding of overtime

Not required by California law, exists when an employee earns overtime on top of overtime already paid.

qualifying event

For benefits purposes, one of several defined events that permits a change of benefits enrollment status outside of open enrollment periods or that entitles an eligible beneficiary to COBRA or Cal-COBRA benefits.

quid pro quo

Latin, meaning "this for that." A type of sexual harassment that conditions job continuance, promotions, benefits, etc. in exchange for sexual favors.

rate of pay

A fixed amount of payment based on a unit of time or a piece of work performed.

reasonable accommodation

Any change in the work environment or in the way a job is performed that enables a person with a disability to enjoy equal employment opportunities. *See also* disability.

regular rate of pay

The calculated amount of an employee's actual earnings, which may include an hourly rate, commission, bonuses, piece work, and the value of meals and lodging.

RMI

Repetitive motion injury. A problematic injury that builds over time, caused by overuse or overexertion of some part of the musculoskeletal system. RMIs are characterized by inflammation, pain, or dysfunction of the involved joints, bones, ligaments, and nerves. Often referred to as cumulative trauma disorders (CMDs) or musculoskeletal disorders (MSDs).

reporting time pay

Payment to a non-exempt employee who reports to work at his/her normal time and is not put to work, or is given less than half the hours for which he/she was scheduled.

salary

A fixed amount of money for each payroll period, whether weekly, bi-weekly, semi-monthly, or monthly.

SDI

California State Disability Insurance. Provides temporary disability benefits for employees who are disabled by a non-work-related illness or injury. Benefits are paid by the Employment Development Department from employee contributions in the form of a tax.

seventh day rule

Non-exempt employees who work on each day of your established seven day workweek are entitled to overtime at the rate of time and one-half for the first 8 hours worked and double time for any hours worked beyond that on that seventh day.

severance pay

Money paid to an employee at the time of termination or layoff, to compensate in part for the sudden job loss. Not required by law.

SIC

Standard Industry Code. System that classifies businesses by their primary activity. The SIC is used for a variety of statistical purposes.

split shift

Any two distinct work periods separated by more than a one-hour meal period.

standby

Time the employee spends on call that cannot be used for his/her benefit. Depending on the limitations on the employee during this time, the standby time may be paid or unpaid.

statute

A law enacted by the legislative branch of a government.

telecommute

To work at home by the use of an electronic linkup with a central office. Employees may use an electronic linkup with a central office or other technology to work from a location away from their office.

TICP

Targeted Inspection and Consultation Program. A Cal/OSHA program that identifies certain high-hazard employers, and requires a fee paid to fund a special inspection unit.

time-and-one-half

The regular hourly rate for the job an employee is doing, plus one-half the regular rate of pay. *See also* double-time, *overtime*.

Title VII, Civil Rights Act of 1964

Prohibits employers of 15 or more employees from discriminating on the basis of race, color, religion, sex, or national origin.

UI

Unemployment Insurance. An employer-paid tax, which is held in reserve for employees in case they become unemployed.

Wage Orders

Contain the instructions for paying non-exempt employees their wages. There are currently 17 Wage Orders, organized according to industry, plus a Minimum Wage Order. The purpose of your business determines which Wage Order applies to you.

WARN

Worker Adjustment and Retraining Notification Act. A federal law requiring employers to give employees advance notice of a plant closing or a mass layoff if the action involves a requisite number of employees. California has a similar law that provides more protection than that of federal law, therefore more employees are covered by state law.

welfare plan

Provides health benefits, disability benefits, death benefits, prepaid legal services, vacation benefits, day care centers, scholarship funds, apprenticeship and training benefits, or other similar benefits. Governed by ERISA.

workers' compensation
A mandatory "no-fault" insurance program, paid for by employers, to cover medical treatment and wage replacement for an employee who suffers a work-related illness or injury.

work permit
A document establishing the maximum number of days and hours a minor may legally work during the workweek. The permit may also impose other limitations on the scope of the minor's work.

Index

A

B

C

D

E

F

G

H

J

K

L

P

Q

R

S

T

U

V

W